How To Raise A Rocket Scienti.. bination of reading gifts. It is both well-written and inspiring. It tells the dual stories of Patience and Courage--both of which are sheltered by Love. If this sounds sentimental -- it isn't. The story it tells--of Katie, a young woman stricken with cerebral palsy and her determined journey and the full-blossoming of her exceptional gifts--is told with careful and caring understatement and lucidity. This is a story for all of us. The father is simply referred to as the father. The mother is simply referred to as the mother. And this understatement allows anyone who has been a parent to enter this story and to care--to tense at its moments of difficulty and to celebrate its moments of victory. It is Katie's story which claims center-stage. And it is the calm and confident telling of this story which welcomes us all into this quite-wonderful book.

--David Kranes, playwright and novelist,
author of "The National Tree"

Katie's story is one of triumph -- how she learned to work twice as hard to accomplish what able-bodied children did, how she persevered and utilized unique solutions to just "get `er done," and how she turned the daily taunts and glares into motivation and understanding, rather than sorrow and anger. But more than that, this story is about what Katie Browne taught her parents, and continues to teach them to this day. If you've heard Steve speak, whether it be his personal story or about customer service or real business development, you won't be able to put Rocket Scientist down. You'll laugh, you'll cry, you'll get angry, you'll feel proud. But more than that, you'll feel hopeful for all of us humans that wish we knew better, could act better, and for whom it only takes a little girl with a stumbling gait and a speech handicap to help us BE better. You will enjoy and be inspired by How To Raise a Rocket Scientist For Fun and Profit. I guarantee it.

--Dennis Conrad, author of "Conrad's Corners"
and "Conrad on Casino Marketing "

THE YEAR'S "MUST READ" INSPIRATIONAL TALE

BASED ON A TRUE STORY

How To Raise A Rocket Scientist

FOR FUN AND PROFIT

Steven A Browne

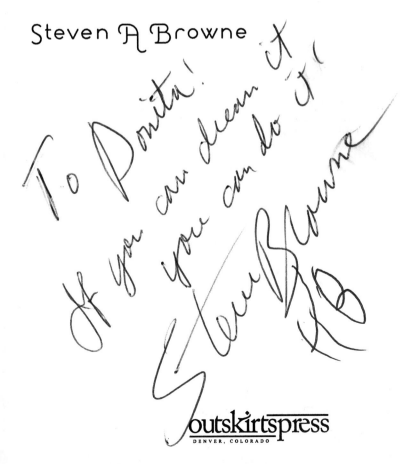

To Donita!
If you can dream it
you can do it!

Steve Browne

Outskirtspress
DENVER, COLORADO

Outskirts Press, Inc.
http://www.outskirtspress.com

ISBN: 978-1-4327-9613-6

Library of Congress Control Number: 2012910799

Outskirts Press and the "OP" logo are trademarks belonging to Outskirts Press, Inc.

PRINTED IN THE UNITED STATES OF AMERICA

To Katie… of course, and to my son Chris.
And to their mother, my wife, to whom I will always be grateful.

The story you are about to read,
the story of a father,
and the daughter who raised him,
is a true story…

However, I consider it a work of fiction, as,
being originally born and raised in Texas,
I am not one to let the facts
get in the way of a good story.

Prologue

42 Steps.

The thought filled her mind, leaving no room for any other thought. Not her speech, nor the people she should thank, nor anything else. 42 steps. That's how long the trip from her seat to the podium was. She knew it as fact. She had paced it off earlier, carefully, while everyone else was busy picking at appetizers, sipping drinks and making polite conversation. 42 steps, three stairs and one podium on a raised stage. She knew the challenge, willed herself to make the trip, without slipping, without falling, without even hesitating. But would she? The speaker's voice droned on and on, talking of accomplishments, mouthing platitudes, listing achievements. And still her mind was focused.

42 steps.

The room was filled to capacity for this, the annual scholastic awards ceremony. The school only held this event once each year. The University was made up of eight colleges, eight separate schools of study. And every year eight students were singled out, awarded with the highest scholastic honor available, first in their class, first in their college, first among their peers.

They were the best and brightest, the cream of the scholastic crop. For four years or more they had labored to complete their course of study, to achieve the highest grades possible. Between them there was not one B, not one course grade below an A. These were not students who dealt in mediocrity; they were the brightest minds on campus. And they were gathered here, in one room, to celebrate their achievement, to receive the adulation of their peers, their family members, the faculty, and the community.

Seven had already been called, been fetched and feted, had made the walk from chair to podium to receive their award, to stand with the one professor they had selected as having the most important influence on their academic career, and glory in the crowd's approval.

One by one the seven spoke into the microphone, making their prepared speeches, the words flowing easily, the memorization of each presentation a simple task to those so academically and intellectually gifted. One by one the pictures were taken. One by one the applause was given. One by one they returned to their seats.

Only one student was left.

One student, the scholastic award winner in the storied College of Engineering, the college representing so many different disciplines, civil and electrical, environmental and mechanical, and, finally, aeronautical and computer science. And for all that, this one last person, this top engineering student could only think of, could only grasp or focus on, one thing… 42 steps.

The room was filled with a myriad of different people. There were the family members and friends of the honorees, people who had come to share in the glory and offer their congratulations. Some were business people, some civil servants, some laborers, teachers and tradesmen. Others were fellow students and friends. One family had come 2,000 miles, across the whole of the country, to be here in this room, at this moment, to celebrate academic excellence.

Then there were the mentors, those chosen by the eight top scholars as representing the faculty member who had most made an impression on them during their years of study. Along with the mentors were the heads of each college, each one a PhD and distinguished professor and academician in their own right.

On one corner of the stage, the chancellor of the university held court, surrounded by staff and invited colleagues. There was a state senator, a congressman, and several community leaders. Eagerly they listened as the accomplishments of each student were repeated and recorded by the alumni master of ceremonies, herself a former scholastic award winner and now leader of a large Fortune 500 company.

The master of ceremonies had done an outstanding job. Her listing of each student's awards and accomplishments had been conducted with just the right amount of excitement and admiration. And now she was about to finish. One student to go. One more award to give out. One more speech to present.

Her voice filled the room as she proudly listed the accomplishments of this final student, this top scholar from one of the most difficult disciplines in the entire school, the College of Engineering...

"...recipient of a prestigious Women in Engineering scholarship," she intoned, "a 4.0 GPA, a course schedule heavy in robotics and artificial intelligence, two internships with NASA, a participant and award winner at the NASA Academy for Future Leaders..."

On and on she spoke, her voice gaining strength as she went, excitement building, the crowd on the edge of their seats with anticipation. For this student had been held to the last, left to the final presentation. This student, above all others, had fought longer, harder, to be seated in this room, on this night, at this time, for this ceremony.

Then it was over, the accolades completed, the introduction finished. The crowd rose to their feet as one body, their hands clapping, the noise louder and louder, anticipation filling the room.

And it was then she knew. She knew it was time. No more to worry about. Nothing more to do. Just rise and walk, rise and take 42 steps.

42 steps.

She was the university's top scholar, first in her class, one of eight scholastic awards winners in a school of over 25,000 students.

She rose to her feet, tottered for just a moment, a fraction of a moment, and then, her eyes steady, her gaze fixed, she began to walk. One step, two steps, one foot in front of the other, hesitating, gaining balance, moving forward, 9 steps, 10 steps, her arms swaying to the tempo of her feet, her head fixed, 16 steps, 17 steps. Blood coursing through her veins, her heart pounding, 21 steps, 22 steps. Here came the stairs, one foot lifted, in front of the other, her hand on the railing, her grip fixed, rigid, unyielding.

Now the most difficult part, crossing the stage, the audience continuing to clap, flash bulbs seeming to pop all around her, 41 steps, 42 steps.

Then it was over. She was there. She had arrived!

She turned to face the standing crowd, gripped the sides of the podium, arms rigid, hands clenched onto the wood as if holding on to her entire life. This was the moment, the moment she had imagined so many years ago, the moment that came from all that work, from all those years of struggling to make it in a world not designed for her, a world not accommodating to her particular kind.

She had written her speech, typing it into her computer one keystroke at a time, then, laboriously committed it to memory, practicing for hours in front of the mirror, recording her voice, working out the pronunciation, trying as hard as she could to make the words intelligible, legible, clear to a stranger's ear.

She had people to thank, others to acknowledge, words to offer for this great honor. For just a moment she panicked. And then, finally, the 42 steps behind her, her mind began to clear, her thoughts to coalesce. She remembered what she wanted to say. Remembered her speech, the typewritten words playing out, as if listed on a teleprompter suspended in front of her, suspended in air, in nothingness.

She looked to her left, to the front row where her parents sat, looked to them for strength and reassurance. She looked to her right, at the alumni master, the chancellor of the university, the congressman. She cleared her throat, leaned forward into the microphone.

She began to speak.

In The Beginning

The hospital was one story, low slung, with a roof line that blended in with the mountain setting. Evergreen trees surrounded the structure on all sides, pressing in on the building, pressing in as if to reclaim the land from a civilization that had come to build, to develop, to intrude upon this mountainous forest. It was a small hospital, serving a mountain community made up of tourist attractions, ski areas, and, yes, casinos, the glitter and neon of the many storied resorts at great odds with the natural beauty of the area. Although small, the hospital offered all the usual services, an emergency room, its porte-cochere covered in snow from a recent new year's storm, small surgical suites, an orthopedic wing for the ubiquitous ski injuries that filtered in every winter. There were even two small wings of in-patient rooms for those too sick or injured to leave.

The date was February 15, the day after Valentine's Day, a holiday in this small community. Snow lay on the ground, mottled and dirt-streaked from being shoved around by the plows continually at work to keep the roads clear. Valentine's Day had fallen on a Saturday, and so Sunday was a quiet day for everyone, everyone except those who served the visitors in the casinos and ski areas. As such, the hospital parking lot was mostly empty, a few cars in the resident lot, one or two in the handicap zone, one truck in the loading zone, its engine running, its heater at work keeping out the winter cold, awaiting some lucky patient being discharged on this cold day.

Over in the emergency entrance several cars were parked haphazardly, as if their owners had arrived too quickly, not wanting to waste a moment by actually parking in a space. One of the cars had its engine still running, its lights on, as if abandoned by an owner too much in haste to actually bother with turning it off.

Inside, just off the emergency room entrance, was a short hallway that led to a cluster of small surgical suites. Only one was occupied. In this room, in the corner of this room, stood a man. He was average in build and height, mid-thirties, his clothes rumpled, his eyes red from lack of sleep, and his face lined but blank in expression, almost as if in shock. Before him was a flurry of activity, of energy and purpose, as others went about their tasks in an almost maniacal fashion.

It was this frantic activity that seemed to explain the jumbled parking scene outside.

Two groups of medical teams were at work, each one huddled over a surgical table. On one table, the one in the middle of the room, lay a woman... dying. And all around her the medical team scurried about, working against time, against nature, trying to save her, trying to stop, even reverse, the onset of finality, of ending, of death.

On the other table, the one over in a far corner of the room, lay another woman, no, not a woman... a baby girl. The little girl lay inert, immobile, not dying, but dead. And all about her the medical crew hovered and worked, trying to revive this little piece of life, trying to bring back the dead, to perform a miracle.

Words and commands flew across the room, like so many disoriented birds. The words and phrases flew this way and that, eventually reaching the ears of the man standing in the corner, standing rigid, fixed, immovable, watching, and, most importantly, listening, listening for any sign of encouragement, of a positive result, of hope.

"...I need more suction over here..."

"...there it is, another bleeder, cauterize that one next..."

"... where the hell's the sutures, I need more sutures..."

"...okay, let's entubate, we need to get oxygen in now..."

"...keep massaging the chest cavity, use small motions, not too much pressure, easy now…"

"…have you got a pulse yet? Check the monitor…"

For the man in the corner this was not an exercise, this was not some assignment or project. He had no duties to perform, no responsibilities, only to watch, to watch and wait, forgotten by everyone else in the room, alone, in a corner. For him this was life and death, the life, or death, of his family.

The little baby girl on the table in the corner was his daughter, born without life, her umbilical cord wrapped around her neck like a hangman's noose.

The woman on the table in the center of the room was his wife, and she was slowly bleeding to death.

Valentine's Day dawned clear and sunny, the sky an intense winter blue made more so by the passage of a cold front the night before. On the ground lay a shallow covering of new snow, a light dusting from the night's fast moving storm, a storm already off over the horizon and moving eastward towards the middle of the country. It was a lazy Saturday, and by noon the day had warmed up to an almost pleasant 50 degrees.

Three people sat at a cloth covered table in a cozy country inn. One was a man, blonde haired with clear blue eyes and a smile that seemed both impish and innocent. The other two were women. One was older, the mother of the young man sitting across from her. She was well built but large, the trim of her figure giving way to the sedentary lifestyle that sometimes comes with advancing age. The other was young and pretty, the wife of the young man at the table, her long hair, brown with a twinge of red, falling easily across her shoulders and down her back. She was visibly pregnant, obviously so and, if truth be told, it was not hard to conclude that she must be near term. In fact she was overdue by a few days.

The father-to-be had decided to take his "girls," his wife and mother, out for a drive in the country and to this small inn for brunch to celebrate the holiday, and, hopefully, the impending birth of his first child.

"I still can't believe," his mother said somewhat in jest, "in this day and age, that you chose not to find out whether you're having a boy or a girl. I certainly would want to know and it would have made the baby shower a lot easier to plan."

"True," he replied, "but I guess we're just being a little old-fashioned. We both like the idea of being surprised when it happens."

"If it happens," his wife said, the irritation in her voice plainly evident. "I don't think this child ever wants to come out into the world. She's gotten way too comfortable in there."

"You said she," he replied grinning, trying to lighten the mood. "How do you know it's a she? Did you find something out I don't know about?"

"Oh it's a she. Women just know these things. Don't ask me how, I just know. It's a she alright."

"So what are you going to name her, or him?" his mother asked. "You still haven't given me a clue and I'm dying to know. I gave you plenty of my suggestions."

"Well, we've decided, if it's a boy, we'll call him Christopher Allen."

"And if it's a girl?" she asked.

"Then we're going to call her Kathryn May, Katie May, Katie for short."

"Really," she replied with a rise in her voice. She was immediately pleased since Kathryn was her name. And May was the name of a favorite aunt, as well as the name of her daughter-in-law's paternal grandmother.

"That's wonderful," she exclaimed. "But why Christopher Allen? I know of no Christopher anywhere in either family."

"We just like the name" he replied. "And Allen is my middle name, as you well know since you gave it to me, even though no one else in our family is called that." He grinned, still trying to keep the mood light, although the pregnancy had definitely put a strain on all of them.

They had been married for not quite three years, this not-quite-so-young couple, still almost newlyweds, although they had lived together for three years before getting married. They met in the casino. He was a casino floor manager and she worked as a cocktail waitress on the casino floor.

He fell in love with her the first time he saw her. He had just transferred from a casino in the city down in the valley below the mountains. He knew few people and was just getting comfortable with his new surroundings and the demands of being a new manager in a new company. She was on a break, sitting in the employee dining room, her cocktail outfit wrapped tight across a body that was strong and lithe and feminine and exuded sex.

But it was not lust that drew him to her, not the appeal of her physical beauty. Not the raw sexiness of her outfit designed to visibly stimulate the gamblers on the casino floor. Rather, it was the way she looked, hair falling over her forehead into her eyes, a pencil lightly pressed against her lips, her face puckered up in concentration as she worked to write a letter to her mother. Yes, she was young and sexy and desirable, but to him she just seemed so vulnerable sitting there, so open and accepting, sitting on the cusp between being a little girl and being a woman.

She was the kind of girl-woman that any man would want to protect, to nourish, and yes, to marry. His heart went out to her immediately and he vowed to make her his alone. He did not say anything to her at that moment, did not approach her or interrupt her concentration. He simply sat, stared surreptitiously... and fell in love.

Later he would discreetly ask around, find out that no, she did not have a boyfriend, in fact had just ended a relationship, that she was single, available, and even knew mutual friends of his. That led to the opening he was looking for. Within a few days the opportunity arose.

She was sitting with an acquaintance, another waitress that had worked with him down in the city. He made his move, barged into their conversation, sitting at their booth without waiting to be invited, focusing on the mutual friend, playing it cool. But that was enough. Introductions were made, followed by small talk, meaningless nothings that are meant to pass time until the break is over. That was all that was needed.

From then on they could acknowledge each other, say "hi" in the hallway, make eye contact on the floor, nod, begin to develop a relationship. When he finally asked her out, it was easy, just an offhand comment. Would she like to see a movie, perhaps get a bite. She said yes, and the chase was on.

"Well," his mother said, breaking into his thoughts, "I for one can't wait for little Katie, if that's to be her name, to join us. Have you been having any contractions at all?"

"Trust me," replied the expectant mother, "I can't wait either. It feels like I've been pregnant forever. I could use a drink. I could use a smoke, and I don't even smoke. And I've been having the weirdest dreams, dreams I don't even want to mention in mixed company."

"That's not unusual," her husband replied. "But Mom, if she doesn't have the baby soon the doctor said they're going to induce labor."

"Yes, you should consider doing that right now," his mother replied with finality. "It's not good to wait so long." She unfortunately knew all the things that could go wrong, the horror stories from her training and years working as a nurse in hospitals throughout the country.

She had been a housewife and mother for many years, a country girl who did what was expected of her in those days. You found a man, got married, had babies, and took care of your family.

She married a doctor, a resident she met while working in the city. He was assigned to care for her brother, a young, strapping boy of a man who had to grow up too fast, who was in the war, the big war, saw the horror of it, and then returned to find he was stricken with a terminal illness. Returned to find a final irony, to find that what enemy bullets and bombs and grenades had not been able to accomplish, his body was quite capable of doing, of giving him a death sentence.

She moved to the city to take care of him and that is where she met the doctor. He swept her off her feet and married her, took her away to another state, another town, to start a medical practice and a family. They had four children, and when the last had grown and gone, they found, like so many others, that they had nothing left in common. They divorced.

It was then that she determined to make something else of her life. To change direction. She enrolled in college, a not so easy thing to do in your early forties. But she stuck it out, learned to study, learned to learn, and within six years she had a bachelor's degree and an RN license. With it she began to travel the world, working in one hospital after another, living almost like a vagabond going where she willed.

There was a great shortage of nurses then, and she had her pick of where to go and where to work. She spent some time on the coast, renting an apartment just steps from the beach, the sound of the waves lapping at her thoughts every night as she drifted off to sleep. She moved south of the border, lived and worked in an expatriate community offering medical care in a clinic. She took a job on an island, where the palm trees swayed, and coconuts fell every night outside her window, going plunk, plunk… plunk.

Then she got the call.

"Mom," her son said the moment she picked up the phone, "we're pregnant."

It was her first grandchild, and all of a sudden the travel and the excitement and the moving and more moving had lost its attraction. She left her island paradise and came back to help, to assist, to be a part of this new life that was building inside her daughter-in-law.

"You know," he remarked during a silence while the others ate, "it would be cool if she was born today, Valentine's Day. She would be a Valentine's baby, a love child."

"Don't even joke about it," his wife replied. "If I could have had her yesterday this would all be over and I could get back to some sense of normal."

She was worried, worried about the delivery of this, her first child. Worried about the pain, the uncertainty, what might happen. At thirty-five she was no longer young, at least in terms of bearing a first child, and she was scared about what lay ahead.

Oh, she wanted children, wanted them in the worst way. Not at first, but she knew that eventually she wanted a family. At first, their life together had been easy, and fun. They didn't marry right away. But by their second date they were practically living together, spending every night in each other's arms, the relationship building quickly and easily, as if each had somehow found their soul mate.

They moved in together within a few months, and for three years they lived and partied, drank and danced, and enjoyed nothing more than the thrill of being alive, in love, and without responsibility. And then, for her, it turned. She wondered. Where were they going? What was the ending to be like? Was this just another fling, another one night stand played out over the years? Heaven knows she'd had enough of those. Or was there to be permanence, marriage, family and all that implied.

There were arguments.

He ignored her, spent time with friends, or on the golf course, or out on his boat. She felt neglected. Discarded. Finally, she'd had enough. The ultimatum came in an act of defiance. She moved out, seeking either to get him to commit or let go. It's me and family and kids, or we give up and try again, somewhere else, with someone else. After all, she thought, my biological clock is ticking and I'm running out of time.

Slowly he came around, understood through the initial pain and hurt of her actions that he was the primary cause of it all, that the fault was with him. He hadn't wanted kids, hadn't wanted the responsibility. After all, he thought, what if they grow up to be assholes? What if I don't like them? What if I am simply not cut out to be a father? But time, and the hurt, and the potential loss of love, brought him to an understanding, to a life change, to a new path. He would woo her again, and this time for good.

They were married in the fall, in late September when the trees still had not changed colors, when the snows were still in abeyance, and the days were still warm and filled with the sun. They set up shop, bought a house, the usual newlywed stuff. They started hanging out with their married friends, getting into the swing of it, learning how to be more than just boyfriend and girlfriend. Kids could wait. Oh, not for long, but they could wait.

Then it happened. One month she was late. More importantly, for the first time in her life, she was not worried, not scared about being late, about what it might mean. This is it, she thought. It's time. He was apprehensive but happy. Okay, he said, here we go.

The pregnancy progressed normally. She quit drinking, quit partying, quit fighting the urge to nest. The nursery was fixed up, books were read. They attended birthing classes together, learning to breathe in unison, learning to feel the rhythm of her body. He placed his hand on her stomach when prompted, marveled over the kicks and jabs of this new life inside her. And for hours on end they would talk of what it would be like, how they would become the parents they wanted to be. How they would avoid their own parents' mistakes. And above all, they wanted a natural childbirth, a natural beginning for this new life.

The time came, the delivery date passed, and still no contractions, no start to the end of this phase of their new life as parents. The words Mom and Dad came easily to them, but it still wasn't quite real, still wasn't quite tangible, or wouldn't be, until the moment arrived.

"Oh."

It came out in not quite the normal way. More like a pause, as if she had been startled by a sudden noise.

And then "OH" again. Louder, more focused.

"What is it babe?" He had never quite seen that expression on her face before, something between fear, bewilderment, and hope.

"I think... no... I'm sure," she replied. "My water just broke."

The moment, the long awaited moment, the moment for which they had planned and thought and worked and studied for... the moment had arrived.

And of course, all that planning and work and study went right out the window.

"WHAT," he shouted. "Your water... what?"

"My water just broke." There was no panic in her voice, no fear now. Just acceptance, and perhaps a touch of determination.

"Okay, let's see, we need to go, no wait, I need to call, who, the hospital, no, the doctor, no... wait should I..." he was flailing around, standing, then sitting, his chair toppling to the floor, the other diners startled, looking at this young couple with the elderly lady, wondering what on earth was going on!

His mother on the other hand, was calm. And ready.

"Have you had any contractions yet?" she asked.

"No, well maybe, oops, yes, just now. Wow. That hurts!"

"Okay, no problem," she said, looking at her watch. "I want you to tell me when the next one starts. We should still have plenty of time. There's no need to rush… SIT DOWN!"

That last directed at her son, willing him to calm down, to act normally.

"You are going to get the car and bring it around to the front door of the inn," she said firmly. "I will stay with your wife and take care of the bill. Then we are going to drive to the hospital. They can notify your doctor. He should be standing by. He knows it's time, past time. Now get going."

He obeyed almost by instinct, with the routine of years, of having always obeyed his mother when she spoke in her mother's voice. It was only a matter of a few minutes before the car was at the front, the precious cargo loaded, the tires squealing in protest as he started out the driveway along the country road back to town. As he drove along, willing himself to calm down, to not speed, to behave responsibly and in control, at that moment, the thought occurred to him. Maybe it will be a Valentine's baby after all, a real love child.

Somehow though, that thought didn't make the drive any shorter.

Valentine's Day came, and went.

Now it was Sunday, a very early Sunday morning. They'd been up all night, the contractions coming and going, the rhythm off, the outcome uncertain. When the contractions started to wane they began to use Pitocin, a drug designed to induce or encourage more contractions and, finally, a birth. It worked somewhat, but not as well as her doctor would have liked. She was fighting it, fighting the process. Things were going slowly, perhaps not badly, but certainly slowly, more slowly than the doctor would like.

The drive to the hospital was uneventful, the contractions many minutes apart. He came screeching into the emergency room exit, and then, at his mother's urging, calmed down enough to open doors, assist with a wheelchair, getting the whole admission process started. The little hospital in the mountains had just finished building natural birthing rooms, with comfortable furniture, a couch, a TV, magazines on a rack. The colors of the room were earth-toned, warm and inviting, the furniture reminded him of his living room at home.

At first the process seemed normal enough. Nurses came and went, her vital signs were monitored, her contractions timed, a baby monitor inserted. Everyone was pleasant, positive, upbeat. This was a natural thing, something that happened all the time, millions of times, all over the world. There was nothing to worry about. The doctor was called, showed up fresh and ready and exuding confidence.

Time came, and time went. The contractions diminished, then started again. Then diminished. The Pitocin was started, then stopped, then started again. Midnight came. And went. And still the process continued, with no outcome, with no finishing, no completion. In the early morning hours she went into hard labor. Hour after hour the contractions hit, coming faster, and still the baby would not move, would not budge, would not give up its hold on this warm, comfortable womb it lived in.

All through the night the soon-to-be Dad held his wife, helped her breathe, felt through his own body her pain and suffering, not directly, but by proxy, willing himself to share in her ordeal.

The doctor began to lose patience. It had been a long afternoon, running into evening, running into night, and now the morning was soon to come. And still no baby. He motioned the expectant father aside for a chat.

"The baby's vital signs are still strong, but I don't like the way this is going," he began. "I don't want you to be alarmed, but at this point I think you two should give up the idea of a natural birth and we should consider surgery."

"Surg.. surgery," he stammered.

"Yes, surgery, a c-section. A cesarean."

He hesitated. His mind screamed yes, anything, just get this over with. But he was tired, and torn, and worried for what his wife would want, for what she would say.

"Let me speak with her," he finally replied.

"Okay, but don't take long. I need to prepare if that's the course we're going to take."

He turned back to his wife groaning and breathing through another contraction. He waited until it had subsided and then leaned in, whispering in her ear.

"Honey... baby..." he started, "the doctor says this has gone on long enough. He wants to do a c-section. He's asking for my permission. How are you? Can you decide? What do you want to do?"

"I don't know. Oh. OOOOH! Don't ask me now. Just decide. Can we... can we try once more... just one more time. Or yes, yes, let's just... yes," she said, "let's just get this over with. I can't take much more." She began to cry. "I just can't take much more." She had been in and out of hard labor for over twelve hours.

He turned and the doctor was there, the doctor heard. "Okay," he said, "I can try once more if you want. I am going to use forceps, but very gently. If this doesn't work we're going to move to a c-section. Alright?"

Numbly, he nodded in acquiescence.

"Okay Mom," the nurse began in her cheerfully professional tone. "Let's really push on this next one."

The doctor grabbed up the forceps, maneuvered them carefully into position, the next contraction almost upon them.

And then it happened.

An alarm pierced the air, its shrill notes dominating everything else in the room. The fetal monitor was screaming in protest, the baby's heartbeat was slowing, stopping.

"Oh god," the doctor exclaimed. "The cord's wrapped. We're going to have to go… NOW!"

The room exploded in activity. The expectant father was shoved aside as a wheeled stretcher was brought in and his wife was transferred to it in one swift, practiced motion by a pair of nurses who seemed to have appeared out of nowhere. "Code C" echoed harshly throughout the room from the overhead speaker.

"Code C stat. Emergency C-section. Code C Room 2!"

Now they were running down a hallway, the stretcher between them. Calls were being made, people summoned. It was a Sunday and there was no staff on site. They were all on call and had to rush to their cars, rush to the hospital, some of them running in at the last moment. There was a delay while the rooms were prepped. And then, without a general anesthetic, with only a local, the expectant mother was opened up, the motions of the doctor quick and practiced, the knife cutting through flesh without resistance, without care. She screamed once, more out of fear than anything else, and then fainted.

He followed the stretcher as it made its way to the operating room. He entered unnoticed. No one had time for him. No one had a thought for the expectant father standing alone, standing in a corner, out of the way, watching, waiting, taking it all in, his mind numbed and in shock from the events of the last hour, the long sleepless night, the breathing and contractions and managing the pain as he held his wife.

The incision was made, the baby retrieved, the umbilical cord wrapped, like some relentless boa constrictor, around her tiny neck. And then the two medical teams, finally assembled, finally ready, began their real work, began to repair damage, began the task of restoring life to one, and preserving life in another.

As they worked, time seemed to stand still. His mind wandered. Being the son of a doctor he was not unfamiliar with operating rooms. He'd seen his share. He'd even worked in a hospital while going to school and during his summer breaks. He'd taken a job in high school as an orderly in the radiology department of his father's hospital, mopping up vomit, running errands, learning whenever possible how to take an x-ray, develop it, examine it for the proper lighting and angle and view. He eventually learned enough, and got good enough, to take on a role as a full-fledged x-ray technician.

He worked on call. Worked in the emergency room. Worked in the wards. He would be called to take pictures of injuries and accidents, people whose limbs had been torn from their bodies.

He'd even once had to x-ray a corpse down in the morgue. A man had been shot and killed. The bullet pierced his aorta and he bled out in a matter of minutes. The bullet, continuing its inexorable path through the soft tissues, finally lodged in the man's spinal cord. During the autopsy the pathologist was not able to find it, to retrieve it for evidence in the case. He'd been called to x-ray the man's spine, to find the bullet so it could be extracted.

Carefully he lifted the man's body to place film beneath, lifting a body whose chest cavity had been emptied, a cavity that lay out before him like an empty vessel. He had never actually, until now, been able to see firsthand what he was taking a picture of. Bones and organs and joints had always been covered in a sheath of flesh and muscle and living tissue. But there it was, the spine, laid out in all its glory. Laid bare by the pathologist's careful extraction of all vital organs during the autopsy.

He almost vomited. But his training took over and he did what he had to do. He took the picture. The bullet was retrieved. The court case was made.

It was this experience, this texture, which kept him anchored in the corner of the surgical suite, kept him conscious and aware of all that was going on, rather than running to wait it out in some deserted waiting room. It was this experience from his past that made the scene before him, if not easier, at least bearable. And so he watched and waited, and let the scene play itself out.

"Okay," one doctor replied, the one in charge of his wife's care, "she's stable. Let's get her to post-op. Then I'll want her in Intensive Care for at least the next 12 hours and I want her vitals monitored every fifteen minutes. There still may be some internal bleeding and I want to be called if there is any change in her numbers, any change at all."

"Yes sir," the surgical assistant replied.

Then she was gone, whisked out of the room almost as quickly as she had been brought in. At that moment the doctor noticed him standing in the corner. He came over quickly and, although brusque, his manner seemed kindly.

"Sir, I need you to come with me. There's nothing more you can do here. Your wife is stable and they're moving her to post-operative care. She's going to be alright, but you won't be able to see her for some time. They're doing all they can for your baby. They have a pulse and the baby is breathing with help. We'll know more later. I want you to come to the waiting room and sit down. Someone will bring you something to drink. Do you want something to eat while you wait?"

"No… no, thank you," he managed to say. "I would like something to drink though. Thank you. Some water. Maybe some coffee."

He turned to follow the doctor into an adjoining small room. There were chairs, a couch, some magazines, the usual detritus of a hospital waiting room. He was sitting as the doctor turned to leave when he remembered something, something important, something he needed to know right then.

He stood up straight and stiff as the thought struck him, struck him like a thunderbolt, made him stammer and almost fall. He righted himself, turned, and called after the doctor.

"Doc," he cried, his voice sounding hoarse, unnatural in the confines of the small room. "Doctor?"

The doctor turned.

"Yes."

"What was it... I mean... what is it?"

"I beg your pardon. "

"The baby. Our baby. What is it? A boy... or a girl?"

"Oh, congratulations," he answered wearily, absently, "you have a brand new baby girl."

The doctor turned and strode out of the room.

The hours seemed to fly by without resistance, without pause. It had been early morning when the fetal alarm sounded in the birthing room, almost mid-day when he collapsed in the waiting room. Now it was approaching evening and the time seemed to slow, to crawl, to creep inexorably towards some conclusion he couldn't fathom.

He wandered from the waiting room to ICU and back to the waiting room. He could not see his wife in the intensive care unit, could not enter her room or speak to her, but he could see where she lay, see the machines above her winking and chattering and letting the world know she was alive, alive and getting better, getting stronger.

At some point the pediatric surgeon appeared as if from out of thin air, his manner direct but measured, his face and body sagging from weariness. This doctor was unknown to him, had arrived in a rush and gone right to work without the formality of an introduction or even a glance. But now he was smiling somewhat, and took the time to introduce himself.

"I'm the pediatric surgeon on call. I've been directing the team working on your daughter."

Your daughter. The words sounded alien to him. My daughter, yes, I have a daughter, or had a daughter. He focused, straining to hear the doctor's next words, the next words that would mean the world to him. Was he to be a parent, father of a brand new baby girl? Or was he to be a mourner, preparing for a funeral, making the arrangements, going through the hellish moments, the days, the weeks, the months of mourning.

"Your daughter is alive," were the doctor's next words. "Very much alive. She is breathing on her own, her heartbeat is good and we have taken her to a special neo-natal intensive care room. It's not far and in a moment I can take you to see her. But first, I would like a few moments to speak with you."

I would like a few moments. To speak. With you. The words reverberated in his brain. They sounded ominous, like a lover stating after a romantic quarrel that everything is okay… but we NEED TO TALK.

"Would you like some coffee? Something else to drink?" the doctor asked.

"No," he replied. "No, I'm fine. What is it? Please, what is it you want to say?"

"Let's sit down, shall we?" The doctor turned. "Over here is fine."

They sat. The doctor paused. And then he began to speak.

"First, before you see your daughter, I want you to understand what has happened. You see, the umbilical cord wrapped around her neck, cutting off the flow of oxygen to her body and brain. When this happens the body tends to shut down, to conserve, to send all of the remaining oxygen to the brain, to protect it and try to preserve life. That's what happened with your daughter."

He continued to speak, to lecture actually. There was a lot to say, a lot of information to process. The body had shut down, the oxygen being sent only to the brain. The heart slowed, vital signs weakened. At that point it was simply a matter of time. Can the newborn be retrieved and her heart and breathing be restored in time to bring her back to life, back to health?

Too much time and the baby dies. If they can get the baby in time, well then it is a matter of how much damage was done. Without oxygen, nitrogen builds up in the muscles, like the bends suffered by a diver surfacing too fast from too great a depth. And the nerves, the nerves that carry the electrical signals to and from the brain, without oxygen they become damaged, they shrivel and die. And nerves cannot be regenerated.

Then there is the danger of seizures. Seizures will damage the brain, damage the organs, cause damage that can last throughout a person's entire life. Even shorten that life and make it not worth living. And, if too much time passes, the brain itself is damaged. Without oxygen the brain suffers, withers away, dies.

The doctor talked and he listened, trying to take it in, understand what he could.

"Your daughter has been very fortunate. As far as we can tell she has suffered no seizures during her ordeal. This is good news," the doctor continued. "Although it could still happen, with every hour the likelihood of her suffering seizures or permanent brain damage greatly decreases. We are monitoring her for that now. There could be nerve damage, muscle damage, possibly brain damage. We just don't know at this point. But without having suffered any seizures, and with a strong heartbeat and her breathing restored to normal, we are very optimistic. As soon as we feel she is completely stable, perhaps within a few hours, we'll send her to a pediatric intensive care unit at the hospital down in the city. They have far more extensive facilities than we have and can better care for her. A helicopter has been put on standby and we'll be using that to get her there as quickly as possible."

The doctor paused to let all he had said sink in.

"So, so you're optimistic." He was finally getting focused,

centered, his senses coming back to him. "She's going to be okay."

"So far," the doctor replied, "but only time will tell what damage has been done. That's all I can really tell you at this time. Would you like to see her now?"

He nodded, numbed, not trusting himself to speak.

They both rose, the doctor leading the way out into a hallway, down to a door leading into an anteroom. Just before entering the doctor turned and once again spoke

"Before you see her, I need to tell you something. You see, without oxygen your daughter's muscles have built up large amounts of nitrogen. It takes a while to flush that nitrogen out. It is very painful, and we cannot at this time give her any kind of sedative or painkiller. I want you to be prepared. She's in a great deal of pain and will continue to be in pain for quite some time."

Then they entered the anteroom, a glass partition dividing it from a small room filled with medical equipment, tables, gauges, IVs and, in the center, a small raised platform, a baby's bed. He peered closer, his nose almost pressing against the glass dividing the two small rooms. And then he saw her, really saw her for the first time, his daughter, a tiny bundle lying naked, heat lamps hovering above the bed to keep her warm. She was screaming, screaming from the very bottom of her lungs to the roof of her mouth. Screaming in pain as her body tried to rid itself of the nitrogen, tried to rid itself of this poison that was causing such unrelieved agony. Her muscles seemed to tense and strain, and then relax, and then tense again, as if going through a never-ending series of spasms.

"Oh my god," he exclaimed. "Can't you give her anything for the pain?"

"I told you, no," the doctor replied. "She has to go through this without drugs. The risk of using painkillers is far too great."

He stood there for what seemed like hours, but was probably only minutes, watching her, watching her scream and shake and shiver. It seemed only a few minutes before, in the operating room, that she had laid still, lifeless, no movement at all. And now her whole body was wracked with spasms, heaving and recoiling from the pain.

He thought to himself, what an awful way to be brought into the world. This, her first few hours of life outside the womb, in the world she must learn to live in, to spend these first few hours in agony, screaming, shrieking. How is this going to affect her? How is this going to impact whatever the rest of her life will be?

He stayed as long as he could, and then fled the room, fled to the hallway, fled back to the waiting room to throw himself down on a chair, to will himself to keep control, to stop the tears that by now were flowing down his cheeks. He had been stoic, controlled, outwardly calm throughout the whole ordeal. And now the raw pain of it surfaced, took over, rushed to overwhelm him.

He sat in that room for a long time, his whole body numb, unable to move. And softly, somewhat gently, the tears continued to flow across and down his face.

Eventually he gained control of himself, began to focus again. He got up and returned to the intensive care ward where his wife was resting. By then they were able to let him enter the room, sit at her bedside, hold her hand. She was not conscious, but her vital signs were strong. She would be okay, they reassured him. "A quick recovery," one said. "She'll be up and walking in a few days." But still he found it hard to believe, to trust in their optimism.

After a while he again ventured into the pediatric ward to see his daughter. She was still crying, but the screams he had seen before were lessened. Her body no longer tensed and strained against the pain, her muscles no longer shook. But still she cried, cried through the pain as it slowly worked its way out of her body.

Then it was time for her to go, for her to move to the hospital in the city. Preparations were made. The baby was wrapped and covered. Her IVs and monitoring equipment were converted to mobile units that could travel with her. He was invited to tag along, to watch the process, although he still had not even had the luxury of touching her, of acknowledging her existence with the most basic of human senses, a touch, a caress, physical contact.

The events seemed to rush at him. One moment she was lying naked in a warmed bed, then wrapped in a protective cloth. Now they were outside, the cold, night air biting at the exposed skin. For it had gotten quite dark on this Sunday night, this day after Valentine's Day, this end to a weekend that had started so calmly, so quietly, so peacefully. The helicopter was standing by, blades quiet and its engine shut off for the loading procedure. The baby was placed carefully in the cabin, straps tightened to make her secure, the medical team finishing last minute preparations, taking their seats and strapping themselves in.

He watched, too numb to feel the cold, as the blades slowly started turning, the engine whirling to life, the wind whipping at his clothes. The pilot leaned forward, his hand lifting levers, turning knobs. The blades quickened their pace, the helicopter rose a few inches, seemed to hover for a moment, and then turned and, swiftly, very swiftly, lifted into the sky and vanished into the darkness.

He turned and walked slowly away. It was quiet again and he was alone, all alone. One foot after another he walked, began the trip back to an empty home, to an empty bed. The sky was still and blank, and he too, like the helicopter, vanished into the dark.

What We Don't Know

The office was large, grey, and sterile. Chairs and desks were left-over government-issue, slate grey metal gleaming against the yellow linoleum of the age-worn floor below. A few pictures hung from the faded yellow walls and the room was faced with two small windows, grime-caked and dirty, overlooking a small courtyard from the second-story of the hospital where the office was located.

This was a big hospital, the city hospital, the finest medical facility within 500 miles of anywhere. The office was at the center of a pediatric and neo-natal intensive care center that was state-of-the-art, its reputation spread far and wide across the western half of the country.

Although the facilities were old and worn, the equipment inside was modern and new and gleaming, the staff well-trained, the doctors at the head of their field. It was a teaching hospital as well. Interns and residents came from far and wide to learn the latest in the care and feeding of infants whose entry into the world had not gone all that well.

Seated at the main desk in this second-story office was a doctor, and he was speaking. "We just don't know," he said with a great deal of seriousness.

Before him sat a couple, their faces lined with worry, their posture stiff and possessed of uncertainty. The doctor leaned forward, fixing the couple with his eyes, eyes that twinkled behind the tired and lined face.

"We just don't know," he repeated.

The baby girl arrived in the night, brought by helicopter from the little hospital in the mountains, its blades beating furiously at the air as it seemed to appear out of nowhere, out of the darkness and into the harsh light of the helipad behind the emergency room entrance.

There a medical team was waiting, their plans made, their equipment at the ready. The baby girl was transferred quickly, her body wrapped in blankets against the cold of the night. She was placed on a stretcher and wheeled into the emergency entrance where a neonatal cart was waiting. She was quickly hooked up to lifelines, the equipment monitoring her vital functions, the IVs keeping her hydrated and fed, the sensors ready to warn of trouble with their shrill alarms.

She was wheeled into the neonatal intensive care center and installed in the corner of a room with three other newborns. One, a baby boy, had been born premature, almost fifteen weeks early, and was struggling to survive. Another, a baby girl born seemingly healthy, had gone into cardiac arrest when only a few hours old and would not survive another day, her heart too small and full of holes to sustain her tiny body. The third, also a girl, was suffering through withdrawal of the drugs her unfortunate mother had taken while pregnant, drugs that addict and enslave without regard for the health of the child to be.

It was into this world that the little girl named Katie was brought. She was stabilized, charts were filled-out, initial measurements taken, benchmarks against the future when she would hopefully leave this room to begin her new life.

On the walls surrounding these three babies were pictures. They were taped and pinned to the wall in no particular order. Some were Polaroids, some were on shiny Kodak paper from a local photo lab, some were simply printed out on paper from a computer printer. They all had one thing in common. They were all pictures of smiling children. Some were in wheelchairs, some standing, some running, some jumping. But they were all smiling and waving at the camera.

They were the survivors, past residents of this room who had lived and grown and thrived. They had made it, and their pictures were testimony to their success.

Many of the photos were written on, written in ink and magic marker, written in crayon, notes of "thanks," and "miss you," and "all is well." They were placed there, these pictures on the wall, for a reason. They were, simply put, hope. Hope for all who inhabited the room, for the workers who toiled in the room, for the parents who visited, for the relatives who came to look. Hope that all would be well, that one day these babies wrapped in their cocoons would someday emerge and grow and thrive, and then take a picture to be sent in, to be included on this wall, to become a part of this collage of hope.

It was in this environment that the newest addition slept, her body twitching fitfully, perhaps from the remnants of the pain that had wracked her body for so many hours, perhaps simply from the memory of that pain, still fresh, still real, in her tiny mind. Her vital signs were stable, her breathing measured and steady.

"Go ahead and insert the feeding tube,." ordered the chief technician on duty. It was early in the morning, not quite past 3 AM. "I want a slow bi-carb push and we'll need to draw another blood spec."

"Right away," her assistant replied.

"She's a fighter this one," remarked the chief technician. "She's a fighter."

"Yes," the assistant replied. "The flight nurse was telling me she was still screaming in pain when they flew her in. She's still shedding the nitrogen. Do you want another blood gas to check the levels before morning?"

"I do," the chief replied, "And we need to keep a close watch on the monitors. As long as she doesn't have a seizure we've got a chance. But I don't like the way she's responding, or rather not responding. I don't like the rigidity. You need to mark that on the chart."

"You mean…"

"Yes, I mean… that. Watch her closely and have the team on alert. The next twenty-four hours will be critical."

"And after that?"

"After that, we'll just have to see. Only time will tell."

In the corner sat an empty wheelchair. The chief technician stared at it for a moment, considering it, wondering if it were an omen. She knew what was at stake. What the possibilities were.

"Only time will tell," she said again… mostly to herself.

Katie's father returned home after the helicopter vanished into the night, returned home alone, his wife asleep in her hospital bed, his new daughter lost somewhere in the night sky. The house was dark, empty, quiet. As he prepared for bed, went through his nightly routine without thinking, his mind numb, his body wracked with fatigue, he thought to himself how sleep would probably not come, how the night would be a long one.

As if to surprise him, his body took another direction. He fell into an immediate, deep, dreamless sleep.

The next few days seemed like a blur as he dealt with all the issues the Valentine's Day weekend had wrought. There were visits to his wife, calls to the family members, both his and hers. There were calls to the city, to the big hospital, to check on the condition of his newborn. There was work to deal with, returning to the comfort of his job, of the routine that he hoped would bring him back to some sense of normalcy.

But even at work there were questions to answer, people to deal with, explanations to be made. And through it all it seemed that, regardless of whatever else there was to say, the only thing he really said, kept repeating to all, was the simple phrase… "…we just don't know."

We will know soon though, he thought. The doctors will be able to tell us and this will all be over. Life will return to normal, or to what he thought should be normal for this time in his life, this time of becoming a father, a parent.

He talked it over with his wife. They spoke to the hospital in the city. They agreed they would wait to go down together, when she had recovered enough to leave the hospital and travel. The next time they saw their new daughter it would be… together.

It would take almost two weeks for that to happen. During that time, his mother became invaluable. She shuttled back and forth, back and forth, between the little hospital in the mountains and the big hospital in the city, her medical training being put to good use, her ability to translate and interpret so helpful in getting them to understand what was happening.

She had not been present during the birth. She had been tired and, being older, had retired on Valentine's Day night to sleep, assuming then that she would awaken the next morning to news of her grandchild's birth. Instead she had discovered what happened, leapt into action, pleased only in that she could now be of real and substantial help to her son, her daughter-in-law, and yes, her new grandchild.

The day came when his wife could go home. She was wheeled out to the curb, weak, tired, but alive. And getting stronger with every day.

She settled into a simple routine at home, talking with relatives, taking it easy, trying to hide the worry, the fear, the sick feeling that somehow she was at fault, that she had done something… something wrong, to cause this tragedy. She prayed every day that the baby would be alright. Vowed to be the best mother she could, to give this child every ounce of her being to make sure she was alright, that she would have… a good life. But, like her husband, she often found herself muttering the same words… "…we just don't know. We don't know what the future will bring. What we will have to do. What we will be faced with."

It was hard living under such uncertainty. Occasionally they snapped at each other, had words. They didn't exactly fight, but they fenced and sparred, each one trying to hide their fears. He refused to fight, conscious of her raw nerves, her belly still swollen and encased in bandages laid over fresh stitches, stitches that held her insides together. She was sore and swollen and still physically miserable.

They felt a separation, a feeling of being apart, being isolated for the first time since they reconciled and got married. And without the ability to touch, to hold her, hug her, cuddle with her in bed at night due to her swollen body, he felt the separation grow worse, more intense with every hour, with every day that passed. And he sensed her worry, her guilt, that she was somehow at fault, that she caused this tragedy.

The day was fast approaching when they would drive to the hospital in the city, and it was then she felt compelled to speak, to bring up what they had only, until now, been thinking.

"I want to talk with you," she said the evening before they were to go. "I don't want to go down there without having an understanding with you about…" She hesitated. "About all of this."

"What do you mean," he asked, knowing full well what she meant.

"I mean us," she replied. "We can't keep doing this. We have to be on the same page. We have to be… to be together in this."

"I know," he replied sadly. "I don't want to fight. I don't want to be this way."

"I didn't do this," she blurted out. "This isn't my fault."

"No, no, no. It's no one's fault. I don't blame you. I don't... I don't know. It just all happened so fast. There really isn't anyone to blame. It just... it just happened."

There was a pause.

"I'm scared," she said finally. "We're scared and we don't know what to do and we're taking it out on each other. I want it to stop."

"Listen," he replied. "I was there, I was there through it all. I saw, I lived it. You almost died. I was scared too. But I saw what you went through... can't believe it. Can't believe you. I'm so proud, so..." He struggled with the words.

And then it came to him.

Grateful.

"I am just so... grateful."

The word flew between them. Then he knew, knew that she knew as well. This would not go away. This would not just melt into nothingness. This would be between them for the rest of their lives. It would have to be dealt with. There would be issues. There would be trials. There would be disagreements and fights. And they would have to be strong, he thought to himself.

But of one thing he was sure. He remembered her on the gurney, her face tightened in pain, her body exhausted, the sweat pouring off of her. He remembered the long hours and the scream she uttered when the surgeon's knife pierced her belly with nothing more than a local anesthetic to comfort her.

And at that moment he knew. Knew commitment. Knew purpose. And he vowed to himself to never leave her. Through the fights to come, through the hard times and the challenges, through it all, he would support her and stand by her and never leave her.

There was love between them now, shared love made stronger by their trial. They could feel it. And there was fear, fear of the unknown, fear of the future. And above all else there was one other thing, one thing that possessed his entire being.

He would always be grateful.

⚜

The day dawned sunny and clear again. Another winter day with almost spring-like temperatures and a sky so blue as to be almost painful. It was the day. THE day. The first day they would see, really see, their new daughter.

The drive to the hospital seemed to take forever, each of them silent, wondering, what would they see? What would they find out? This trip was their future, was their future in a way that no other event in their life had been. They were going to see their new child, and they were going to hear just what that would mean to them for tomorrow, and the next day, and for the rest of their lives.

So they didn't speak, just drove and wondered. And through it all they felt not alone anymore. They felt unified, coupled with a bond stronger than any that had existed so far in their short time together.

The hospital was big, and at first they got lost. But eventually they found their way to the right wing, the right room. Slowly they walked in, noticed the tiny beds with their tiny cargo. There were now only two babies in the neonatal care unit, the preemie and their new daughter.

The first thought that occurred to them was that she seemed so… so normal. She was laying quietly, her eyes open and searching, wandering from one face to the other, checking out these new faces, these new people in her world. She reached out with one tiny hand, one tiny arm, to her mother, not knowing it was her mother, not knowing who or what she was. Reached out, and then it happened.

She smiled… and the world fell away.

The new parents stood and stared, amazed. This smile was different, strange coming from one so tiny and new. It was full and knowing, it was mischievous, it ebbed and flowed, it possessed the entire room, consumed the very air they were breathing.

It was tiny, and yet it was huge.

And at that moment, the fear, the uncertainty, the future... vanished. There was only this day, this moment. That's what the smile told them.

They felt filled with warmth, and love, and hope. That smile said it all. That smile seemed to say, "Hi guys, where you been?" and "Everything is going to be alright."

It was the smile that did it.

It was the smile.

And it made them smile, made them laugh out loud. It broke the ice, broke the tension, broke everything. They smiled and laughed, reached out to touch their daughter, to hold her gently through the IV tubes and machine monitors. To hold her and talk to her, to coo sweet baby things, things neither of them ever thought they would say.

It felt so natural, like it was supposed to be. Like the events of the past two weeks had simply melted into nothingness.

It was the smile that did it.

THE smile.

They spent the next few days in the city. There was a large casino with a multi-story hotel tower that offered very good rates on a standard room. At least that's what they were told. But when they checked in later that first day, after they spent several hours with their new daughter and her beautiful smile, they were told there was a problem.

"I'm sorry folks," the front desk clerk said resignedly. "but there's a problem with your reservation."

"Oh no," they both thought to themselves. "Not now, not after what we just experienced. Not... NOW!"

"Yes," the clerk went on. "Your reservation was for one of our rooms with a special mid-week rate and we don't have any left. They've all been given out."

"You've got to be kidding," he replied with alarm. "None? Are you telling me you are completely sold-out?"

"Not completely, but almost. We have two conventions in, and three unexpected busloads of gamblers from out of state showed up. That's who got the rooms you were supposed to have."

"Well, that's not our fault. Please, can't you do something? We've just come from our daughter's hospital room. You see she was born… born with trouble." He just couldn't bring himself to go into details. "This is the first time we've even gotten to see her… hold her. Please tell me you can do something?"

The hotel clerk looked at the couple standing in front of her, saw the worry, saw the lined faces, sensed the trials and tribulations they'd been through. In that moment her heart went out to them.

"I'm a fairly new mother myself," she said. "I'm sure we can take care of you. Just give me a moment."

The clerk returned within a few minutes.

"I have you all set. I just got approval to upgrade you, and at no charge. We have a small honeymoon suite available. It's really nice with two rooms and a great view. I know you'll love it. Would that be acceptable?"

"Well, sure," he gulped. "We'll take it. We'll take anything at this point."

The deed was done, the credit card swiped, the keys given out. They took their small overnight bags and made their way to the elevator through the throngs of bustling gamblers all hurrying from one point to another, one machine or table to another, seeking fun and excitement, bent on another encounter with chance, and oblivious to the couple moving through them like wraiths.

The elevator ride was swift, there was no one else onboard and they reached their floor quickly. They made their way down the hallway to the front of a double door with lettering carved into the wood and highlighted in gold leaf, signifying to all that this was no ordinary hotel room, that this was a suite.

"Oh my," she said, "this must be quite a room."

"It is," he replied, smiling. "It is the Honeymoon Suite my dear, and just for us. Don't you feel like a newlywed again?"

He put the key in the lock, turned the handle, opened the door and held it for her. She stepped in, he followed, and then they both froze, neither one able to move.

There, in front of them, lay the main room of the honeymoon suite. It was decked out in gold lace, and fancy red wallpaper. And in the center of the room was a heart-shaped bed, a waterbed covered in plush brocaded slip covers and quilts. A canopy hung around the bed, with drapes flowing in folds along the contour of the bed frame.

And there, above the bed, affixed to the ceiling, shining and polished, as if awaiting the anticipated arrival of newlyweds with only one thing on their minds, was a mirror, a beautiful full length mirror.

Instantly he thought of his wife's tender belly, the stitches from her surgery carefully covered in gauze and tape, her belly distended and her whole body tender and raw for the past two weeks. He turned to her, a big grin slowly spreading across his face. "Welcome to the honeymoon suite my dear," he said.

"Don't even think about it," she replied.

The next few days were filled with visits to their daughter interspersed with visits to doctors and the reading of reports.

The first meeting was the most daunting. They were sitting in another office, with unwashed windows, the window shades hanging unevenly as if forgotten by some late night cleaning person, the sun filtering between the blinds to play in random patterns upon the far wall. The doctor had been precise but somber in his remarks.

"The patient of course suffered from extreme perinatal asphyxia at birth. A lack of oxygen, lowered heartbeat, no respiratory activity." He droned on. "Her apgar scores at birth were basically zero. She was born, for all intents and purposes, without life. Resuscitation was performed, a heartbeat established and respiratory function restored. Luckily, the patient was nine pounds and nine ounces at birth, giving her a far better chance of survival. A preemie would have been lost at that moment."

They listened, trying to understand. The doctor's sterile use of the words "the patient," his manner that of one who was simply reading from a report or chart, bothered them, but they said nothing. They were focused, trying to understand.

"What you have to realize is that while stable and apparently healthy now, the patient has certainly suffered neurological damage as a result of the oxygen deprivation. Nerve damage, possibly other damage, we won't know much more for some time."

"But she's alright," he blurted out. "She will be able to go home with us. We were told…" his voice trailed off.

"Of course," the doctor replied, but there was a seriousness, a finality in his voice. "She will be able to go home with you. But you must understand there are complications, issues to watch for. Our diagnosis for now is that the patient has a form of rigidity that might be cerebral palsy… nerve damage, possibly brain damage."

It was not the first time they had heard those words, heard cerebral palsy. But it was the first time they had heard them here. The first time they had heard them in reference to "the patient," to their daughter.

The room grew quiet. It seemed they'd been given a death sentence. Visions of wheelchairs, invalids, sanatoriums, special wards flew through their minds in unison, as if they were imagining them as one person.

"Of course you will get far more information at the final briefing before you take the patient home." Again he used the words "the patient," and those words grated on their ears. "That's all I'm prepared to say at this point. When we process her out you can meet with the chief and ask your questions."

Finally the day came, the day when they could take their daughter home. Once again they found themselves in another doctor's office.

The Chief, as he was referred to affectionately by all who knew him, was a kindly man. He had been practicing pediatric medicine for well over 40 years. His face was tired and lined, his shoulders stooped, but his eyes were alive and bright, they twinkled with excitement, as if in possession of some secret known only to them.

He was head of pediatrics at the hospital, the top man in his field, well-versed in counseling and, he often thought, educating anxious young parents as to the conditions plaguing their newborn babies.

Now, sitting across from him, were the new parents of the little girl brought to the hospital several days ago. They looked both rested and tired, alert and dazed, understanding but not comprehending. It was all too new, too strange, too far outside their expectations for what should be happening now, as parents of a newborn.

They weren't supposed to be here, the chief thought to himself. Weren't supposed to be learning about seizures and oxygen deprivation, immune systems and bodily functions. They were supposed to be changing diapers and learning how to survive without sleep. They were supposed to be feeding and cleaning, holding and hugging, and showing off their new addition to a world of family and friends.

And none of that was happening. Instead, they were sitting in this room, this office, in this hospital, in a city in which they did not live, talking to strangers, listening to doctors and specialists and staff members, trying to piece it all together. Trying to make sense of it all. Trying to… understand!

"I want you to know," the chief began, "that your daughter has responded wonderfully. Her signs are strong and so far we have not found anything physically to alarm us. She is growing stronger with every day."

But then he turned serious.

"And now I must speak to you about the future."

Here it comes, they thought. The future. The bad news.

"We believe your daughter has a condition we call cerebral palsy. While this diagnosis is usually made later when developmental abnormalities surface, the rigidity of her muscles and muscle tone coupled with the circumstances surrounding her birth lead us to this conclusion. While there are many causes of this, and many we cannot explain, your daughter's form of cerebral palsy is due to oxygen deprivation at birth. I believe this has already been explained to you. The body shuts down and sends what little oxygen it gets to the brain to try and protect it. That is what happened in this case. Should the brain suffer seizures, then the damage can be quite far-reaching. However, this did not happen to your daughter and so we are hopeful. It may have resulted in a form of damage we call spastic, or athetoid, cerebral palsy."

"What does this mean?" he continued, "Spasticity refers to the inability of a muscle to relax, while athetosis refers to an inability to control the movement of a muscle. Infants who at first are hypotonic like your daughter, may later develop spasticity."

"Of course at this point all of this is academic. For all intents and purposes your daughter is behaving like a normal infant. Spastic or athetoid cerebral palsy conditions, as well as any brain impairment, will only become apparent as she grows and begins to go through the different stages of her development. These stages, unfortunately, may be affected. She will not develop in what we would call a normal fashion."

"But for now, we are going to recommend that you treat her as a normal baby with a few exceptions. All of this will be written up for you so you can take the necessary precautions. And of course we will recommend a regular interval of follow-up visits, and there will probably be a need for certain physical, respiratory and vocal therapy regimens."

The chief paused to let all that he had said sink in. There was a long and a great silence in the room. Finally, the new father spoke.

"This, this cerebral palsy," he stammered. "What does it mean for her growth. Will she be able to walk?"

"We don't know," the chief replied.

"Will she be able to talk?"

"Probably, but how well… we just don't know."

"Will she be able to ride a bike?"

"We don't know."

"Drive a car?"

"We don't know."

"Go to school? Learn like other kids?"

"We don't know."

He looked at his wife, struggling, wondering. She looked back with a blank stare, as if uncomprehending the magnitude of what they were being told.

"So she may be in a wheelchair for the rest of her life?"

"We don't know," the chief replied again, patiently. And then his voice changed, became deeper, became stern and implacable.

"Young man, I want you to listen, and listen carefully. You've been given a gift. Your daughter is alive. She is healthy in all basic respects. As to what she will be able to do, or not do, what kind of life she will have, we don't know. In reality, no one knows. Regardless of how a baby is brought into this world, things happen, things beyond our control. A perfectly healthy baby all of a sudden develops blindness, or deafness, or a heart condition. Medicine is as much an art as it is a science and there are many things we simply do not know. We can predict. We can prognosticate, we can guess. But we are not psychics. We cannot know the future."

He paused for just a moment, took a deep breath, and continued.

"My best advice to you is this. You two are going to have to take each day as it comes. For the recovering alcoholic, every day is a new opportunity to not drink. And for you, every day is a new opportunity to help your daughter learn to live in this world in whatever manner she was meant to live. If she shows any signs of being able to do something, something simple, like kneeling, or standing, or yes, even walking, then by all means help her, push her, help her to gain whatever abilities she can, whatever they may be. And rejoice in that. Be thankful and understand that there is no one way, no ideal condition in this world, only what we are capable of, and what we are given. Your daughter has been given life. Use it to make her strong in whatever she can do. Never deny her."

He paused and then continued, his words rushing at them like a river.

"Do not coddle her. Do not shield her from the world. For in whatever ways she manages to fall down while going through her life, it will only be her ability to pick herself up, in any way she can, that will make her life worth living. You won't always be there for her. Do you understand?"

"I, I think so," her father replied after a long pause. "Yes, we understand."

"Good, then take your daughter home and forget about the future. The only thing that matters is right now, today, and then tomorrow, and then the day after. One day at a time."

"She's alive and healthy. But as for the rest of it…" he said simply, "well, we just don't know."

School Buses and Other Things

"**Y**ou need to come home... NOW!"

It was late afternoon. The shadows were just beginning to lengthen and grow, the light through the window beginning to dim. He was sitting in his office, going over paperwork, when the phone rang.

Perhaps it was his imagination, or a reflection in hindsight, but he seemed to remember that the ring had a certain urgency to it, a tone, frantic and demanding. It seemed to say "you need to answer me now."

He picked up the receiver and heard his wife's voice on the other end.

"You need to come home now," she said. "Right away."

He noticed immediately the urgency in her voice, the insistence. But there was no alarm, no fear or panic, and so he remained calm.

"I need to come home now," he repeated. "Honey, I'm still working. I've got more here to wrap up. Besides, it's still early."

"I don't care. You're the boss, you don't have to ask. Just come home now."

Still he hesitated.

"Please, oh please, oh please, please," she said. She was practically begging. "I need you to come home now, as quickly as you can. Believe me, you'll thank me. Just come home."

She hung up abruptly and he was left to ponder what that was all about. But he was a realist and he understood that the right path of action was to, well, to come home now. Married life was certainly teaching him things he never learned in school.

So he wrapped up what he was doing, did it quickly, and hurried to the parking lot. It was only a matter of a few minutes before he was winding through the streets of the small town in the mountains, winding his way along the familiar neighborhoods to the home he shared with his wife and daughter.

He pulled into the driveway and she was waiting for him at the front door, screen thrown wide open, beckoning him onward. She was waving, her arm pulling him, pulling him forward.

"Hurry," she said. "Come on. Quickly. I need you in here now! Before it's too late!"

Now he began to worry. The short drive home convinced him that something was wrong, something was off. He didn't feel quite right. Was his daughter okay? Had she fallen out of a chair or bed, hurt herself? Had her condition somehow taken a turn for the worse? Had their worst fears come true? So far they had been lucky. Their daughter was generally healthy, although it was clear she had many physical problems. Was all that about to change?

He had just enough time to turn the engine off and slam the door when she hurried to his side and practically pushed him into the house. They entered the foyer, the living room off to the right, the dining room off to the left, the old familiar coat rack standing forlorn in a corner of the entryway.

She steered him into the living room, let go of his arm, turned and spoke.

"Well," she said, a smile slowly spreading across her face. "Well?"

He looked into the room, to the familiar furniture, the TV beside the fireplace, the chairs and couches as he had left them. What was it, he wondered? Did she buy something new, a new addition to the room? Was there a fire somewhere, a bug he needed to squash? What?

Then he saw it, or rather, saw her.

His daughter was in the room. She was over by the coffee table. And she was standing, her legs unsteady, her whole body swaying.

She was using the coffee table to balance herself, her tiny arm outstretched. After all this time, he thought, now, after years of one-day-at-a-time, of holding his daughter, of feeling the rigidity of her muscles, her inability to do much more than lie about or affect a simple type of crawl, after all this time, she was standing.

She was three years old, and she had never stood on her own before.

The months that followed Katie's return home from the hospital were quite uneventful. Except for a few subtle indicators, she seemed, to anyone who bothered to notice, to be a normal child. She ate and slept and pooped. She cried a little, smiled a lot, and learned fairly quickly how to sleep through the night, or most of it. Learned to sleep without waking her parents every few hours.

But there were signs, signs known only to her mother and father, and to her grandmother, signs that she was… different. Her muscles would tense and then relax, there seemed to be no middle ground. She was either rigid or flaccid. She had trouble holding her head up long after most babies would be able to do so. And she could not turn herself over, could not roll around or slither about when placed on the floor. When most babies would be exploring their new world, she seemed content to just lie about and not move.

Then there was her smile.

It was the same smile they had seen the day they arrived at the hospital to meet her for the first time. But it had grown in size and stature.

Her smile lit up a room, lit up the whole of the air around her.

When others saw it they melted. They smiled in return. They laughed out loud. It was the smile that did it. And she smiled a lot.

Oh, she had tantrums, loud bouts of screaming and yelling, those times even more painful to her father as it brought back the memories of her birth, of her screaming in pain as the nitrogen left her body. Oh yes, she could cry and scream and complain, her voice filling the entire space around her.

But it was the smile that became her signature, that defined her as something different, something special.

At seven months, when most babies are starting to crawl, to roam and explore their small world, Katie remained immobile, stationary, content to lie about and let the world come to her. She still could not roll over on her own, or lift her head any great distance.

But she could smile, and her eyes took in the world with a constant, persistent wonder.

At one year old, when most babies are starting to experiment with walking, start processing the tools needed to stand upright and take their first steps, Katie was still immobile, still fixed in place.

And still she smiled away the world around her.

The doctor visits continued, the evaluations, the prodding and poking by specialists. She was healthy as a horse they said, but her development was, well, delayed. Certain milestones were not met, certain actions not completed. Her mind seemed active and bright, but it was still too early to tell what damage, if any, she had suffered through her birth.

Then, at two years old, a hopeful sign. She began to creep, not crawl, but creep. Slowly at first, and not like a regular baby would creep, her hips splayed out, her legs pushing outward but not forward, her arms still not functioning quite right, but she was beginning to move, and for a while her parents were hopeful. Still there was no sign she could do more than just creep about the space around her.

Doctors came and went. The diagnosis was confirmed. She was atehtoid cerebral palsy. Her muscles were spastic and non-controllable. Her range of motion was rigid or flaccid, with little in between. Her parents went to clinics, read books, studied up on the subject.

And still there were no answers, no prognosis beyond the simple "we don't know, take it one day at a time."

Through it all she continued to smile, to meet the world every day, to greet the people in her life every day, to face every situation every day, with a delightful, delicious smile.

Her body grew, not quite normally, her limbs tiny and thin, the contours of her body straightened by the lack of muscle definition and tone.

And still she smiled.

She could not grasp objects like her peers. Could not handle tiny toys, or dolls, nor manipulate the knobs and dials and levers of the educational toys placed in front of her.

And still she smiled.

The doctors would poke and prod, tsk and tsk, make notes on charts. The list of things she couldn't do, but should do were she normal, grew longer. Crawl, grasp objects, stand upright, walk, control arms and legs, feed herself. The list grew and grew.

And still she smiled.

Well, her father thought one evening as he cleared the dinner plates, if nothing else this kid can grow up to be a professional optimist. She can smile her way through the world. He turned to look at her propped up in her high chair. She looked back, and, as if reading his mind, her eyes locked with his and... she smiled.

A great big full wonderful wide smile.

And the world seemed, at that instant, to grow brighter.

At least that is what her father thought as he slowly turned back to the waiting dishes.

"You know," Katie's mother said, almost wonderingly, "I've noticed something funny when Katie and I go driving."

"Really," her husband replied. It was another evening, another day in late spring. The air outside was fresh and new, the world was starting to turn green and the sun was hanging longer and longer into the evening sky. "What's that?"

"She loves school buses."

"School buses?"

"Yeah, school buses. I don't know if it's the color, the bright yellow, or the shape, you know they're so much bigger than anything else and she can see them from her car seat. But whenever we pass one, or they pass us, she goes nuts. She smiles and waves and gets excited."

"Are you sure it's the school bus that's doing it?" he asked.

"Pretty sure," she replied. "It happened again today, three times. Each time I repeated the words to her as she saw them. I told her, 'that's a school bus Katie.' I think she even recognizes the words."

She was driving her daughter a lot over the first few years of her life. The motion of the car seemed to soothe her, sometimes it was all that would do it. For all of her smiling and sunny disposition, there were times, and sometimes for a long, long time, that Katie would scream and yell, her body tensing as if reliving the pain of her birth. She would fight sleep, fight her nap times, throw tantrums, and scream and cry and generally shout at the cruelty of the world around her.

It was during these tantrums that her mother found, quite by accident, that taking her on long car rides would soothe her and calm her and lull her to sleep. Sometimes she would drive for hours at a time, wandering around mountain roads and through the small towns nearby, Katie in her car seat, sleeping a deep, untroubled sleep, the car wheels going swoosh, swoosh, swoosh, the motion gentle, much like a rocking chair.

It was those times, when she was driving and nothing more, that her thoughts again turned to the future, and the unknown of the future, and the fear would once again rise to the top of her stomach, rise into her throat, and spread throughout her entire being. Those drives, while comforting and soothing to her baby girl, were times she had come to dread.

Katie's father turned to his daughter sitting in her high chair. He caught her attention and tried the words, looking for recognition.

"School bus, Katie?" he asked excitedly. "Did you see a school bus today?"

Katie smiled, laughed, waved her arms, tried to speak, made cooing sounds of recognition, or so he imagined.

"I think you're right," he replied. "Maybe it's an omen. Maybe there are school buses and school days in her future. Maybe school is going to be something big in her life."

They looked at each other, their faces full with the look of that old familiar pain, the pain of not knowing, not knowing about the future, about what the future would hold for their daughter. It was that which brought them closer together and drew them farther apart. There were many times when they would fight and argue, but there were times when they would hold each other close, knowing they were in this together, knowing that no one else could share their joy and their pain.

Would she walk or talk? Be in a wheelchair for the rest of her life? Would she be able to learn, go to school, do all those things the "normal" kids did? It was the unknowable and unknowing that defined them, defined their relationship, their lives, everything.

Katie had not even been home for a year when they had their first big fight. It was over the birth and the doctors and, well, just everything.

She wanted to sue, sue the doctors and the hospital, sue for her daughter's condition. She was lashing out, looking for someone to blame and she was worried, worried again about the uncertain future ahead.

Katie will need therapy, she argued, will need doctors and who knows what else. Where is the money going to come from, she asked. They should be responsible for helping with all of that. After all, they knew she was big, so big at birth. She was nine pounds and nine ounces. They must have known that would be a problem. And why did they wait so long to make the decision, to order a c-section. Why had it taken so long? And then the delay, while the team was called. It was negligence. They should have been ready, been standing by. If they had, if they had... BEEN THERE... then the time would have been lessened and Katie might not have suffered this damage, suffered any damage at all.

No, he argued back. It's nobody's fault. It just happened. Everything is easier to figure out in hindsight, he said. But it was their choice to have a natural birth, to try again and again when they could have made the decision at any time. Not the doctor.

They went back and forth, the words harsh and getting hasher, voices accelerating and growing in volume. He was a doctor's son. He didn't believe in suing doctors unless they were malicious or negligent. He had been there the whole time. The doctor tried his best. He was competent and conscientious. And tired. It was just bad luck.

No, she argued. They should have known. They should have been better prepared. They're the experts, have gone through hundreds, thousands of births. They should have been prepared. She's going to need help, help we may not be able to afford to give her. We should sue for her future.

Inside he knew she was probably right. That it was about the child. But he couldn't help thinking that by suing he was trying to profit from his daughter's misfortune, from his wife's ordeal. And the idea sickened him. He had made this bargain, made this decision with her, to bring a child, this child, into the world. And that decision, he knew at the time, bound him, bound him to love and protect, and... *provide for*... that child from his own resources, his own sweat and toil. He would not do that from a courtroom. It seemed too easy a way out.

But she was right. He knew, a part of him knew, that she was right. It was about the child. It wasn't about profit, or anger, or revenge. It was about the child.

Still they argued back and forth, the words harsh and mean, the fights pulling them apart, building a wall, separating them from each other, and in some ways, separating them from their daughter.

In the end they let it lie. There was no agreement, no consensus. Just a lack of action.

They knew it would never be settled, this argument, would be another wedge between them, to remain long after this and for the rest of their lives. It was just another thing that drove them apart, kept them isolated from each other. But it was also a shared thing, and even though they could not agree, it also brought them closer together, made them feel even more connected in some bizarre way. It was bad… and good… and incomprehensible.

In the end, they didn't sue.

They talked about other things, about possibilities, and potential.

They talked about small victories.

They talked about her smile, the smile that warmed and comforted them every time they saw it.

And they talked about school buses.

Bright, shiny, yellow school buses.

Even with Katie's lack of mobility they took her everywhere. Oh, it was difficult, was even almost unmanageable at times, but they did it. The doctor's remarks would replay in their heads, his advice to push her, to expose her to the world, to not coddle her. So they would pack up the normal baby things, the diapers and the bottles of formula and the blankets and cribs and the strollers she would need in order to sit up for long periods, and they would go.

They explored the mountains, Katie perched atop her father's back in a special hiking pack. They took her boating on the nearby alpine lakes, Katie in harness and attached to something solid and braced, so she wouldn't go flying, wouldn't slip off into the water and a sure trip to the bottom.

They took her to birthday parties, not just her own, but other kids' birthday parties. She didn't know any of the children whose parties she attended, couldn't visit and play with them, socialize in any way, but they took her to the parties just the same. Her father would often bless himself later for having had the foresight to do so, for it was at just such a birthday party that something momentous happened. Although at the time he didn't know it would be momentous, could not have imagined what it would mean for the future, that unpredictable future they so dreaded, it was, nevertheless, momentous.

Katie was about to turn three and they took her to a birthday party. Another friend, a couple they had known for many years, had brought two daughters into the world, two girls, cute as buttons, cuddly as teddy bears, a few years older than Katie, and yes, very much normal.

And one of them was having a birthday.

The house where the party was held was full of people. There were kids of all ages, from babies to toddlers to pre-teens. The birthday girl herself was turning five. The kids were playing all around, running through the house, gathering in the girl's bedrooms, rolling outside into the yards. They were running and laughing, pushing and shoving, playing with new toys and old. And making an infernal racket all the while.

There were the adults, the parents and grandparents, friends and neighbors, some single, some long past child-rearing years. They stood in groups, talking, eating, drinking. They herded kids, refereed fights, tried to keep some order in the maelstrom that surrounded them. They organized games, formed groups, and set up toys. It was a big party, a huge party, and the house hummed and throbbed and growled with the pent up energy of so many people having so much fun.

Through it all, Katie sat and watched, or crawled about from one spot to another, trying to take part, trying to participate, but not really being able to. Trying to fit in, but not really fitting in. Her mother set her up to play with others, but they quickly lost interest and moved on to more physical activities, more movable pursuits.

Then one of the parents put a video in the tape player, a movie, a story about a mermaid, a little mermaid named Ariel.

It was a new offering from Disney, it had just been released on video and someone had brought it as a present for the lucky birthday girl. As the movie began several kids gathered around the TV, their little eyes glued to the screen, their ears trying to hear through the cacophony of sound going on around them, as mermaids sang and swam and danced under the sea.

Sebastian the Crab conducted as an orchestra of marine life played the tunes and coral reefs sang the songs. It was catching, this tale of a mermaid, enrapturing to those small children who watched, believing, believing in the world of magic being played out in front of them on the small screen.

Katie sat with the group. Her mother finally found something Katie could participate in with the others, something she could do that made her feel she belonged, was part of the group. She sat Katie down, pointed out the screen and beckoned her to watch, to watch and enjoy.

It was only a short while later, the story still in its infancy, when her father walked by... and stopped. He was startled, wasn't sure why, but he noticed something, something different, something significant. He turned to look at his daughter, to watch her watching the video.

There she sat, transfixed, her eyes glued to the screen, her smile ever-present, large, inviting and fixed, her whole being focused on the story before her. It was strange and wonderful, this little scene being played out on the living room floor, the party surging and ebbing around her, the world rushing by as she sat mesmerized by the story playing out before her.

Katie has no eyes for anything else, he thought, no notice of any other motion, or sound, or activity. She was inside the story, inside this magical world. She would try to sing with the crustaceans, wave an imaginary baton with Sebastian. She cooed at Ariel and she shrank in fright from the menace of the sharks. She laughed, she smiled, she cried, all of the emotions playing across her face, simple and easy to interpret, to understand.

For the first time, for just a moment really, her father felt that she was free, liberated from the confines of her body and the real world around her, that she could swim, and dance, and sing, and yes, fly, with the characters on the magic screen. That she was... normal!

The magic of Disney, he thought to himself. Is it really magic? Is it really... that powerful?

He remembered his childhood, the memories of Sunday evening and the Wonderful World of Disney on the TV. Oh, he would wait for that show, wait all week, anticipate watching, long for when it would be time to turn it on and lose himself in the adventures of Daniel Boone and Huckleberry Finn, of Peter Pan and the sword fights with the dreaded Captain Hook, of camping in far off and exotic places like Yellowstone and Yosemite. He thought of his coonskin cap and the musket he had received at Christmastime, a gift from another magical person called Santa Claus. But it wasn't Santa he remembered so much as the image of that kindly old man, an uncle really, Uncle Walt, talking of imagination and wonder and dreams from the confines of his television screen.

Was it really that powerful? Really that real? He wondered. And then he looked again at his daughter, at the look on her face, in her eyes, her mind off in some far away world under the sea... under the sea.

Was she swimming with the dolphins? Was she really singing with the marine band? Was she falling in love just as this little mermaid was doing? He wondered.

When the movie was over, when the story had ended, the problems resolved, the challenges met, when the happily-ever-after had become happily ever after, Katie started to cry. One thoughtful parent pressed the rewind button and started the story over, played it again for the children whose appetite for wonder and magic had not been fulfilled.

While most of the other kids finally got bored, saw the same scenes twice, started to wander in their minds as little ones will, left to find other more profitable activities, still Katie watched and wondered and dreamed in front of that two foot by two foot screen. It was a world she was discovering for the first time. And for the life of him, her father could not help but cry inside, just a little bit, for the joy his daughter had found.

Is it real? This magic? This make-believe world? It certainly was for her, he thought, just as it had been for him.

Later, when the party was over, the food put away, the toys scooped into the closets, when good-byes had been said, children rounded up and herded into their respective cars and seats and strollers, later, when they were driving home, Katie asleep in the back, safely tucked in her car seat, her eyes closed, her mind at rest, he turned to his wife as if to say something, as if to speak over the distraction of driving.

"Yes," she asked. "You were going to say something?"

"Oh, I was just thinking," he replied. "Just thinking out loud."

"What?" she asked again. "Can you tell me?"

"It's nothing," he answered. "Nothing really… I just thought…"

"Yes," she prompted.

"I just thought that maybe it was time we got some movies. You know, for the house, for Katie. Maybe it's time we got her some movies… just for her."

"What kind of movies?" she asked.

"Disney movies," he replied, simply.

By two to three months babies can lift their head from a supine position. At seven to nine months they can control trunk and hands, sit without support and crawl about. At ten to twelve months they can control legs and feet, stand, creep, and grasp objects with control of thumb and forefinger. From one to one and a half, they can creep up stairs, walk for 10 to 20 minutes, and make lines on paper with a crayon. By two years they are capable of bladder control. By three years they can ride a tricycle, and by four years they can even jump up and down on one foot. By five years they are using language in an almost adult fashion.

One by one these developmental steps came and went, came and went. By the time Katie was well over three she could control her head, crawl in her own fashion, and even creep, and yes, she had even accomplished a modicum of bladder control. Thank goodness for that, her mother and father often said. Diaper patrol had become an ongoing commitment, you could even call it a career, at their house.

But grasp objects? Stand? Walk on two legs? All of these were beyond her control.

While other kids were rejoicing in their first tricycle or bike, Katie was still crawling over the floor of her world. While other kids were drawing and building with blocks, she was still trying to simply hold onto something. While other kids were running and jumping and playing ring around the rosy, she was trying to sit up without rolling over.

She began to speak. To make sounds. It was clear she could understand things, follow commands, respond to her name. And her attempts to talk seemed to make sense, even if the sounds themselves were only approximations of what it seemed she must be trying to say.

But it was the walking that mattered most, mattered so dearly to them. For it was the simple act of standing on one's own two feet, of balancing, and, yes, walking, that seemed to elude her. And that seemed to her parents to be the one thing most important to her future. They began to research wheelchairs, braces, walking aids of a fashion, not that much was available, or even practical.

So when the day arrived, when that one single day came, the day when his wife called him at the office, when she commanded that he come home… right NOW… on that day, the world changed. Time seemed to stand still. The earth stopped spinning, the stars winked out, the universe took a pause.

SHE WAS STANDING!

His heart almost stopped. He turned, and his wife was smiling, laughing, and crying at the same time.

"She's been doing it all afternoon," she cried. "She started an hour ago. I was talking on the phone, I came in and there she was, standing by the coffee table."

"I don't believe it," he replied. "Has she been standing all this time?"

"No, she stands for a bit and then falls down. And she gets back up. I've counted it out now. She's pulled herself up five times. I can't believe it."

This was momentous. This showed promise. If she could stand, then maybe she could walk. And if she could walk, then who knew, maybe she could run. And then maybe, just maybe, she could learn how to fly, and to soar.

He thought of what had happened at the birthday party so many months ago, of how Katie had watched, watched the story of that littlest of mermaids, how he felt she had become free in that magical world, free to walk, free to run, free to swim and dance and sing.

And this, this sign, this moment of hope? It would take magic, it would take a belief in the unbelievable, it would take faith, and yes, it would take more magic. But he could see the future and there was hope for his daughter, hope that she too would feel the magic of walking and moving through the world on her own. At that moment he knew just where the magic was going to come from, knew it deep in his heart. After all, where do you go when you win the World Series? Where do you go when you win the gold medal at the Olympics, when you finish the marathon, or win the big prize? That's what walking meant to his daughter, to him and his wife. It was the World Series, the Super Bowl, an Olympic gold medal... all rolled into one!

"You know what this means," he said, turning to his wife with Katie swinging in his arms and smiling that smile.

"What?" she cried.

"It means she's going to walk, and when she does... *we're going to Disneyland!*"

Learning to Walk

It was shiny!

That was his first thought, how shiny and bright it was gleaming in the rays of light from the morning sun streaming through the windows of the little shop on the corner. The shop had all sorts of shiny things, wheelchairs and stools, braces and motorized scooters, all made out of bright, highly polished metal. Shiny, he thought again.

They were looking over a walker, a brand new walker that was shiny and bright and big, sitting there on the showroom floor. It was obviously made for a grown-up, for a senior citizen with mobility problems, made for the support of adult legs and knees and hips weakened from years of use.

It was certainly too big for Katie, he was thinking.

As if reading his mind, the little shop's proprietor spoke up. He was a kindly older man with a twinkle in his manner that told the world he loved what he did, believed in it, and knew the value of it to the infirm and immobilized that he served day in and day out.

"Oh, we can cut it down to any size. Heck, we do it all the time, you know, for little people. Of course we don't get many kids in here for customers. You understand," he stammered quite apologetically.

The walker came in multiple sections, each one made of shiny, polished stainless steel, and each piece attached to others with sturdy rivets and bolts. It had two wheels on the rear legs, small round pieces of rubber molded into sturdy axles that attached to the frame. The front legs had no wheels, were simply straight and reinforced at the ends with rubber caps. Each leg had a telescoping feature that allowed one to raise or lower the height depending upon the person using it. The walker was open in the back, so you could step into it, grasp the sides, lift and step, lift and step.

Katie sat in her stroller, watching the adults, looking, wondering. She had enjoyed the ride to the little shop, the car swooshing and sweeping down the mountain roads, down to the city in the valley. Now she sat looking at this shiny new object, this shiny new toy. For surely it must be a toy, a new toy for her to play with. And with that thought she smiled, smiled wide and long, the power of it washing over the people in the room, washing over the shop's kindly old proprietor.

"What a sweetheart you are," he cried delightfully. He leaned down to look her in the eye, to take in that smile, to feel the warmth and the power of it. "You are just a darling. What's your name?"

"I'm Katie," she replied without shyness. At least that is what she tried to say. The words came out garbled, not quite intelligible without one being practiced at the art of deciphering them.

"What's that?" he asked again, looking from Katie to her parents still inspecting this shiny new toy, this walker. "Kathy, did you say?"

"No, Katie," she replied again without irritation, with the patience that came from often having to repeat herself. She was getting used to repeating herself as she got more involved in playing this language game that adults seemed to want to play.

"Katie?" he guessed. "Okay, Katie," he said with finality. "Katie. That's a pretty name for a pretty girl. So how do you like your new walker, Miss Katie?"

Katie nodded and continued to regard the proprietor with a sense of somber wonder and concentration. She knew this trip was for her, that this store, and this shiny metal object, were for her, but the why of it she had no clue.

"So how long does it take to cut down?" her father asked. "How long to fit it to her?"

"Oh, not long at all. I just need to take some measurements, you know, of her arms and legs, and we can do it in a jiffy. I have the equipment right here in the back of the shop. Takes a welding torch you know." He smiled. "Have to learn to weld and cut and all sorts of things in this line of work. As I said, we can fix you up in a jiffy."

"Hon," he asked, turning to his wife. "What do you think?"

"We'll take it," she said directly to the storekeeper.

The proprietor got right to work. He pulled out a tape measure, had them hold Katie's legs out straight, and then her arms, worked quickly taking measurements and jotting them down on a small pad with a worn stub of a pencil.

"There, that should do it. I'll be right back folks."

The proprietor vanished into the back of the shop, took the walker with him, leaving them for a moment all alone in the store. There were no other customers.

"Well," he remarked to his wife, "that was easy."

"Yes," she replied. She reached out to take Katie, to lift her up and check that everything was all right, a mother's check.

As she did, he wandered the store looking at the wheelchairs, the motorized scooters, the leg and arm braces and other prosthetics on the shelves. It was a store the like of which he had never seen, never been in before, never had reason to.

At this moment he was not to know, not to truly understand just how intimately he would become acquainted with this walker, how involved with it he would be. There would be countless times when he would fold it, pack it, and carry it. Countless times that he would unfold it, set it up, adjust it. That it would become a part of his day-to-day existence. He would repair it when it broke, try to polish it when it had become dull from the oil of human hands and the grime of the outside world, and times when he would have to pick it up and put it down, and right it when it had tumbled over. All those times were yet to come.

At this moment all he could think of, as the glow from the

welding torch reached out from the back of the store to illuminate the corners of the little shop, was that it sure was shiny.

Very shiny.

The moment came, and passed. Katie could stand. Maybe not for long, maybe not totally by herself, not without the tenuous support that came from that outstretched arm... but she could stand. And if she could stand, then maybe she could walk. It was like a revelation. It gave them hope, focus, determination. Oh, and it gave them a project and a goal on which to focus. Teach Katie to walk.

They talked it over, discussed it when they went to bed at night, mentioned it casually over coffee in the morning, referred to it during brief phone conversations.

They agreed that the first trip would be back to the doctors. There was advice to get, suggestions, recommendations. How should we proceed? What should we do? What precautions should we take? How far could we... push her in this new endeavor?

The ride to the specialist's office in the city was filled with anticipation. Katie's father took off from work for the whole day. Her mother arranged for someone to cover her shift. She had been working in a local tavern, a neighborhood bar where everyone knew your name and the locals came to talk and gossip and play.

They had the whole day and night to begin this monumental task.

Teach Katie to walk.

The specialist was not long in making time for them, although for him it was turning into a busy day of appointments and rounds. He heard the excitement in their voices, heard the news about her standing, on her own, without being propped up or enticed into it. Truth be told, he was excited himself. It was a good sign, a sign that she was beginning to reach her own developmental milestones, not the ones published in all the "raising baby" books, but rather her own.

"Well," he began. "Katie has been standing up for you, I hear."

"Yes, I've been working with her on it every day," her mother replied. "And it seems she's getting better and better at it. Yesterday I timed her for a whole minute, without support, just standing and balancing."

"So now you want to see if she can start to learn to walk. I want to caution you, this does not mean she will be able to, at least not without assistance, but it is a very promising sign, very promising indeed."

"What do you mean without assistance?" she asked.

"Oh, that's easy. She'll need a walker to start. Maybe forever, but certainly to start. A walker will give her the support, the balance she needs to start learning to walk on her own. Now that she can stand, you can place her in a walker and work with her for as long as she can stand it."

"But we don't want to overdo it," her father replied. "Just how far do you think we should push her?"

"That will be up to her. I think she will have no problem in letting you know when she's had enough. But by all means, you can push her a bit. She's taking on a big task, a monumental task in her case, and it is going to take a lot of effort and determination."

"How long will she need the walker?"

"Hold on now, don't get ahead of yourselves. It's enough that she can start to learn to stand and walk with support. Walking unaided, well, let's cross that bridge when, or if," he added sternly, "we ever come to it. Look, I don't want to alarm you, or dampen your enthusiasm, but the chances of your daughter being able to walk unaided are still very slight. You have to understand that."

"Now," the doctor continued, "I am going to want you to invest in some pads as well."

"Pads?" Katie's father asked.

"Yes, pads and a helmet. You have to protect her. Her body is still frail, not weak, but frail. Those thin arms and legs, thin from lack of muscle tone, will be vulnerable to fractures and breaks. So you are going to need knee pads, elbow pads, and a good stiff helmet. I'll write a prescription for the walker, your insurance should cover at least some of it, and you can probably get the pads and helmet at the same place."

They finished with the doctor, received written directions for additional exercises, and purchased the walker and pads at the little shop on the corner, a shop the doctor was quite familiar with and directed them to. The helmet was another thing all together. The shop didn't have one and they could not find one anywhere else in town. They finally ordered one from far away through a catalog that specialized in adaptive gear for handicapped children.

And with that they were ready, felt it, felt they were ready for this monumental task. Teach Katie to walk.

They had the pads.

They had the helmet.

They had the walker.

There was only one question left.

Did they have the will?

So the quest began, the quest to teach a child whose muscles were not under control, whose muscles would strain and tense and go from flaccid to rigid seemingly instantaneously, to teach that child how to stand, stand and walk, one foot in front of the other, one step after another, while leaning on a metal contraption that weighed at least half again as much as she did.

It was a fun project, frustrating, maddening at times, but fun. For it brought the two of them together again, united them in a common effort, a common goal. The future didn't seem quite so scary now, so unknown. They had something to focus on, something positive, something important, so very, very important.

Katie's mother began to take notes on Katie's progress, how long, how many steps, kept a log which she would share with her husband every night when he came home. And once again he marveled at her resilience in the face of such an exasperating task, admired her determination and focus. He remembered back to the night of Katie's birth, that long night, oh so long ago it now seemed, when she had strained and struggled so. And again he felt... grateful. Grateful to her and loyal, and steadfast in support of everything she was going through.

Katie delighted in the task. She would smile, crawl to the walker, grasp the sides, and pull herself up as her mother held the metal cage steady. Then she would start to walk, to move forward in an effort to reach a certain prize, a favorite toy placed a few feet in front of her, perhaps a blanket or sweet treat from the kitchen.

Hips splayed apart, feet pointed at different angles, her spindly legs wobbly and unsure of themselves, Katie would push ahead, delighted in this new game, and the attention she would get for playing it. There were times she would fall, would come crashing down, the pads bearing the brunt of her collision with the floor, the helmet called into play, her head constantly banging into the carpet.

There were times she would cry, scream even, when the falls really hurt, or when she grew tired and irritable and all she wanted was to sink back to her comfortable sitting position, the one she had learned to maintain for hours at a time. Her tiny body was constantly covered in bruises from the falls because the pads only protected certain areas.

Some days she didn't even want to try, was irritable and colicky and didn't want to play this new game that took so much out of her, that made her sore, and hurt, and bruised all over.

Months went by, and Katie grew stronger, more stable, more sure of herself. Her muscles, worked constantly under the strain of moving upright, began to take some shape, to grow and mature. The walker became a staple in their preparations for outings into the world. Along with the blankets and bottles and strollers and backpacks, wherever they went, the walker went.

Her toilet activity became more regular, more predictable as she began to move throughout the house, not crawling, but walking, stumbling ahead, her hands tightly gripping the metal of her walker, and always under the watchful eye of her mother or father, always within reach, ready for those times, and there were many, when she would come crashing down, crashing into a heap, the walker tumbling over, her head protected in a cocoon of plastic and cloth.

Spring came, and then summer. They took her to the mountain trails they knew so well. Had her practice on the level spots along the path. They took her to the parks and playgrounds where before she had simply sat and played with whatever toys were in reach. They took her to the beach at the nearest lake, where the sand challenged her movements, but also cushioned her fall. It was there they first tried to take the walker away, tried to get her to stand and walk without the comfort of that metal cage. At first she was scared, wouldn't move, would sink to the sand and cry for the comfort of her mother's arms. Then she seemed to get it, seemed to get the idea that walking alone, unaided, was really a very cool thing to do. She tried, tried again, and again, and again, and made progress, slowly, over days and weeks and months.

Her parents noticed other changes. Her whole body was growing stronger. She could grasp objects with her fingers and thumbs, hold cups and utensils, although she couldn't really use them. The cups had tight fitting lids to prevent spills, and straws to assist with her drinking. She would make use of straws for the rest of her life probably, but that was okay, they thought. That was okay. They were learning that there were ways to fit their daughter to the world, since it was obvious that the world would not fit itself to their daughter.

This walking project was teaching them other things, what clothes would allow her to dress herself, the power and beauty of Velcro over shoelaces, how to open doors, and even brush her teeth, an oversized toothbrush handle clenched firmly in her little hands.

Day after day, the days turning to weeks, the weeks turning to months, the months signaling the change of seasons, Katie continued to work, to strain, to use this new toy, now getting worn and nicked and bent from the falls, the shiny finish wearing off to be replaced by a dull film of grime and use.

Winter came, and with it her fifth birthday. It was an important year, a year when most children start off to kindergarten, start the long journey down the path of public education. And she was… getting there. She could now walk unaided, her pads still affixed to her tiny frame, because the falls would come even more often now, more often without the comfort and support of her once-shiny steel cage.

Her gait was clumsy, jerky, and not always straight. But it was hers, and it worked, got her where she wanted to go, got her to whatever prize waited at the end of the trip.

They took her to the store, the park, the mountain trails. She would fall and they would help her to get up at first. But eventually they began to back off, to withhold help, to push her even more, even though it broke their hearts inside, broke their hearts to see this little girl, this tiny body falling, and struggling to get up, to learn to live in a world not meant for her, a world of gravity, and hard floors, and sharp objects, and obstacles.

At times they were vilified by the people around them, accused of being child abusers for not letting others help her to her feet, for not letting others help this tiny girl to get up, to get going again. They became hardened to the insults, the accusations. Hardened to the sight of people who would cross the street twenty feet ahead of this tiny bundle of energy waddling down the street encased in a shiny steel cage. Hardened to the sight of people who would cross the street so they wouldn't have to walk by her and acknowledge that such a thing as a crippled little girl like this could exist in their perfect world.

When other girls were starting to take piano lessons, she was in her walker.

When other girls started learning the basics of the ballet, she was in her walker.

When other girls took to the fields to play soccer, their new uniforms shining brightly under the sun, she was in her walker.

When other girls were riding bikes and skipping rope and learning to play hopscotch across chalk squares marked in the cracked sidewalks of the neighborhood… she was in her walker.

It seemed to her parents that Katie lived in her walker.

It was her only home.

Finally, on the evening of the night before her fifth birthday Katie's parents sat and talked, and agreed they'd been successful, that they had won, or rather, that Katie had won.

She could walk.

Oh, not well, and not without some danger, But she could walk, alone, unaided. She could brush her teeth, put on shoes fastened with Velcro, drink through a straw without spilling. She was becoming independent, in her own way, in some ways, not all ways, but enough.

She could walk. Maybe she couldn't run, or skip, or play ball. But she could walk.

And for them, that was enough.

Disneyland

The café seemed small and intimate for being located in such a big place.

It was situated outside, on a roped off patio. There were tables and chairs, bright shiny umbrellas to protect from the rays of the sun, and there were waiters and waitresses moving about among the tables, their arms lifted high, their hands supporting trays filled with plates of odd-shaped pancakes and waffles, eggs and toast, milk and juice.

The tables were all full, the breakfast parties in different stages of eating, some waiting for their food, some ordering, some happily shoveling forkfuls of sweet breakfast cakes into their mouths. And there were the kids, kids everywhere, kids eating and ordering, kids playing and running, kids resting comfortably in strollers.

To complete the scene, there were the characters, great big costumed characters roaming from one group to the next, from one table to the next, from one gaggle of delighted children to the next. There was a big duck, with big black eyes and a shiny orange bill sticking out from his feathered face. There was a dog, goofy-looking, with droopy ears and a big, really big, nose jutting into the air.

Over in the corner, somewhat off to the side, separated a bit in space from all the rest of the activity, was a little girl. She was standing, holding on tightly to the rails of a shiny metal cage, a walker. The little girl's face was lifted to the sun's rays, lifted to the sight before her, a smile playing wonderfully across the whole of her face. She laughed, she giggled, she grinned. Sitting beside her, the object of her attention, the recipient of her smiles and laughter, was another girl, no, not a girl, but rather a mouse, a female mouse.

This mouse was very large, and she was garbed in a beautiful red dress covered with white polka dots. She had on big, clunky, white high heel shoes, and she carried a small black purse around her left wrist. Her name was Minnie, and Katie was meeting her for the very first time.

Minnie threw up her hands and shook her head from side-to-side. Katie threw up her hands and shook her head from side-to-side. Minnie stretched out her gloved hand, holding forth two fingers and went tsk, tsk, tsk. Katie stretched out her hand, stretched out her tiny thin arm, held out her fingers as best she could, and went tsk, tsk, tsk.

Her parents stood to the side, watching, wondering, smiling. It was the first morning of the first day of their first trip to Disneyland, that magical place that held so much hope for their daughter and her dreams. They were having breakfast with all the Disney characters at Goofy's Kitchen. They had entered the restaurant and, almost as if on cue, as if by magic, Minnie appeared at Katie's side. She seemed to know just what to do, just how to act, just how to capture this little girl's whole attention.

Katie and Minnie continued to gesture and talk and communicate in that magical way that so captures small children's' imaginations. And then, as if out of nowhere, as if by magic, an attendant appeared beside Minnie. She had a picture in her hand, and she had a pen, a big, shiny black magic marker. Minnie carefully took the pen and proceeded to write across this picture, a picture of Minnie herself, dressed in that same red dress with white polka dots and the purse and the big, shiny-white, high heeled shoes.

She finished her task, took a moment to look over her handiwork, then shook her head vigorously, up and down, up and down, as if to signify that she was very pleased with the result. Carefully she leaned forward and handed the personally signed and autographed picture to Katie. It said, "Best wishes and love to my best friend

Katie," and it was signed, "Minnie Mouse."

That picture was to become, in the years that followed, her most prized possession, destined to occupy the place of honor on the shelf above her bed. It would be the last thing she saw every night before drifting off to sleep, and the first thing she saw every morning when she awoke. But at that particular moment in time, at that very instant, to her parents, it was simply a picture, a little piece of magic in this magical place.

Watching Katie hold that picture in her hands, hold it with fingers rigid and twisted, the paper wrinkling under the pressure of her grip, pressing that picture to her breast, hugging it, they knew they had done the right thing, brought her to the right place, at the right time.

Brought her to a place where she could just possibly walk, and run, and fly, with Peter Pan... on his magical flight.

It was a celebration of sorts, this trip to Disneyland. Ever since her father had witnessed that scene at the birthday party, ever since her parents had started to bring home movies about the magic of this world, they had known that one day they would take Katie to see it firsthand. It had only been a matter of when.

They talked it over more than once, argued back and forth. Her mother wanted to wait until Katie was older, stronger, maybe until she could walk. After all, they were focused on the walking project and it consumed all their time and energy. He was more impatient, wanting to go just as soon as possible, eagerly anticipating, with all the will of the little child within him, the trip and the wonders they would experience together.

In the end, her common sense won out and they waited, waited for the right moment, waited for that time when Katie would be stronger and could walk for short periods without any aids or assistance. It was well past her fifth birthday and the time was soon coming when she would begin to go to school. First grade loomed over them, as did all the challenges school would put in front of them.

So this trip, this carefully planned trip, was both an ending and a beginning. It was the end of one phase of Katie's life, the pre-walking phase, and the beginning of another, the go-to-school phase, the explore-the-outside-world phase of her life. And again, the uncertainty of the future weighed heavily upon them. Would she be able to go to school? Regular school? Public school? Or would she have to go to a special school, a school designed for those children facing certain challenges in life? It was another momentous time in their lives, a time when they would again find out if theirs was to be a more normal journey along the path of parenthood, or if it would be filled with special needs and special schools and special programs and special problems. After all these years, one-day-at-a-time was still the order of the day.

Katie was possessed with the kind of fanatical excitement most children develop when being told they are going to Disneyland. She had watched the movies, been a fan ever since that birthday party several years past when she first saw the wonders of the littlest mermaid and her adventures under the sea. She knew throughout the long ordeal of learning to walk that the prize at the end of that effort would be this trip, this visit to a world she was quickly coming to know and delight in.

The ride down the mountain to the airport in the city was uneventful, and normally she would have enjoyed it and wanted it to go on and on. But now she was impatient, wanted to get going, wanted to get to this world she had only seen on TV, or in the movie theater, or in her own imagination. The airport and waiting plane were not new to her, she had flown before, visiting relatives in far off places with strange names and stranger customs. She was already, at five, a somewhat experienced traveler. But this trip would be different. On this trip she would be walking on her own. She packed her own suitcase, with her mother's help of course, a small pull bag with wheels and decorated with images of the mermaids from under the sea.

They were taking her stroller, and yes, her walker, ready for any eventuality. Boarding the plane would be a real event with everything they were carrying. But in the end it was done, Katie pre-boarding with her parents, walking proudly, if somewhat slowly and unsteadily, down the gangway to the waiting entry port of the big jet, the flight attendants smiling and welcoming her, delighting in the wonderful smile with which she returned their hospitality. For Katie's smile continued to grow in presence and power with every year.

The flight down was uneventful, the taxicab ride from the airport routine. It was only when they exited the highway, turned on to the side streets and saw the tip of the Matterhorn looming up out of the distance, peaking out over the tops of the hotels and motels, the restaurants and diners surrounding the park, it was only then that the excitement began to build anew, the anticipation causing them all to laugh and point and giggle together as one.

The Disneyland Hotel was everything they hoped it would be. It had both an air of nostalgia and a feel for the future, an aura of magic and a sense of wonder to it. It seemed to suggest that magical moments awaited those who stayed there. And throughout their first night they were riddled with a feeling of excitement and anticipation for what lay ahead, for what waited in a place that was so close, just a few feet away, and yet so far, an eternity of time from when the sun had set until it rose again in the morning and they could rush pell-mell into their first day's adventure.

The breakfast at Goofy's Kitchen was the first real feeling of being there. The costumed Disney characters were the first sign that, yes indeed, the magic was real, the place was all that had been promised through the movies and the books and the fairy tales they had watched and read and shared with each other.

They finished breakfast, returned to the room to put away the treasured photograph that Minnie had provided, picked up their last minute items, and headed for the park entrance. The shuttle buses, open trams with canopies the like of which Katie had never seen before, whisked them away to the park entrance, the driver cheerfully speaking over the intercom about some of the wonders they were about to experience. At the entrance they handed over their gaily colored tickets to the smiling attendant. And it was there that they knew this was to be a special time, a time for Katie, a time of magic.

They were wheeling Katie up to the entrance in her stroller, both to save time and what energy Katie had, for she still expended huge amounts of effort in her attempts to walk unaided. Just before they reached the turnstiles they stopped, took Katie from the stroller, folded it up and made ready their tickets. Katie swayed for a moment as she was released, swayed on unsteady feet, gained her balance, and with steely determination started to walk towards the ticket takers. One step after another, her gait unsteady, her feet splayed apart, she moved with determination… forward.

The gate attendant took in the scene in front of him, took in the presence of this tiny twig of a girl walking unsteadily towards him, and never missed a beat. Without hesitation he came out from behind his station and approached Katie, a shiny glittering something in his hand.

"Young lady," he said with mock seriousness, "Young lady, do you know what this is?" He held out the glittering object.

Katie regarded the attendant with wide-eyed wonder mixed with curiosity and not a little bit of fear. She shook her head.

"This is a tiara, and it is only to be worn by a princess. Can you think of anyone here who should be wearing this tiara, any princess in the crowd?" he asked, his eyes, his face, his whole body bearing down on Katie with serious intent.

Katie shook her head again, solemnly, slowly, her eyes fixed on the attendant as he towered over her.

"Well, of course, this is for you, " the attendant replied. "You are our princess for the day. This tiara belongs to you." He gently but quickly placed it on her head, where of course it seemed to fit perfectly. After all, this was the land of magic.

Katie stood for a moment, unsure of just exactly what to do regarding this new development, this pronunciation of her royal state. And then she did what she did best, what she always did when not sure what she should do.

She smiled.

And once again, the world fell away, and seemed a brighter place.

The attendant was speechless for a moment, unable to utter a word as the power of Katie's smile washed over him, made him smile in return, and then laugh out loud.

"Come this way folks," he finally managed to continue. "Quickly now, let's have those tickets. We must not keep her royal highness, the princess, waiting anymore. Her chariot awaits, her castle is open, and her subjects desire her presence."

He quickly took the tickets, processed them through the turnstile, and escorted them a few steps as he pointed out the way to go.

Katie and her mother ambled ahead in the direction indicated. Katie's father held back for just a moment and turned to the young man who had so wonderfully anointed his daughter a princess.

"Thank you," he said, eyes glistening with moisture, "thank you so much. I can't…"

"No matter my dear fellow," the young man replied with an air of seniority that belied his young age, "it's what we are here for. Please, enjoy your day and take care of that beautiful little girl. She really does have a wonderful smile." He turned and walked away, back to his station, back to his post, back to the real world of his duties as gatekeeper of this magical place.

As Katie's father turned to catch his wife and daughter and enter this fantasy world, at that moment, the magic seemed to take hold, and for the first time he truly felt it, felt that in this world anything was possible, and that fairies really must exist, and they really must be able to fly. And that other magical things must exist too, like mermaids and unicorns, and yes, princesses.

Little princesses named Katie.

The visit to the park was everything they hoped it would be. They spent two days there, two full days and nights of experiencing the magic and the wonder. Katie wore her tiara proudly throughout the entire time. It rested next to her on her pillow at night, sat by her placemat at meal times, rested perfectly on her head between rides.

On that first day, their first stop was Disney's City Hall, a two story brick building that, according to legend, housed Walt Disney's personal apartment, living quarters he would occupy whenever he stayed at the park. It was just off the town square that visitors first enter when coming into the park. There they received a magic pass. The magic pass, the attendant behind the counter said, was made especially for a princess like Katie. No one but a special prince or princess could have one. It was created by mysterious incantations and a magical potion. It allowed her to go to the head of any line in the park. It allowed her access to any area, any place, that her little heart might care to go. And she could take her mother and father with her.

They used it to visit all the places they had read about, Peter Pan's magical flight, Mr. Toad's wild ride, journeys that went up and down, and around and around. They sat on the back of Dumbo, the flying elephant. They marveled at the wondrous landscapes of Fairyland, got wet in the jungle boats, and laughed and sang along with the incredible figures in a journey through a small, small world. Katie braved the dangers of the pirates as they laid waste to the Caribbean islands that she floated through. And everywhere she went she was greeted with a fuss and a bother, with broomsticks and fiddlesticks, and a fantasy world that seemed to be made just for her.

Here people did not cross the street just to avoid walking past a little girl, her arms and legs twisted and rigid, her hands gripping frantically at her walker. Here people did not stare and wonder what's wrong with this girl, what's her problem, why is she like that? Here, the people who populated this world, who worked within the confines of this magical place, knew just what to do to make a princess feel like, well... feel like a princess. When they saw her they lit up like a candle on a birthday cake, and they came running, bearing little gifts, telling little stories, performing little tricks, paying homage to the princess who had come to visit.

On the second day, just around noon, they stopped at a sidewalk café to have lunch, to get a bite and take a rest from the rigors of their journey. Katie had been walking some all by herself, she had been using her walker at times, and yes, when tired she had surrendered to the comfort of her stroller. It was tiring, this visit to fantasyland. It took all of her strength to make it through the first day. And it was quickly taking all of her strength to make it through this second day.

She was enjoying the rest when another princess entered the café. This princess had on a tiara just like Katie's. It was bright and shiny and the sun sent rays of light reflecting off of it into even the darkest corners of the small café. But there the resemblance ended. For this princess was not walking, nor even strolling. She was in a wheelchair, her arms and legs twisted and wracked with that familiar rigidity, that familiar tenseness that so marked Katie's movements.

Her head was braced with a padded steel bar that wrapped halfway around her skull.

Her parents slowly maneuvered the wheelchair next to a table in the far corner of the cafe. They busied themselves with plates of food and glasses of liquid, and tended to the process of trying to feed their daughter, a girl who could not feed herself, who could neither walk, nor run, nor even crawl.

At that moment, for Katie's parents, the magic vanished and reality set in. They looked at each other, their eyes expressing what their mouths would not say. There but for the grace of god go us.

"Did you see that?" Katie's mother asked. "She has a tiara just like Katie's."

"Yes," he replied. He had been thinking it, but hadn't wanted to say anything. "I see it. Do you think she knows she's princess for a day?"

"I don't know," she replied. "You remember what we read, about the other forms of CP, the more serious forms, with brain damage and seizures. She must have suffered through those as well."

"I know. It's such a different world, different from the one we lived in before Katie. I could never have imagined, never understood what that was like before. You know, we are very, very, very lucky."

"Oh yes," she replied sadly. "Yes, I know how lucky we are. I say prayers everyday for that, for Katie, for all the ones that suffer the way she does and those who suffer even more so. And it feels so... so..." she grasped for the words.

"It's okay," he said reassuringly. "It's okay. We have our own Princess to worry about. And I think she may be ready for another round of magic. Say the island of Tom Sawyer for instance?" There was a twinkle in his eye, but it was met with alarm in her face.

"Katie," she exclaimed. "Oh god, where's Katie, she's gone. Katie?" That last a cry, a shout, an alarm. "Katie, where are you?"

She looked about frantically, they both did. They had forgotten about her during their brief conversation, taken their minds elsewhere, paid no attention. And now she was gone, her chair vacated, the walker beside it standing empty and alone.

"KATIE!"

They got up, started to search the room, looked outside the doorway to see if she had gotten distracted by something outside. They looked up and down the pathways outside the restaurant. They came back in, looking, searching, peering into every dark corner of the large room. All of a sudden her father stopped, reached out, put his arm on his wife's shoulder to stop her frantic searching.

"Look," he said. "It's alright. Look, over there, over in the corner."

She turned to look where he was pointing.

"I think our little girl had other ideas."

Katie was standing by the little princess in the wheelchair. She had gotten up, quietly, without her parents noticing, and she had made her way slowly, carefully, across the café to where the little girl was perched in the corner of the room. Now she was talking to her, her little arm reaching out, her hand caressing the little girl's arm as it lay rigid across the armrest of the wheelchair.

As her parents came rushing up, concern, relief, compassion in their eyes and on their faces, as they approached, Katie turned and in a small voice that nevertheless seemed to ring throughout the room she cried, "Mom, look. She's a princess too."

They spent the rest of that afternoon together, the two couples chatting, getting to know one another, sharing experiences, sharing feelings, sharing the pains and joys of their lives as they warmed to each other. And the little princesses also talked and laughed and made faces at each other, one in her wheelchair, one in her walker, moving slowly, sharing the magic around them.

They walked. They strolled. They stopped to stare and to gawk. They rode rides, what rides or attractions that would fit them, two little princesses and their parents. They shopped. They ate. And they talked, and talked, and talked, the world around them opening up, parting, making a path for them to travel along, their own path, a smooth path, a timeless path, a moment when nothing mattered but this certain time in this magical place.

Others looked on in wonder. There was no pity on their faces, no fear or disgust, just wonder, wonder at the sight of these families sharing a world that seemed to have been made just for them. If truth be told, many were just a little bit envious, jealous of this scene of intimacy and family, and yes, of love.

And when they finally parted, had to leave and take separate paths, these two special families, there were tears and hugs, the exchange of numbers, promises of keeping in touch, of continuing to share even though they lived worlds apart.

Later that night, as he was tucking his daughter into bed in their hotel room, Katie's father thought of those moments and how funny fate could sometimes be, to throw them together like that, at that time, in that place. He cried inside for the little girl so crippled and knotted in her wheelchair, for the understanding he now had about people like her, and like his daughter. NO, not quite like his daughter, he thought.

He was lucky. He knew. He could not even begin to imagine how he would handle such severe incapacitation in his own daughter. And once again the fear of the unknown, of the future, gripped him. Could she somehow regress to that state? Could she have come as far as possible? Was the rest of her life to be one of limitations and disappointments?

Katie looked up at him, her eyes wide, her smile ever present, even through the tiredness of a day that rested so clearly on her face.

"Dad," she said.

"Yes, Katie," he replied gently. "What is it?"

"Are there more princesses like us in the world?"

"Oh yes, Katie," he said. "There are many, many princesses in the world. It's what makes the world such a special place. Because every princess and prince in the world is a very, very special person."

He tucked the covers around her carefully and turned to go.

"Dad," she said sleepily.

"Yes, Katie," he said, turning back to look at her.

"I'm glad I'm a princess."

And with that, she fell into a very deep sleep.

All good things must come to an end, and so it was for their first Disney adventure. The next morning they carefully packed up the mementos, the gifts, the things they had bought. The picture of Minnie was carefully rolled up and placed in a cardboard tube for transport. The tiara was packed in tissues, lots and lots of tissues, and tucked neatly into a corner of Katie's mermaid suitcase. Clothes were folded and placed inside, toothbrushes and combs wrapped up and stowed.

They said one last goodbye to the park, waved from the hotel's porte-cochere as they boarded their taxi and began the long ride to the airport, to the waiting plane, and their home in the mountains.

Once again the taxi ride was uneventful, their mood happy, but also solemn and even a bit sad for having to leave this sunny paradise where magic lived. At the airport their tickets were printed, their bags checked. They had lunch at one of the restaurants, waiting for their flight, killing time. Finally their number was called.

Once again, Katie proudly walked down the gangway, her gait unsteady but her motion determined and forceful. She was getting better at this walking game, getting stronger, more assured and confident. She had on a pair of mouse ears and she carried a magic wand in one hand. Between that and her ever widening smile, as she made her way on to the plane, the flight attendants burst into smiles themselves. They welcomed this little bundle of light and joy into their world and fussed over her. She let them know she was a princess and where she had been and about her royal adventures, her voice garbled, but just understandable to one who listened carefully.

As the plane lifted off into the dark of the evening sky, they settled in for the flight home, Katie instantly asleep, exhausted from this, her first real big trip, her head resting comfortably upon her mother's pillowed shoulder. Her mother, like her daughter, also fell into a deep sleep as the plane climbed for its final cruising altitude, leaving Katie's father alone with his thoughts.

"What does Disney sell?" he thought to himself.

They sell magic, magic in a world in which there is no magic left, and they sell it to people who desperately need it, he thought. Like my daughter. Like the little girl trapped in her wheelchair. For a princess like her.

And although at that moment he was not to know that this place, this magic kingdom, this land they had just left, would become the most favorite destination in the world for his daughter, a place she would return to again and again, through her adolescence, into her teenage years, and even beyond, nevertheless he could sense the importance of it.

Why?

Because the magic works, he thought. Because at Disneyland she can walk, and she can run, and she can fly. Second star to the right, and on till morning. Isn't that what Peter Pan cried on his magical flight?

"Katie," he said softly to himself as he watched her sleeping comfortably by her mother's side, "you're headed for the second star to the right and you're on your way." No matter what the future would bring, the big bad unknown future, somehow he knew he was right.

"Sleep tight little princess," he whispered under his breath.

You're on your way.

School Daze

It was flat, and gunmetal grey, with perhaps a touch of blue in it.

It was long, rectangular, and surprisingly light and easy to carry. The case was plastic but sturdy, unbreakable they said. It had a small screen, two lines of display only. It had keys, letters and numbers, and other more mysterious symbols.

It was not a computer. It was not a toy. It was not a phone, nor an Internet portal. It was not a radio. It didn't play music. It didn't offer games.

It had one purpose. It was a tool for writing. An electronic writing machine for those who couldn't write themselves, who couldn't write by hand, who couldn't put pen or pencil to paper to make long, flowing strokes, shapes, and letters. It could hold several pages of words and numbers in its memory. And it could print them out when attached to a printer. It was a simple, unbreakable, portable, word processor.

And its name was Alpha.

Katie regarded the little keyboard with some amount of wonder. She had been using little toy computers, her fingers learning how to carefully punch buttons, one at a time, her efforts slow and her fingers often missing the mark. Oh, she knew what to do, knew how to do it. But doing it was another matter. And now she was being given this, her first computer, although not really a computer, the closest thing to it she had ever possessed, ever been encouraged to use.

"Katie," her third grade teacher said slowly, "this is yours and yours alone. We got it just for you. You can write your homework on it, put in numbers and enter answers to your math problems.

You can use it to write notes, to write letters, to write anything you want."

Katie nodded solemnly. "Can I take it home, or do I have to keep it here?" she asked.

"Oh no, this is yours. You can use it here and at home. Just don't lose it," she replied with a grin. "Come on, let's try it out."

It was early, before the regular school day began. None of the other children in the class had arrived yet, just Katie and her teacher, and the Alpha.

For an hour she tried typing, using the middle finger of her right hand, the index finger of her left, her motions erratic, slow. She would type, one letter at a time, her eyes searching the screen to ensure she had done it right. It took her a good three minutes just to type the first word. The second was shorter and took half the time. As she typed, she began to move her arms, slowly at first, but then faster, faster, her arms circling above like a bird of prey, then sinking to strike, and then recoiling, her eyes searching the screen. Did she hit the mark? Would she have to erase and start over? Or move to the next letter? Faster and faster, her arms circling, her fingers punching keys, the teacher close by, watching, observing, looking at Katie's face to note the concentration there, the focus.

And Katie was focused. She was entranced. This was a new kind of magic. This was awesome. The possibilities were just beginning to creep into her consciousness. She could write! She could... communicate, without having to wait for someone else, for someone else's hands to make the motions, put pen to paper, write down what she said as she dictated her work.

The other kids arrived, class was starting. Still Katie focused, she typed, she made words. She couldn't follow the sentences yet, for the screen would only display a few words at a time. But she was making words, and delighting in the freedom of it.

The other kids gathered round, watched, also fascinated, some talking about their own computers, those who had them, those whose parents had the wherewithal and resources to supply them. They watched fascinated at Katie's arms as they dipped and swooped, round and round, plunged to depress a key, then drew back in a great arc, her muscles rigid, her fingers outstretched.

In the back of the room, her parents watched the scene, absorbed in the moment. They had been there all along, quietly staying out of the way, out of the moment, watching, observing. It seemed to her father, as she typed away, her arms swooping and flying in the air above the keyboard, that Katie had found another bit of magic, another way to walk and run and fly. She was free, free to express herself, free to communicate, free to work without bonds, without limits.

He turned to his wife.

"Let's go," he said simply.

"Shouldn't we say goodbye, let them know we're leaving?" she asked.

"No," he said. "No, let's slip out. They don't need us now. They're doing just fine."

Quietly they walked out the door, into and down the hallway, the voices of children from the other classrooms reaching out to them as they made their way out of the schoolhouse.

"You know," he said thoughtfully.

"What?" she replied. "You know, what?"

"I think we'd best go shopping today," he replied.

"Shopping?" she asked. "Shopping for what?"

"A computer," he said.

"A computer?"

"Yes, a real computer. A computer for Katie. A computer just for her."

"Yes," she replied simply. "Let's do that."

The public school system in Katie's town was not bad, not by any means. They were progressive, they tried, with the resources they had, in this small town in the mountains, to stay current, to be on the cutting edge of the nation's education system. But it wasn't easy. With small facilities, and not a lot of students, they had not the resources of their larger, more substantial sister schools in other parts of the state.

But they tried.

So it was that their first reaction to the idea of Katie going to public school was not a favorable one, but they were willing to listen. There were concerns, of course. Could she keep up? Could she do the work? And what about liability? What if she fell in the hallways, injured herself? What if the other kids pushed her, teased her, bullied her? It was possible, they said. And so discussions were held, long discussions, about Katie, about her needs.

"I want you to understand," said the school superintendent somewhat sternly. "I want you to understand all the ramifications of your daughter's condition and her ability to go to our school."

They were sitting in his office, Katie's parents, and they were meeting with several school officials, the superintendent of schools, a first grade teacher, a special education consultant. The office was cheerful, bright, there were windows overlooking a small park that bordered the playground of this elementary school that Katie was applying to attend. She would be in first grade. It was time. And they were discussing all the prospects of such a momentous phase in her life.

"I think we can appreciate your concerns," her father answered back. "But you have to understand, with Katie it's one day at a time. I don't know if she can do this, but we have talked it over, and we want to try. Only that way will we really know what she can and can't do."

"Of course," the superintendent replied, not unkindly. "I couldn't... we couldn't agree more. But you must understand it may not work. We may have to try different alternatives, different approaches. It may be better to start her on one of those and ease her into the school system when she is older and we know more about what she can and can't do."

"No, I don't agree with that," her mother replied. "We've never done that with her. I think it would be a mistake. We challenge her. And this is what we want to do first. We think she's ready. You don't know how tough she is, how far she's come. And bright? She's completing every task we put before her. She's reading, she knows her alphabet, she's soaking it up."

"My biggest concern," Katie's father broke in again, "is that she not hold the others back. I understand your position. We know she is bright, that she is testing off the scale. The question for us is can she do the work without holding the others back, without holding up an entire class? We wouldn't want that. It's not fair to the other kids, the other parents, and we would be the first to want to take her out, to... find other alternatives. But we think, with reasonable accommodations... and we really don't know what those are... that she can do this."

"Well, of course, we can try," the superintendent responded. "I would like our special education consultant to walk you through the program Katie will work under for her entire school career, a program that will take her all the way through the twelfth grade, that is, if she is successful. But I want to warn you, this may have to change."

The special education consultant was a young woman. They had been thankful for that. She was progressive, and full of energy and optimism. She was all about "can do" and she wanted Katie under her control in the worst way. Katie would be her first real triumph, her masterpiece, the ultimate proof of her belief that you could do anything, achieve anything, it was only a matter of how. She had been their ally in the fight, Katie's mother's fight, to get her into the school.

"We're going to put Katie in a special program," she began. "Don't worry; to everyone else it will seem she is just another student. But this program allows us to provide the reasonable accommodations that we spoke of before, that you just referred to. It is called an IEP, or Individualized Education Program. Every semester we will meet with you to go over her progress, her issues, and what special accommodations are available via the school, state or federal government, to facilitate her education. It will all be handled under the IEP."

"So this will happen every semester? Twice a year?" he asked.

"Yes, I have prepared her first one here, based on the tests we performed and the questionnaires you filled out. We can go over it with you but let me point out the most important parts. Katie will enroll in first grade as a regular student. Her mother has agreed to volunteer as a classroom assistant under our PTA program."

That part, the volunteering, that was the final straw, the deal maker, the final piece with which the school was ready to try and accommodate Katie. Volunteers were hard to come by, and here was one willing to spend a great deal of time, not just with one student, but with all the students in class.

"She will not only assist with all classroom activities, but also be able to provide special assistance to Katie as needed," the consultant continued. "At this point we are talking about activities that require the physical coordination she does not possess, writing, drawing, PE activities, handling classroom supplies like staplers and scissors, and so forth."

"Yes," Katie's mother replied, "I can do that. I have already arranged to drop most of my work schedule. I can be there every day."

"Good, because until we know what the limitations are, your

presence will be very important. As the semester goes on, we will readjust as needed and set another IEP evaluation for late fall. Is that all acceptable to you?"

"Oh yes," they both replied, almost in unison, drawing forth a grin from everyone in the room. They were eager, eager to get started, eager for the challenge.

The meeting broke up, goodbyes were said, and they found themselves outside the administrative building, walking slowly to their car. Katie was at home, her grandmother staying with her. Babysitting had become her grandmother's favorite thing. She had given up her nursing, given up her wandering ways to be close, to be there, to be a part of this little girl's life.

"I want to thank you again," he started to say as they walked across the grounds of the school. "Volunteering like this, giving up everything, to be with her, I want you to know how… grateful I am."

There it was again, that word between them. He was grateful, had never stopped being grateful, as she had risen to every challenge, fought for her daughter in so many ways over the years, was still fighting. The school did not want her to start in first grade. The school wanted her in a special program, a special home school program. But she fought them, fought them to a standstill, made them take a chance. And her presence in the classroom, not some of the time, but all of the time, swayed the group and won the argument. Katie would be going to school with all the other first graders.

Katie would be going to school.

"No," she replied. "You would do the same, if the shoe was on the other foot, you would have. But I'm going to need you, need you at home, need a lot of help."

"Of course," he replied. "Whatever… whatever you need."

"Good," she said. "Then you can start now."

"What?" he said, surprised.

"Yes," she said. "You can start now."

"How?"

"First, we're going shopping… then dinner… a movie… and then," she smiled as they stood by the car, "and then, whatever else I want you to do tonight!"

And with that, she opened the door and hopped into the car.

Better call grandma, he thought to himself, it's going to be a long, long night!

That was a pleasant thought, and he couldn't help smiling as he got in the car and drove them away, into the rest of the day.

The first two years of school were almost routine. Katie excelled in all the work, although truth be told, the academic demands of the first and second grade are not all that strenuous. Through it all her mother was there, was in the classroom, every day, until it became clear that some days could be missed. But she hardly missed any. It was exhausting work, the demands of a bunch of six and seven year olds was enough to keep three teachers busy, much less an assistant, a volunteer.

She wrote for Katie, handled all the physical tasks like cutting out paper, gluing together projects, writing out math problems. Katie would talk out the problem or task, and she would write it down. It was to become a custom between them for many years and many grades to come.

During recess, when the other kids rushed outside, to freedom, to play, to physical activities, Katie remained behind. She worked on special projects, games and puzzles, with her mother. It was tough at first, the other kids would look and point, or whisper at times in the corner. She was different. They weren't really equipped to handle different. Not at that age.

Some understood, some reached out. But they were busy, busy

with cub scouts and girl scouts, busy with piano lessons and ballerina lessons, busy with sleepovers and parties. Katie didn't fit into
that schedule, didn't fit into that life.

Riding a bike was out of the question. Ballerina lessons, soccer
practice, these were beyond her. She still wore a helmet and pads
when the conditions warranted. She still fell, stumbled, bruises
marking her arms and legs more often than not. But she was there,
she took part, and her schoolwork excelled. She spent a lot of time
reading, reading and doing puzzles with her mother. She took physical therapy, voice therapy. She spent time in a horse riding program,
her tiny body perched atop a huge horse, an attendant walking along
beside her, holding her, steadying her. She took swimming lessons at
a private pool, her instructors holding her carefully, teaching her to
dog paddle in her own fashion, her own way, her tiny arms and legs
splayed out into the water, her muscles tensing, straining, and then
relaxing completely.

She still used her walker at times. And every night, when she
went to bed, she was asleep before her head hit the pillow, tired,
exhausted from a day spent trying to be normal, a day spent expend-
ing five times as much energy as anyone else just in the simple act
of putting on her shoes, brushing her teeth, putting on and taking
off her clothes.

She spent many hours with her grandmother. They would read,
watch TV, play games and take walks. Her grandmother was a strong
woman, her small-town, country upbringing making her tough, her
independence, her travel, her work making her a source of strength
for Katie. She would often tell Katie that she could do anything she
wanted, "and don't ever let anyone tell you different."

Katie would come to her in a bad mood, depressed. She wouldn't
talk about it, but it was clear something had happened, something
at school, something having to do with the other children, her classmates. Only her parents knew the reason for it, the times they would

spend holding Katie close as she cried over the cruelty of others, the cruelty of small children who don't know the hurt and pain of words, words like geek, and spaz, and freak. Yes, she had to suffer from the ignorance of others who simply couldn't leave alone the fact that she was different, flawed in their minds, not like everyone else.

It was during one of those visits to her grandmother, a time when Katie was silent, subdued, unhappy with her school day, when her grandmother took it upon herself to intervene. They were making popcorn and getting ready to watch a movie, and she asked Katie the question, the question that others were afraid to ask, the question only her parents had been able to deal with until now.

"Katie," she asked, "do the other kids make fun of you? Do they say things, mean things? Do they bother you?"

Katie hesitated, as if she didn't want to answer, as if she didn't want to say.

"Sometimes," she said finally. "Sometimes they make fun or say something that isn't... nice. Not all of them. Only a few. But everyone stares at times, they stare at me when they think I'm not looking."

"What do they say?" her grandmother pressed her. "What do they do?"

"They call me names..." Katie said slowly, her eyes starting to swell, her tiny face devoid of the smile that so lit up her features. "They call me stupid... or retarded. They make fun of my walk... and my pads. They sometimes call me little Miss Spazz... or spaz-ma-tazz." Katie stumbled over the word, her lips trembling, her voice garbled and just barely audible.

Her grandmother paused, searching, searching for the right words, the right answer to something that wasn't really answerable. She took Katie by the hand, led her to the couch in her living room, sat down with Katie standing in front of her. She grabbed her by the arms, held her for a moment, and then drew back, looked long and deep into her eyes.

"Katie," she said. "Let me tell you what I want you to do. The next time someone treats you that way, says something mean, I want you to get right in front of them. Just like I am with you now. Get right in front of them. Do you understand?"

Katie shook her head slowly, up and down, up and down.

"And Katie, I want you to say to them, I want you to say it loud and clear, you say, 'Stop it! You stop it right now. That's not right.' Do you understand Katie? Can you do that?"

"Yes, grandma," she replied. "I can say that."

"Good," her grandmother replied. "Good. You stand up for yourself little missy. Because if you don't, no one else will. Do you hear me?"

None of them was to know, later, if she ever acted on that advice, ever confronted another child, ever said those words. But from that time forward, Katie never seemed to have a problem, never came home depressed or in tears, never mentioned the subject again.

The addition of the Alpha to Katie's life opened up a new world to her. She could type, answer questions, solve math problems. She could print out her tests and assignments. She was free, free to do her own work.

Oh, her mother still helped her, still wrote out her math homework, especially as, later in fifth grade and middle school, the math would become harder, more complicated. For years to come her mother would patiently wait while Katie worked a problem in her mind, and would then write out what Katie had computed, what Katie had worked out in her head.

She could do complicated formulas without a worksheet, could do them in her head, slowly verbalizing the solutions so her mother could write them down accurately. She took tests the same way, doing it in her head, figuring it out without pencil or paper or scratch pad, the assistant carefully writing down her responses, writing down her answers.

They got her a computer, a laptop she could carry around as she got older, although she continued to use her Alpha every day. But the computer offered another form of freedom. She could play games, write, read, explore the new world at her fingertips. The Internet was growing, becoming more powerful, and she was dialed in.

She made friends of a sort, cyber-friends, joined discussion groups, explored the world made small by the miracle of technology. When the computers began to make it to the classroom, she was ready to help, to teach her teachers about this new device, teach the ones that were supposed to be teaching her.

One by one the grades fell away, fourth grade, then fifth. She entered middle school, began to have to walk to different classes in different buildings, her backpack weighing her down. Her helmet, now painted and decorated with drawings of colorful flowers, would still make an appearance, would continue to provide her with protection from the inevitable falls that continued to plague her on a daily basis.

But through it all she excelled. Her grades put her at the top of every class, her teachers delighted in her performance. The accommodations she was provided did not slow down the others, her presence did not disrupt the flow of class or the work of her classmates. If another child needed twenty problems to learn a concept, she did it in five. If it took another child an hour to master a formula, or memorize a table, she did it in half the time.

In mental exercises she was quick, quicker than most, but the physical world still weighed her down, still caused challenges for which there were no easy answers. If it took another child an hour to write a paper for an assignment, it took her three hours, one letter at a time, one keystroke at a time, her arms whirling in the air, her fingers trying to hit the right key. But she was getting practiced at working her keyboard, at making the right motions. She became a whirling tornado of movement on her computer, arms flailing, fingers poking, her body swaying to and fro as if conducting a symphony, a symphony of movement and effort.

The day came when she was to graduate from middle school, to finish that part of her education and get ready to move to the real challenge, to the new and challenging world of high school. It was a spring day, not unlike other spring days, the air cool but the sun warm, the sky cloudless and promising the arrival of a hot blue summer to the little town in the mountains, a town until only recently still covered in snow and frost.

Katie's mother was working at the sink, washing dishes and preparing dinner, when Katie's father arrived home from work.

"Have you heard," she exclaimed as he walked in the door. "Have you heard about Katie?"

"No, what's up?" he said.

"She got an award at school today. She has to get up at the graduation ceremony and make a speech."

"Really," he replied, not sure if this was a good or bad thing. It had been enough for both of them that she was even able to attend a regular school, much less win awards and engage in public speaking. He wasn't even sure she could do such a thing. Her voice was still garbled, her words slurred, her meaning hard to deduce unless one were practiced in deciphering it. "Do you think she can do it?"

"I know she can do it," she replied. "She's already working on the speech with her Alpha. She's going to print it out and practice with it."

"But the award," he asked. "What is it?"

"She got top student in the school," she beamed as she spoke. "She's graduating first in her class."

The Sporting Life

It was a small room, a classroom that had been turned into a conference space, with a mishmash of tables cobbled together, chairs scattered around in haphazard fashion, and blackboards lining three of the four walls. On the blackboards were various scribbles left over from past meetings, past groups. The fourth wall held windows open to the outside world. In the corner was a small hutch with a coffeepot and condiments, a column of Styrofoam cups stacked neatly off to the side.

Katie's father sat at a table in one corner of the room, perched in a chair slightly too small for him, feeling slightly ridiculous as a result. His wife was on his left, Katie seated to his right, a seeming wall of people sitting opposite them.

There was the special education consultant for the high school, a middle-aged woman with grey-streaked hair pulled tight at the nape of her neck. She wore black-framed glasses and had the look of a rather stern schoolmarm of old, but her manner and expressions were kindly. There was the principal of the school, well past middle-aged, his bald head shining under the fluorescent fixtures hanging from the ceiling. There was a school counselor, young, eager, dressed sharply in a suit and tie, his long straight hair worn in a ponytail, his hairstyle at odds with the business attire that hung loosely on his rather gangly frame. And there was another sitting to his left, a teacher, and although he had been introduced as a health and physical science teacher, he had the look of a high school football coach with his tight fitting t-shirt, bulging forearms, and crew cut hair.

It was an early fall day, still summer really, the room hot and stuffy even with the windows thrown open to the afternoon breeze. That made it hard for Katie's father to concentrate, hard for him to focus on the conversation flowing around him. They were talking, each one in turn, about Katie, about her tenure at this new school, this high school that she was about to attend. Talking about accommodations, about her… program. About the challenges that lay ahead.

The special education consultant was holding court at the moment, referring to a document of many pages that she held tightly in one hand.

"Katie's IEP from past years is impressive, very impressive," she said. "I am extremely pleased with the comments and observations from her last year in middle school. I am, of course, referring to the right most column on page 2 of the IEP."

Idly he glanced at the copy of the document she was referring to. It lay in front of him open to the very page she was referencing. He read it again, the comments seeming to jump off of the page.

When compared to her peers, Katie is rated in the "very superior" range of achievement. Her weakest area is factual knowledge (art, music, and literature) and in these areas she is still rated in the very high average range for her age grouping.

The wording seemed dry, clinical to him. He wondered about the literature part. The way that child read and read and read, he was surprised she was only rated a "high-average." He read on.

Poor motor skills and her orthopedic impairment limit Katie's abilities in the academic setting. She is able to overcome these weaknesses through her intelligence and academic diligence. She is well accepted by teachers and peers. Teachers refer to her as "…a joy to have in class."

Academic *diligence*. He liked that word, liked the sound of it, mulled it over in his mind as the consultant droned on.

Diligence.

She certainly has that, he thought. If he had to use one word to describe Katie when it came to her schoolwork, diligence was it. But then, he thought with momentary sadness, she had little else in her life to distract her from the pursuit of academic diligence, little else in the way of activities or social contact to lead her astray, to provide her a substitute to the diligence with which she attacked her schoolwork.

Katie is well adapted and her ability to read, solve problems and her outstanding work ethic serve her well in the academic setting. Katie is incredibly intelligent and hard working. She is a wonderful young woman with boundless good humor.

Someone, he thought, some school clerk or assistant somewhere had gotten carried away in writing that last. But it was true, all true. He had given up thinking of limitations for his daughter when it came to matters of academia. Oh, there was plenty she couldn't do, couldn't ride a bike, couldn't play the piano, couldn't pick up a glass and drink from it without spilling most of it all over the floor and herself. Couldn't tie her shoes or write a legible word with pen and paper.

But she could think. She could read. She could solve problems.

She could solve complicated algebraic formulas in her head without breaking a sweat. At that moment, the incongruity of the whole thing seemed to overwhelm him. The simplest physical tasks any four-year-old could handle were beyond her. Yet, she could dance academic circles around anyone within a few years of her, could cite passages from a Shakespearean play, solve a quadratic equation in her head, figure out how many miles Bus A would have to travel to catch Bus B with a half-hour head start, a quartering headwind, and a road to tire friction coefficient of 4.75, whatever that meant, he thought to himself, smiling.

She was an enigma, a definite enigma.

The special education consultant continued her patter, the pages of the report being turned as she read on and on.

Katie will need 122.5 credits and to pass all parts of the proficiency exam to earn a standard diploma.

Katie will pass all aspects of the High School Proficiency Test.

Katie will improve general science knowledge in the areas of Geography, Biology, and Chemistry, receiving no less than a C on all assignments and tests.

No less than a C, he thought to himself. Are you kidding? The kid hadn't made anything but A's since the third grade. Why, if she made a C he honestly believed she would have a nervous breakdown, would need psychiatric help just to get over the shock. He remembered when she had come to him one night, to both of them, her face serious, her eyes already beginning to fill with wetness, the tears not far behind.

"Mom, Dad," she said solemnly.

"Yes, Katie," they replied.

"I just want you to know," she continued, "I just want you to know, to be prepared, okay?"

"Prepared for what, hon," her mother replied, the concern evident in her voice. "What's wrong? Tell me."

"I'm not going to get an A in Geology," she stammered, almost crying, relieved she had finally gotten it out. The words came rushing one after another with barely a pause in between. "The teacher pulled a surprise test and she told us to study the wrong thing and I wrote down the wrong pages and she wouldn't let me take a make-up and it's not fair, and I'm probably going to get a C, or even worse."

"It's okay, Katie," her mother replied. "You don't have to get an A in everything. Why are you so worried?"

"Katie," her father had chimed in, "your mother's right. Did you try? Did you do your best? Then that's all you can ask of yourself. Let the grades fall where they may. Just do your best and be proud of that. Besides, are you sure? Are you sure you haven't made a mistake? There's plenty of time left in the semester. Besides, if you get a B or a C on a test now, you could still get an A for the semester, couldn't you?"

"No," she replied. She was emphatic, a C it was going to be. There was nothing else for it and she was devastated.

Then the time came, the end of the term, the end of the grade period, the time most children dread, when report cards come out. They hadn't known at first, had to ask her if she received it, where it was, what she got. When he looked at it, of course he wasn't surprised, but feigned surprise anyway, his eyebrows rising, his look one of confusion.

"Katie," he exclaimed. "This is all A's. Where's that B you promised me?" he said with a grin. "Where's my C? What was it, geology? Or no, maybe math? Where's the C?"

"Dad, stop it," she cried.

"Not a chance, little girl. I want my C. I want my B. What is this with all A grades? What are you? Some kind of smarty-pants? What's going on here?"

"Alright Dad, I get it. I get it."

It would become a joke between them for years to come. Katie, where's the C you promised me? And he hoped it would remain just that, a joke, for he dreaded the consequences should she ever receive one.

The consultant droned on, the report in her hand. He continued to glance at it, to read the words.

Katie will improve math skills in the areas of Geometry and Algebra, receiving no less than 70% on all tests and exams.

These were the targets and objectives of this, her ninth Individualized Education Program, her IEP. She'd received one every year since first grade. Every year they set the objectives. Every year she blew them away.

Katie will improve broad-based knowledge by reading essays on a variety of subjects and answering questions on the given topic at 80% or better as determined by teacher-developed probes and standardized testing.

They were almost done, he thought, almost through it. In the beginning he paid very close attention to these evaluations, these goal setting sessions. Now they were getting to be routine, their expectations far below what his daughter was actually achieving. He thought they were almost an exercise, an exercise they continued to fulfill because it was required, because it was procedure, because it was the law of the land.

"Now to Katie's accommodations." The consultant paused. Took a breath. Her father leaned in. This was the important part. This was the reason for all the other busy work, the routine assessments, the procedures, to justify their making changes to the normal, ordered world in which they operated. Without the justifications you simply couldn't ask the school system to change, to adapt to one individual when there were so many others to be served.

This was where they needed to understand what changes were necessary, how they needed to change their ordered world, adapt it, make it fit a girl, no, a young woman the report had referred to her as, make the world fit a young woman who was having to work every day to fit herself to that world, a young woman with muscles that wouldn't work right, nerves that wouldn't regenerate, a body that wouldn't cooperate.

Katie will use the Alpha Smart in classes, with a volunteer to write for her during math (notes, assignments, and tests). She may come to the resource room to take tests and complete assignments in coordination with resource staff. She is allowed extra time to finish assignments due to disability and/or teachers may shorten assignments so that she can complete them in class. She will have a study period each day and be left free to work on her assignments as she sees fit.

That last was important, and he broke in, interrupted the teacher's monologue, finally, with something to contribute, something important.

"Yes," he began, "I want it understood that her study hall is not a formal study hall. I know most of the kids in study hall are there because they are slow learners and need help with their studies. But Katie doesn't need that kind of instruction. She really needs to be left alone to complete her work during that time."

The teacher who looked like a coach spoke up at that point, he had been silent since the meeting began.

"Yes, we are aware of that," he said. "I spoke with her homeroom teacher from middle school and she assured me of that. I handle the study hall and she will be in my class. I will see that she gets the time she needs and isn't bothered. You can rest assured on that."

"Good, sorry, didn't mean to interrupt," he stammered. "I just want to make sure you understand her situation. She doesn't need to be coddled, as some think when they look at her or listen to her speak. She's not slow, she needs to be pushed, pushed hard, or she'll

get bored fast. So please, go on, continue. I didn't mean to interrupt," he repeated himself, feeling awkward for a moment.

"Okay, Katie," the consultant concluded. "That just about
does it. Oh, one more thing. You also don't have to take Physical
Education, you know, PE. We've got that waived for you. You don't
have to earn the required number of PE credits in order to graduate
from this school in four years."

Katie looked up quickly, she had been examining the report as
the consultant read, and the relief in her face was clearly evident at
this good news. She worried about PE, a subject she'd never taken,
never had to take, never been able to take. In high school it was a
required subject. You needed two full years, four credits, to graduate. And just as she was about to respond, to thank the consultant
for granting a very important wish of hers, just then, the study hall
teacher once again broke in.

"However, Katie," he said with a grin, "you could earn that PE
credit if you wanted to."

"How?" she asked. "How could I do that?"

"You could come out and be the manager of the girls softball
team," he replied. "I'm the coach, and I think you'd make a great
manager. And you'd earn two PE credits for every season you manage. How about that?" he finished, with a flourish in his voice.

Immediately her father saw the look of concern, no, fear, in her
face. She didn't know those girls, those ball players. Hadn't ever
known them. They were jocks. They could walk and run and throw.
They could slide in to a base, swing a bat and make a catch. She
couldn't do any of those things, never had. When they were learning
to swing a bat and kick a soccer ball, she was learning how to walk,
with a helmet on her head and pads on her extremities, memories
of her walker, now discarded in a closet, still immediate and fresh
in her mind.

She's afraid, her father thought, and unsure as to whether she can even do it. After all, what does she know about baseball, about any sport, about a manager's duties, about what she would have to do?

Katie turned. She looked at her mother. She looked again at her father. Her chin jutted out in just that certain way she had when she was determined to do something, her lower lip curling out and over her chin, her face set with purpose, as if getting ready to take some foul-tasting medicine. At that moment, Katie's father seemed to read her mind.

"Yes, Katie," he said, knowing what she was asking with her eyes, "Yes, we'll help you any way we can."

Katie turned back to the teacher, the teacher who'd made this proposition, the smile still on his face. She thought of the risks involved. Could she do it? Did she even know what was required?

She thought of the early days of her education, her first few years in elementary school when the other kids had been, well, had been cruel at times. The comments, the stares, the occasional bully she had to put up with, to suffer through, the taunts and jokes made about her... her condition. She thought of her sometime nickname... spazz-ma-tazz, and the old pain resurfaced, raw, unresolved, hurtful.

Kids at that age are not socially adept, not trained to hide what they are feeling. And many was the time she had borne the brunt of those feelings, their reactions to her condition, her manner, her way of walking and talking and interacting with the world around her.

Even today people would stare, stare when they thought she wasn't looking, and she felt the pain of those stares resurface in her mind and in her heart. She felt her muscles tighten, the rigidity taking over her body as it often did when she was stressed or in fear from some sudden movement or noise. She was afraid, afraid of the unknown, of the risks involved.

Then the moment passed, for it had only been a moment, a momentary pause. Her father saw her tense up, saw the rigidity that others didn't see, didn't notice. He sensed her fear. Then he saw her relax, the rigidity fading to nothingness, watched the expression on her face change as she turned again to face the teacher who'd thrown her this curveball, this challenge.

"Okay," she said simply. "Okay… I'll try."

It was at that moment, that one second in that hot, late summer classroom, perched in a chair two sizes too small for him, that her father knew, knew that somewhere, somehow, his daughter had learned that things are only worth it if you earn them.

As the special education consultant took pen in hand to make the notation, to add to the report that Katie would act as manager of the softball team, at that moment, he realized just how much she wanted to earn that PE credit.

He realized just how much she wanted to earn everything… to earn it all.

Baseball.

For as long as there has been a child throwing a ball towards another child swinging a stick, there has always been a game of baseball. Called by different names over the centuries, from rounders to stool ball to goal ball, the game transcends the modern era by many generations of time. But in 1845, a man from New York named Alexander Joy Cartwright created the first modern baseball field, put in writing the first set of rules, and without much fanfare, could be said, as well as anyone, to be the inventor of the "modern" game of baseball in America.

Several years later, in 1887, a bunch of young college men hanging about indoors after a football game, started what was to become the modern game of softball. One of those men, by the name of George Hancock, tied a boxing glove into the shape of a ball, chalked a diamond on the floor of the gym where they were lounging, grabbed a pole for a bat, shouted "let's play ball…" and a new game called softball was underway.

Well over one hundred years later, Katie stood at the edge of one of those softball fields. This field was part of a larger sports complex at the only high school in the little town in the mountains where she lived. She stood, silent, motionless, and contemplated her fate.

It was only fall, and the season's schedule of games was still several months away, in the spring. But fall was a time for practice. Fall was a time for recruiting players, holding tryouts, welcoming the returning veterans, sizing up the new rookies, and playing a schedule of tournaments and games that would pave the way for the real season to come.

It was also a time when the team managers got very, very busy. There was equipment to sort, supplies to be ordered, repairs to be made. There were lessons in scoring and keeping stats, there were team meetings to prep for and attend. It was a busy time in the life of a team manager, much less a player.

It was all new to Katie, all foreign to her world and her way of thinking.

Yet, in she jumped. If she was going to do this thing, then she was going to do it. If she was going to earn her PE credit, then she was going to earn it. She studied the game, learned the rules, began to watch the professionals on TV, their season winding down to just a few playoff games in far away cities. She became a fan of one of those teams, studied the players, got to know them from their bios and stats.

She picked up the language, the lingo. She learned the meaning of certain statistics, and the importance of them, and why batting average was different from slugging index, and on base percentage, and earned run average, and on, and on.

She learned how to keep score. She learned how to keep statistics on the players. No, she couldn't write them down on the forms provided. A pencil, paper, and clipboard were beyond her attempts to master. So she sat down at her computer and she developed her own forms, her own shorthand. The computer was portable. The computer was moveable. The computer was the perfect instrument to record and write and maintain the information she needed to manage.

She downloaded forms, developed her own files from spreadsheets and word documents. She learned to keep player lists and notes and other information in the computer, organized in a way that delighted her coaches and made her something of a hero in the organization. For they had never been quite so... organized, the coaches thought. That is, until Katie came along.

She hauled the equipment out before each practice. She helped haul it in. In and out, in and out, her muscles straining, her fingers grasping and holding the odd shaped gloves and pads and bags of balls. She staggered under the load. Occasionally she fell. But she refused help, laughed off any physical miscues, and the others learned to leave her to her own devices, her own efforts. Not that they didn't try to help. But Katie could do it herself, thank you.

During the practice games she stood inside the dugout, her computer at the ready, entering the day's quota of data. She occasionally stepped out onto the field, once she gained confidence, stepped out to chase down an errant ball thrown in from the outfield before the start of play, to corral an errant bat carelessly tossed aside by the previous batter on their way to first base, or thrown aside by the next batter getting ready to hit.

Through it all her smile never wavered, never left her face. In the end, it wasn't so much the hard work, the falling without complaining, the picking herself up and dusting herself off that did it. It was the smile. The smile endeared her to everyone on the team. The big and little, the rookies and the pros, the jocks and the wanna-be jocks, they all grew fond of this girl, this freshman, this manager who worked so hard, so selflessly, who fell and got hurt and shrugged it off as nothing. And who always seemed to light up their world with her smile.

It was infectious, that smile. It was contagious. It was there when they lost. It was there when they won. It was there when the coach ordered extra calisthenics. It was there when the snows came and forced them inside, to the hot and stuffy gym, where practice seemed to be nothing more than the drudgery and pain of doing exercises and running laps. Whatever the occasion, whatever the circumstances, Katie was there, there with a smile, a word of encouragement, an example to all who struggled and fought to excel in this game that demanded of these young women the sweat and exertion, the scratches and gouges, and yes, even the broken arms and wrists and elbows that went in to forming a team.

Throughout that long fall, into winter, and even to the beginning of the spring season, when the real competition with teams from other schools would begin, Katie's team worked and practiced, sweated and ran, threw and caught, swung and hit, and came together. Throughout it all Katie's smile was the common denominator, the fundamental element, the foundation of all their efforts to meld into a single unit, a single... team.

And she was making friends. Real friends.

For many years she had enjoyed a sort of notoriety at the schools she attended. It started in elementary school. Her father noticed that whenever he picked her up from school, everyone who walked by her on the schoolyard would shout out a "Hello Katie" and "Hi Katie" and "See you tomorrow, Katie." That she was popular was evident. Everyone wanted to know her, to pay her some acknowledgement at those times. After all, she was different, she stood out, almost as if she was a favorite mascot, a signpost, a differentiator.

But the invitations to parties, the invitations to sleepovers, the trips to see a movie, the shopping sprees at the mall, those never came.

It was a faux fame, he thought to himself at the time, a sort of celebrity status without any real meaning or content behind it. It was lip service. Not that he begrudged them their actions. It is hard for children to deal with something so outside their normal world, when everything else in their world is so new. At that age the world is unfolding, and learning to live in it is not easy, not easy for anyone, much less those youngsters learning to socialize with their peers for the very first time in their lives.

So Katie had acquaintances, many acquaintances, but no real friends, no hang-out-on-a-Sunday-afternoon-and-do-nothing friends, no sleep-over-and-sleep-in-on-Saturday-morning friends, no go-shopping-at-the-mall friends. She studied, she read, she explored the world inside her computer, but she spent little or no time simply playing and socializing with friends.

Now, baseball was changing that. These players, these teammates were becoming friends. Oh, not all of them, but enough. For once Katie was beginning to get invitations, to parties, to trips to the mall and the movie theater. She was beginning to fit in, "fit in" in a way she never had before. For once, she was feeling like a part, a true part, of the world she moved through. This school was becoming more than just a place to go and study and learn. Baseball was doing that for her. Sports, the one thing above all others that her parents thought was beyond her reach, beyond her situation, sports was paving the way to a real sense of community, of belonging in the world.

She was beginning to make actual friends.

So the time came. After all the work and practices and meetings, it was time for the first real game of the season, the first game that would count towards the league standings and entry into the end-of-season tournament. Katie arrived early, the excitement carrying her away as if she were to be out on the field swinging and throwing and running with the others. It was a home game and she had equipment to haul out, a field to prepare. She had pads and bats to carry, bags of balls, her computer and printer, and all those scoring sheets and forms to fill out.

The other girls began to arrive, to work out and loosen up. They were in high spirits. The team was favored this year to win it all. There was excitement around the beginning of what many thought would be their best year, a championship year. Katie was caught up in it all, running from place to place as best she could run, providing a glove here, a ball there, a bandage when it was called for to bind up a scrape from an errant slide or catch.

Her parents arrived early as well. They were keyed up in anticipation. This, after all, was a new experience, one they hadn't ever expected to be a part of. They suffered through the early days of fall practice, of Katie coming home tired and bruised, worn out from the exertion of trying to handle all her duties. They saw her grow and mature, saw her attack her role with the same diligence she applied towards her schooling. They began to think of her as one of the team, almost as if she too was a player.

So they looked forward to that first game with a great deal of anticipation. Schedules were checked, arrangements made. They would be there, would be there for the first pitch and the last out. They would be there to cheer and root like any other parent, any other player's proud mother or father. They chose the best seats in the bleachers, just behind home plate and high enough up to command a view of the entire field. They arranged seat cushions, broke out the peanuts and drinks from a small cooler they had provisioned that morning, and settled in for the duration.

The rituals of game time began, the colors presented, the anthem sung, the players introduced. The first pitch was thrown and the contest was on. It was clear this game was going to be a close one. The other team was rising to the challenge of playing one of the top seeds in the division. At this time, so early in the season, the bats on both teams started hot, while the fielding suffered. The pitchers were nervous, threw a lot of balls, walked a lot of players, threw easy strikes that a willing hitter could do much with. Many runs were scored. By the bottom of the fifth, the game was tied at ten runs apiece.

With only two more innings to go, the home team coach went to her ace in the hole, her closer, the senior pitcher who had been named an all-star the season before. The game was fast-pitch, and this senior had an arm like a tree trunk, with blazing speed out of the wind-up. She could move the ball up or down, in or out, but it was the speed that made her so hard to hit.

In the top of the sixth inning she mowed down the competition in order... one, two, three. The first she retired on three strikes, three straight fastballs too hot for the opposing batter to handle. The second batter managed to foul off two pitches before she too went down swinging, swinging at nothing but air, the ball already having passed on into the outstretched glove of the catcher. The last batter managed nothing more than a weak pop-up that was easily caught by the third base fielder.

In the bottom of the sixth, the visiting team, sensing doom, also went with their best pitcher, one they had held in reserve as well, for just such a situation as this, with the score tied and only one and a half innings left to play. It was another three-up and three down performance, as each of the home team's hitters were unable to connect, unable to manage a hit against this new pitcher's fresh arm. Going into the seventh and last inning, the game was still tied at ten runs apiece.

In the top of the seventh, the home team pitcher kept up her winning ways. She fanned the first batter on three strikes, worked up to a 3 and 2 count on the second, and put her away with a fastball down the middle. Then, the opposing team tried one last trick, one last chance to win. They sent in a pinch-hitter whose size and stance seemed to suggest power beyond what any of the others on the field could even imagine. She was big, tall and sturdy, her arms long and well muscled. It was clear she was a stick, a bat, a pinch-hitting specialist, a girl who knew how to swing, how to connect with any pitch and send it flying into the stratosphere.

She was held back, was kept on the bench, in reserve, for just such an opportunity as this. Last at bat, last chance to break open the game and win it all. And she was ready.

The home team tensed up, called encouragement to their pitcher, their ace. The outfielders moved back, the infield as well. The crowd, sensing a pivotal moment in what was becoming a fantastic contest, shouted encouragement from the bleachers. For just a few moments it was bedlam on and around the field as the noise swelled to a crescendo in anticipation of the duel to come, a duel between these two, this ace pitcher with the blazing speed, and this powerful batter with the muscled arms.

The pitcher squared up to the mound. She shook off the first sign. Shook off the second. She wanted a fastball. She wanted to challenge this batter right out of the gate. Finally, she nodded. She had the call she wanted. She wound up, she released, the ball sailing to the center of the plate, the speed growing and growing, a fastball right down the middle.

And sure enough, with a mighty swing, the batter launched this very first pitch and sent it flying into the left field gap. Up, up, up and away the ball went, a home run for sure, the crowd gasped in unison. This could be the game.

Then, running, leaping, jumping, stretching all the way from center into the gap, her arm outstretched, her leg lifted to the fence, her foot propelling her body up into the air, her glove rising over the edge of the top of the outfield fence, the centerfielder made an incredible catch, a gravity defying catch, a leaping running twisting catch... a game winning catch.

The home team crowd erupted, the cheers rolling over the field like some giant wave, and the players came skipping and running and cheering off the field. At the dugout they mobbed their team-mate and congratulated her on the amazing catch. They knew now they had one last chance to break the tie and win their first game of the season, a season they were supposed to dominate.

Bottom of the seventh.

Last inning.

Score still tied, ten all.

The first two batters went down swinging. The visiting team's pitcher was still just too hot to hit. With nobody on and two outs, the last batter got ready to head to the plate. Katie was standing at the spot her coach had designated for her during game time, just in-side the dugout entrance, her computer immediately to her left on a small stand up against the dugout fence. From here she could man-age the score and the stats, collect pads and gloves from the players returning from the field, and be in a position to handle anything else that might come up during the game.

At that moment, something else came up. An opportunity arose. The last batter was getting ready to take the field, getting ready to hit. She had been in the on deck circle, warming up, but returned to the dugout at the last second to change bats. As she walked by the benches, and began to pass out onto the field, at that moment, Katie reached out, touched her arm, and gave her a smile, the smile, the smile that the whole team had come to know, that great big wonderful smile.

"Hit it," she said through her smile, the other girl locking eyes with her for just that moment in time. "Kill it. Knock it out of here."

Then she smiled, again.

The other girl, her teammate, smiled back, smiled, laughed, and went out onto the field, her words trailing behind as she went. "You got it, Katie," she said as she walked. "This one is all yours."

Up in the stands, Katie's father saw the brief exchange between his daughter and the batter. Saw the smile, the return of the smile, saw the batter's lips move, although he couldn't hear what was said. But at that moment, he had a feeling, a hunch. He turned to his wife as the batter took her stance.

"This is it," he said. "First pitch, a home run. Katie put the mojo on her. She's gonna knock it out of the park."

"Yeah right," his wife replied. "You've been watching too many movies."

"Wanna bet?" he shot back, a grin playing across his entire face.

Before she could respond, could even draw another breath to speak, it happened. The pitcher made her wind-up and released her first pitch, the ball rifling towards home plate, a perfect strike, right down the middle.

There was a crack, a loud crack, as if someone had smashed a stick against a solid metal post, as if a gun had been discharged, its explosive burst of gunpowder echoing across the surrounding mountains.

Bat met ball, and the ball went away, soaring, rising, reaching up to the sky, arcing out over the players, over the infield diamond, straight for center field, straight for the longest part of the outfield. The opposing team's center fielder went back, back, back, her arms stretched, her body straining, her legs pumping furiously. She jumped up, reached out, got her glove on the ball...

The ball, the glove, and the top of the fence came together in one unifying impact, one massive collision, all three arriving at the same point in space at the exact same moment in time. The glove hit the fence, the ball hit the glove, the ball hopped up, and lazily, as if in slow motion, popped over the fence and dropped into the field beyond.

A walk-off home run.

Game over.

The crowd burst into cheers, the players swept out onto the field, eager to be at home plate when the winning batter finished her victorious romp around the bases. They wanted to celebrate this incredible finish, and this wonderful beginning to what was to become a great season.

But Katie's father was to remember it for something far more important than the thrill of that final home run. With the game over, his wife left quickly for the long walk to the parking lot, her car, and home. She had errands to finish and dinner to start. But he hesitated, stayed in the bleachers, watching and waiting, for what he did not know.

As the dust settled, with the game finally over, the teams huddled in front of their respective dugouts. They began preparing to step out onto the field, to walk past the other team, player by player, to shake the other team's hand, player by player, a time-honored tradition going back dozens if not hundreds of years. And at that particular moment, something happened, something that no one else might have noticed.

You had to be watching. You had to be paying attention to just the right spot, and to just the right people. And he was. He was watching Katie, his daughter, the team manager, the one girl who had not set foot on the field as a player, had not caught one ball, swung one bat, or fielded one hit. He was watching her as the two teams started to shake hands in single-file, the players stretched out into one long line on each side of the diamond.

She was standing by the dugout, in her appointed place, just inside the entrance, when it happened. One of her teammates, the hero of the game, the one who hit the crushing, soaring, arching home run, that teammate turned, saw Katie standing alone, and stopped. She walked over to Katie, grabbed her by the arm and started to walk her into the line of players.

Katie pulled back, resisted the gesture. Her father could see it from where he sat alone in the bleachers. He could see it as if standing only a few feet away. He could imagine what she must be saying, must be thinking.

"No, I don't belong out there, I shouldn't be doing this, I'm not a player, I'm only an assistant, a manager."

He could also hear the other girl's voice, imagining her response as she pulled and tugged at Katie's arm.

"Yes, you are. You are a part of this team. And you will walk out and shake the other team's hand at the end of the game, win or lose, because it's the right thing to do... and you are a part of this team."

So Katie walked, succumbing to her teammate's gesture, her hips splayed apart, body shifting from side to side. She walked across the field, last in line, her arm outstretched, her fingers grasping at the hands as they came her way.

The other team's players looked at her in surprise, some startled, some unsure how to proceed. Who was this girl that was bringing up the end of the line? She was not a player. She could barely walk, her hand outstretched, rigid, grasping at air. What was this? What was going on? The first player to reach her stopped for a moment, paused, as if wondering what to do. And then, after an awkward, oh so awkward, moment, she reached out, took Katie's hand, and shook it. Her teammates followed her lead and one by one they passed Katie, shaking her hand, nodding, accepting her presence as if it were the most natural thing in the world.

As he left the field, as her father climbed down from the bleachers and turned to make the long walk to the parking lot and his car and home, as he turned to walk away, he knew he would never forget that sight, never forget the sight of his daughter and her teammates, shaking hands, wishing well, in this, the first game of the season.

He would go to many more games, watch her walk across the field many more times over the years, shake many more hands. But never again would he feel the way he did at this moment, in this place, at this time.

She was a member of the team. She belonged. For the first time in her life, she truly belonged.

And the fact that he cried all the way to his car, really didn't bother him at all.

Weeks flew by, and then months. The games came and went, some at home, some on the road. Katie attended every one, standing at her post, attending to her duties, her presence a talisman of sorts, a good luck charm for this championship team. And champions they were. They finished the season in first place, won the season-ending tournament, went to sectionals. It was there they finally came face-to-face with defeat. It was there they lost in the final game, lost a chance to go all the way to the state championship game. But that was alright. They had succeeded beyond their wildest dreams. They had become champions, heroes in this little school in this little town in the mountains.

And through it all, Katie belonged, she was a part, a part of this team, a part of this championship season.

Spring turned into summer, the days grew longer. The snow melted and everything began to turn green. Katie finished her first year of high school. Her academic record remained unblemished, every class completed, every grade an A. And she earned two PE credits in exchange for her success as a manager of the softball team, manager of a championship team. It was, they all decided, a successful year, a great year, a sporting year.

Katie's father began to travel for work. He would fly to faraway places with strange names, traveling all around the country, help-ing businesses to operate better, to market and sell their products better, to offer better service to those they served. He developed a consulting practice that was becoming increasingly more successful, which meant he spent an increasing amount of time away, away from his wife, away from Katie, away from the little town nestled in the mountains.

He loved the work, found it satisfying, enriching. But the time away was difficult. He missed being at home, missed being able to participate in every event, every significant moment in his family's lives. It was during that lazy summer, the summer after Katie's first year in high school, that he found himself half a continent away, working a project, when his daughter called, her tiny voice carried across the country by the magic of the airwaves.

"Dad," she asked, "when are you coming home?"

"In a couple of days, Katie," he answered. He could hear the excitement in her voice, could feel it through the static of his cell phone. "Why?" he continued. "What's up?"

"Because we won, Dad. We won. And I got a trophy. My first ever trophy. And I want you to see it," she said.

"Oh, Katie," he exclaimed, "That's great. That's wonderful! I'll be home in a few days, just a few days. I promise. You can show it to me then, okay? I'm so sorry I wasn't there. So sorry I missed it. But I'll be home soon. Okay?"

"Okay, Dad," she said. "Hurry home."

After that winning season, the coaches from her high school formed a summer team from among the players on the school squad. They wanted to keep the team together, keep them playing, keep them sharp for the coming year. The team played some local games, but their big plan was to attend an out-of-town tournament, a tour-nament that featured teams from all over that part of the country. Katie was invited to join as team manager. They wanted her with them, wanted her smile, her energy, her spark.

They agreed, her parents, agreed to let her participate, to travel with the other girls on chartered buses to a city far away. Her mother even made arrangements to go, to watch a few days of the week-long tournament, to assist the team along with a few other dedicated parents. But he was not able to attend. He had to travel, had to be away. It was another in a long line of disappointments he had to endure, traveling for business, missing those moments, those times that you could never get back.

That was the hard part, the missing, the lost moments. They won the tournament, were victorious, and every player was given their own trophy, Katie included. He thought back to a time when he was in school, when trophies were a part of any normal child's life. He thought of his friends, friends with children, and the times he would visit in their homes, tour their rooms, see the trophies for tennis and soccer, for baseball and football, trophies for ballet and dancing, heck, they even had trophies for piano recitals, he thought.

It was something he never really even considered for Katie. A trophy? Maybe for school, maybe for her academics. But it was beyond his wildest imaginings, his and his wife's, that she would actually join that group of kids proudly displaying their trophies along the walls of their bedrooms.

Now it had happened. And of course, he'd missed it. It was these times when the travel seemed most hard, seemed to take too great a toll on him.

It was hard on his wife as well. She felt like a single-parent at times. There were still therapy sessions to go to. A busy schedule of specialists, yoga classes, voice classes, physical therapy classes. It was not easy doing this alone, handling it all without assistance.

"I know you have to travel," she said. "I know you do it for us, but it's hard when you're not here. I have to handle it all. And she needs her father around."

It was another chasm between them, another thing for them to deal with. They argued and fought. They would make up. He felt powerless to change things. At times he felt resentment. After all, he was sacrificing, missing out, so they could all have a better life, a better existence. But she was right again. He knew it in his heart. He should find a way to be there, to be present.

Once again, there was no solution. They had to simply let it lie, to deal with it, to find a way to incorporate it into their relationship without it dividing them, fracturing them beyond repair. But he was all too often saying those words, those words he had come to dread saying. "I'll be home soon… really, I will… just a few more days."

The pain of Katie's birth, that time of near death, was always there, always between husband and wife, between mother and father. Her condition was a constant reminder of that experience. It drew them together, it pulled them apart. It bound them, and it created boundaries between them. The future continued to be unknown, the victories they experienced the only shield they had against the uncertainty of the future, of Katie's future, and theirs. The failures, and there had been many, the failures brought back the pain, the pain of knowing what might have been, what might have occurred if they hadn't waited, hadn't insisted on a natural birth, if they had just decided sooner, just a few minutes sooner. The regret, the guilt, was like a crushing, smothering blanket ready to suffocate them at any moment.

Their daughter still could not do many of the things others simply took for granted. She could not write out a signature on a piece of paper, couldn't tie her shoes. Her voice was often garbled, you had to concentrate to understand her, asking over and over for her to repeat herself, repeat herself until you could figure out what she said. She still couldn't ride a bike down a sidewalk, or bake cookies on a lazy Saturday afternoon. She had few friends. No boys would call. That was probably a blessing, they both agreed. The softball team was a start, but she was still struggling to have any kind of a social life, any kind of a relationship that other kids simply took for granted.

Would she be able to drive, to work, to be self-sufficient once school was over and the world called to her to make her own way, to start her own life? Would she be able to marry, to have children of her own? Would she be able to work, to keep up in a world that was moving ever and ever faster?

They wouldn't always be around to help, to protect her, to shield her from a world that didn't give a damn. There were simply too many unanswered questions, too many unknowns. And they sometimes felt they were drowning in those unknowns. The doctors said to take it one day at a time, and they tried. But it was hard, hard to deal with, with the unknowing, and the unknown.

His traveling didn't help, didn't solve anything, just drew them farther apart.

But through it all he still felt gratitude, gratitude for this woman he loved, for this woman who bore this child and met every challenge, who fought for her daughter, fought to get her into school, fought to get her into therapy, fought to find answers, fought to make as normal a life as possible for this little girl who was anything but normal.

She had been at the game and he hadn't. She had been at home every night, and he wasn't. She was the one Katie came to when others were cruel or mean, when Katie was frustrated by her inability to do something, something simple. She was the one who held her at those times, when Katie would cry and shake, her fragile reserve broken by the sometime cruelty of others. She was the one who tended to this young girl while he flew about the country, taking care of business, making the money they needed for the clothes and the therapy and all the other things that would insulate them from the evils of the world.

Through it all, through the fights, the disagreements, and the arguments, he remained grateful. As he traveled home from that trip, home to see his little girl's first trophy, he thought of that word. Yes, he was grateful, grateful for his wife, grateful for his daughter, even grateful for her condition and everything it entailed. For it defined him, defined who he was, defined him in a way he had never understood before.

The drive home from the airport seemed to take longer than ever before. The plane was delayed, and he was running late. He had promised his daughter he would be home by suppertime, home to see this new trophy, the first trophy she had ever won.

Suppertime came and went and it was getting on into late night. He flew into the driveway, barely remembered to put the car in park, and raced to the kitchen door. There was no one in the kitchen, nor in the first floor of the house. He called out.

"Honey, I'm hoooooome," he cried. "Daddy's home!"

There were voices from above, from upstairs. He raced to the landing, rushed to the top, turned and swung into the doorway of Katie's bedroom. They were both there, his wife and daughter, sitting on the bed. She was combing Katie's hair, the brush flying through the thin strands in short, quick stokes.

"Hi, Daddy," Katie cried. "You're back."

"Welcome home, honey," his wife said as a smile played across her face. "You made it just in time. Your daughter is about to burst. I never would have gotten her to bed, much less asleep."

They both grinned from the bed. He took it all in, enjoying the high spirits, the jovial mood in the room. This was home. This was domestic bliss, this scene, these two women sitting on a bed, welcoming, smiling. This was a calm moment in a sea of constant storms, and it washed over him, bathed him at that moment in happiness, the kind of happiness you cannot define, the kind you can only feel, if just for a moment... pure, sublime, blissful.

Then he saw it. It was sitting there in front of him, standing really, as it was so tall it seemed to be reaching for the ceiling. It was perched on her shelf, in that certain position of honor right above her bed. It was sitting right next to the photo that he knew so well, the photo from their very first trip to Disneyland, the personally signed and autographed picture of Minnie Mouse in her red and white polka-dot dress.

It was a trophy all right, sitting on a large base of solid wood, the wood stained dark and faced with a brass plate that said FIRST PLACE in big bold letters, the only part of the writing he could read from where he stood in the doorway.

Rising up out of the base was a column of silver and gold, an octagonal support that rose at least several feet towards the ceiling. Perched atop that column was a large replica of a softball player, her hair flowing around her neck and shoulders, her body twisted and straining as the bat she held seemed to swing for the fences.

It was a fine trophy, a good trophy, a solid trophy. More importantly, it was hers. She had won it, earned it as much as any other player on the team. At that moment they all felt it, felt a closeness, a togetherness that transcended all the pain, all the fights, all the differences between them.

They were one.

They were celebrating a moment that happened over and over again, in households all across the country. A child brings home a trophy, a symbol of accomplishment, of having achieved something on a field of play. It was a proud moment, a close moment.

It was a normal moment, in an abnormal life.

In the fall, when school started up again, with Katie beginning her second year, her sophomore year, they held an awards banquet. It was an award ceremony for all the spring sports teams whose seasons had finished too late in the prior semester to be properly recognized. It was a big event, the baseball teams, the field and track teams, the soccer and volleyball and tennis teams, all attending.

The banquet was held in the gym, the floor of the basketball court having been transformed into a dining hall. There were ribbons hung from the rafters, balloons filled with helium, tied into bunches, and strategically placed around the large room. At the front was a temporary stage with a podium where the speeches were to be made, the awards presented.

They were all there, the students and coaches sitting at their respective team tables, the parents seated at tables in the rear, the school officials located at a special table in front, the principal and assistants, the athletic director and staff, all present for the festivities.

The softball team had won their division, been champions, came one game away from the state championship, and they were being singled out, the most successful of all the teams present. With dinner over, the time for the awards came. Speeches were made, then the presentations. One by one the team members stood, formed a line, and began to march across the stage to receive their medals and certificates of participation.

Katie's mother and father were sitting towards the front of the parent section. They had again arrived early, not wanting to miss a moment of this spectacle, an event they never thought they would be participating in. They strained to see as the team lined up for their awards, strained to catch a glimpse of their daughter, to make sure she was accorded enough time to make her way to the stage, to ensure someone was there to help her climb the few steps to the raised platform. She was at the end of the group, second to last, another teammate helping her along.

There were cheers from the crowd as each player received their award, polite clapping, murmurs from different parents as they spotted their children. Katie's turn was like all the rest, polite applause and congratulations from some. She was simply another member of the team, a part of all that was going on.

With a flourish the last player was awarded, the last team received their accolades. The party broke up, parents collecting the kids too young to drive themselves, the others, the juniors and seniors off to celebrate on their own. Katie came walking up to her parents, excited, smiling, her medal clutched in one hand, her certificate in the other.

"Katie," her mother scolded, "be careful, slow down. You know you're not supposed to walk that fast with your hands full."

"Yes, Mom," she replied, groaning as any teenager will when being scolded by a parent.

"Mom, Dad, can I go with the team to a party? I can get a ride, and they'll bring me home. Please, oh please, they want me to come. Can I?"

She was still just a sophomore, and most of the girls were juniors and seniors. They had worried about this, about Katie going out with others who didn't understand her needs, understand the dangers she faced, dangers that were nothing more than routine actions to others.

"I don't know, hon," her mother replied. "We were planning on taking you out to celebrate ourselves." She was hesitant, still getting used to the idea of her daughter being out of sight, out of her protection, running with kids she didn't really know, hadn't had a chance to get to know through the years of isolation Katie had experienced. This socializing was new to her.

"I suppose it would be alright," she hesitated. "What do you think, Dad?"

"Sure, Katie," he replied. "You go ahead. Just be careful."

He turned to his wife to reassure her with a look. He was becoming far more confident in Katie's ability to handle herself.

"We'll be okay, I'm sure we can find something else to do this evening."

He smiled at his wife, took her hand.

"Oh thanks, guys, thanks a bunch." She rushed off, just barely remembering to hand the medal and certificate to her parents. "Thanks, I'll be home by midnight?" This last more a question than a statement.

"No, young lady," her mother replied sternly, "you will be home by ten, you got that?"

"Yes, Mom," she managed to gulp as she rushed off, glad for her freedom, happy to be away, on her own, with her teammates. It was tough, this high school life, this being a teenager with overprotective parents, parents that worried about every little thing.

"You know," his wife said, turning to her husband. "That's the first time I can think of when we had to set a curfew for her."

"And it probably won't be the last," he replied, grinning. "She's growing up, Mom; she's getting her legs under her. I think this is the start of all those teenage horror stories we've heard about."

"I suppose," she said. "It's always later with Katie, but then better late than never. Still, I can't help but feel we're losing her, losing her to the world we've protected her from all these years."

"We knew it had to come," he said. "She's learning, learning to deal with friends and activities, learning how to live. At some point we're going to have to let her go."

It was a sad moment for both of them, but also a proud moment, a moment they both had looked forward to, hoped for, for many years.

As they walked to the parking lot and their waiting car, he couldn't help but think to himself that in some way Katie had crossed a threshold, had passed from one life to another, from a life of introspection and isolation, of academics, of therapy and specialists and learning how to deal with the world, to one full of the world around her, of a social life she'd never had.

He was not to know, not at this point, on this night, that this would be only the first of many banquets, many awards. Katie would spend four years managing the softball team. She would earn four medals, four certificates, and two varsity letters for sports. And, even more important, she would graduate with eight PE credits, twice the amount needed.

She would graduate having made friends, true friends of those other players, those teammates of hers.

Against all odds, he decided, it was going to be a sporting life for her after all.

A very sporting life… indeed.

Growing Up

If her early years were a period of development, of working and striving to simply survive and exist in a world not made for her, then the teenage years were like a coming out party for Katie. She was growing more independent, more sure of herself. Softball had a lot to do with it. Her time with the team was something she could call her own, something she had achieved all by herself. But the years ahead held many other milestones, many other achievements, achievements that would define her as she grew to young adulthood, define her as her own person, capable of living in the world and being a part of it.

First and foremost, there were the friendships that had so eluded her in the past.

She was making friends. With age and a bit of maturity, others were beginning to discover Katie as a friend, a confidant, a companion. Oh, the faux celebrity status continued on in to high school. People would call from across the campus grounds, on the way in or out of class, shout out a "Hello, Katie" and wave, or when passing in the hallways of the school, acknowledge her and smile. Most all of those who called were still simply acquaintances, people you knew, but don't really know. She was like a mascot, a symbol, a fixture that made the other students feel a sense of community and closeness, of familiarity, like a long lost hometown revisited in one's older years.

But there were a few that called, that went on trips to the mall or the movie theater, who spent the occasional night at a sleepover. And there was one girl, one young woman, who was to become her very best friend ever, a BFF the girls called it… Best Friends Forever.

Her name was Amy, and she was the daughter of Katie's father's business partner. They met as children, they connected, and became acquainted. But she lived in the big city in the valley, went to different schools and hung out in a different community. So for several years they simply knew one another from afar, saw each other at holiday gatherings, or at the business functions and parties of their parents.

It was at a holiday party during Katie's first year of high school when they really connected, when the bond grew stronger and more lasting. They were sharing a holiday dinner, the two families, and everyone was there. The meal was completed and the party broke into small groups. Katie and Amy slipped away to Amy's room to look at the gifts Amy had received that year, gifts that had, a few short days before, been mysterious, gaily-wrapped presents under a tree. Amy was showing off the best of those holiday gifts, a new computer, a laptop, her first, a present for her schoolwork, and for emailing and communicating with friends.

She had just unpacked it, charged it up, and was trying to unlock the secrets of its mysteries, when Katie showed up. It started as a simple question about the operating system, about how to perform some simple task, how to place a background picture on the desktop, the main screen of the computer.

Amy was amazed when Katie took the computer from her, placed it on her lap, and, with arms poised and ready, the digits of her fingers extended into that familiar rigid pattern, began to type. Around went her arms, down came the fingers, one keystroke at a time, a symphony of movement, awkward and balanced, chaotic and controlled. Katie's fingers flew, the computer obeying her commands, the screen changing with every keystroke.

"Katie," she exclaimed, "how on earth did you learn to do that?"

"It's simple," Katie replied, smiling. "You just right click anywhere on the desktop and the commands come up. Here, watch this."

Quickly her fingers raced across the keyboard, her arms pumping up and down furiously, her fingers unerringly going to their mark. Occasionally she would miss, would have to backtrack and rekey the command. But it was a world Katie had lived in for years, a world she knew well, knew how to manipulate and control. Amy was awestruck.

"Can you show me how to set up an Internet connection, how to get online?" Amy asked.

"Of course," Katie replied. "It's easy. Here, let's see if any wireless connections are present."

Once again her fingers flew across the keyboard. For the next two hours they sat, engrossed, working with this new toy that Katie knew so well, talking and laughing in between, Katie showing Amy shortcuts, secrets, ways to connect with friends, how to email and Facebook.

When the party was over, when all the other guests had said goodbye, when her parents were ready to leave, the last ones to go, the girls still sat and talked, and talked and laughed, and talked some more. They had to be pulled apart, her father shouting from downstairs that "someone was going to get grounded if she did not come down RIGHT NOW."

Slowly Katie turned the laptop off, lowered the cover, placed it carefully on the bed. Amy reached out, they hugged, and then Amy whispered in Katie's ear the words that she knew she would never forget, words that would come to mean everything over the coming years.

"Katie," she said, her mouth pressed close to Katie's ear as they hugged. "We're going to be best friends forever."

She'd never had a best friend, much less a best friend forever. It left her dumbstruck, speechless, yet possessed of a feeling of warmth and happiness that washed through her like a river rushing through some deep and mysterious canyon. She hesitated, took in a breath, and began to smile that wonderful smile, her smile.

"Yes," Katie said simply. "Yes, we are."

It wasn't easy being best friends forever, because they lived in different towns, worlds apart. But somehow they managed. She would beg her father to take her into the city when he went to work. She would go for sleepovers during the weekends. Amy was a year older, and so got her driver's license while Katie was still a sophomore. Then she could make the drive to the little town in the mountains, could plan trips and outings, to the mall, to the movies, to parties. It opened a whole new world for Katie, a new set of friends in a faraway place, a different city, a different school. And, if they were to truly be best friends forever, if they were to truly be so close, then Katie knew that one day they would have to share her most favorite place in the world, a place of magic and make believe.

It happened in the winter of her second year in high school. It was a cold January, there was snow all over the ground, and school was just starting up again after the holiday break. Katie had just received her report card for the first semester of that sophomore year. She was taking three honors classes, one in math, one in science, and one in computers. She had a full schedule and was working constantly, doing homework at study hall, in the afternoons, and at night, her fingers furiously typing at the computer, trying to keep up, to keep up with the work that took her so much longer to complete than others.

But the work paid off. Once again she brought home a report card full of A's, another perfect semester, another academic achievement. Her parents were once again amazed at what she had been able to accomplish. They were sure the rigors of high school would begin to put a dent in Katie's grades, in her work. But she met the challenge, from freshman year to now, her perfect record of perfect marks continued unblemished.

They were all standing in the kitchen, Katie, her mother, and her father. Katie's father was looking at her report card, marveling at the grades that his wife had already examined, the straight line of A's marching across the page, the comments from teachers jumping off the remarks column of the form.

"Excellent work!" one said.

"A joy in class," another remarked.

"Superior ability," read another.

As he read through the report card, a feeling passed through her father. He wasn't exactly sure what it was, but it was equal parts of pride, and joy, happiness, and yes, even a little jealousy. He had stopped being able to help her with her math homework for some time. It was simply beyond him. She had surpassed whatever academic prowess he had ever accomplished in the areas of math and science.

The feeling continued to grow and build, welling up from somewhere within his very center, his core. It was powerful, consuming, and inspiring, and it finally reached a peak and came rushing out of him, rushing out in a way he hadn't even planned.

"Katie," he said. "We are so proud of you, so blown away by this. We're so proud... so..." he reached for the right words. Then it occurred to him, came over him so fast he simply blurted it out without thinking.

"Katie," he exclaimed, "we're so proud of what you've done that for your birthday coming up next month your mother and I want to give you whatever you want. You can have anything, go anywhere, do anything... whatever you want for your sixteenth birthday."

His wife turned to look at him, her face a mask of horror. It seemed to shout, "are you crazy, are you out of your mind? This is a teenager after all. Forget the disability, forget the handicap, she's a teenager. What on earth are you thinking?" She was startled at this offer, shocked if truth be told. She knew the danger of it, the insanity, or so her face seemed to convey, as she stared at him, startled beyond words.

Katie's reaction was somewhat different. She heard the words, heard the offer, and processed what it could mean, what the opportunity was. She leaned forward, her eyes bright and shining.

"Anything," she replied, repeating and slowly stretching out the word. "ANYTHING!"

"Yes, anything," he said with bravado, false bravado he admitted to himself, as he began to understand just what he had done. He was beginning to comprehend the magnitude of his mistake.

Anything! What, are you nuts, he thought to himself, echoing his wife's sentiments. Anything could mean, well… anything! And yes, this was a teenager, a very cool, very hip teenager, he had come to discover. No longer were the clothes at Wal-Mart good enough, oh no, not for this girl. She had to have the trendiest clothes, the coolest shoes, even if she couldn't wear half of them.

"Anything" could hurt, he thought to himself again. Hurt big time. He could feel the wallet in his pocket grow warm, his credit cards starting to melt from the prospect of excessive use. A trip abroad? A shopping spree at Macys? Anything, after all, was, well, anything.

Then Katie spoke. She had paused a moment, she had to think about this gesture, this magnanimous offer she was being given.

"Well, Dad," she replied, grinning from ear to ear, "if I can have anything for my sixteenth birthday, well, then, I want to take off from school and go to Disneyland, and I want Amy to go with me!"

There it was, the magic again. That was it, he thought to himself. If she could do anything she wanted, then a visit to the land of magic was her request. And he wasn't really surprised. The mysteriousness of far off lands held no allure for her, the thrill of a shopping spree couldn't compare to the place where she could be a princess. He should have known. But at that instant, there was something he did know, knew for certain, that he would honor his promise. He would take her to Disneyland, and her best friend too. It was the least he could do.

She'd been back to Disneyland many times since that first trip, many visits, but always with her family, never with friends, never with another child, a peer, a companion her own age to share the magic and the wonder.

He turned to his wife, a smile playing across his face.

"Well, honey," he said, "I guess you know what this means?" He held up the report card as he spoke.

"Yeah," she replied with equal parts of resignation and disdain. "It means we're going to Disneyland... again!"

"Okay, put a divisor here."

"Now, put a left squiggle here… and here."

"Put a right squiggle there… and there."

"I need a 2475.36 above the tent…"

"Okay, now wait for the next number… it's going to go under the tent."

Katie's fingers flew over the keypad of the oversized calculator sitting on the table in front of her. She was dictating, and her mother was writing, patiently, her fingers poised over the paper, pencil in hand, trying to keep her mind blank and receptive to the next directive from her daughter.

It was a tough thing, Katie's father thought, this writing out homework, especially math homework, or rather, advanced math homework. He was standing in the kitchen, hiding almost, standing to the side of the refrigerator, and he was eavesdropping on this strange ritual, listening to the words, a secret code developed by his daughter and his wife, a language indecipherable to him, but plain as day to them, a language that used words like "squiggle" and "tent" to represent strange mathematical symbols and functions.

As the words flowed out in an almost sing-song rhythm, he was reminded of a day many years ago, when the extent of her homework was learning things like… "put your left hand out, put your right hand out, put your left hand in and you move it all about." He smiled as the song played across his memories. It was a far cry from what he was listening to now.

There was much Katie could do on a computer, much she could figure out, jury-rig, adapt, to her needs. But there was much that the computer could not do. The computer could not take pen or pencil to paper and write legibly. The computer could not fill out forms, sign documents, take tests. The computer could not write out complicated mathematical formulas. Nor could Katie. She could think them, create them in her head. But to write them out legibly was beyond her abilities. Someone else had to do it for her.

And so, sometimes for hours on end, her mother would sit patiently at the kitchen table, writing from Katie's dictation, writing symbols and lines and numbers she did not understand. She learned to write it as she heard it, without thinking, without playing any other role than that of mechanical dictation machine.

Along with computers, Katie was getting more and more into the mysterious world of math. Not simple algebra and geometry as he had in high school, her father thought to himself, but complicated stuff, algorithms and calculus, and predictive analytics. He knew it had progressed far beyond his understanding, and his understanding had been, he thought, more advanced than most. After all, he'd taken calculus in college, had passed trigonometry and spatial geometry. But that was a long time ago and many brain cells in the past. He found he was not as good a dictation machine as his wife, his inability to shut off his mind getting in the way of Katie's efforts.

He would challenge a statement, question an equation, dispute a number, much to Katie's growing frustration.

"Dad," she would say, "Just write it like I say it."

So her mother took over the duties, took on the task of learning a secret language, shorthand that they developed for each of the symbols and constructors that Katie used in her formulas and equations. It would not be until later that she would discover the software, even write some code of her own, that would allow her to use a computer to construct these mathematical symbols and print them out for her classes. So her mother would sit, and write, sit and write, sometimes for hours on end, as Katie figured out her problems, and completed her work.

It was all part of a larger picture, her father thought as he watched them from the corner of the kitchen. So many ways in which she excelled, so many ways in which she was limited, was deficient. By now many of those shortcomings were a given. Riding a bike was not going to happen. Playing piano, singing in the choir, these were not going to happen. Learning to dance was out of the question.

That was a sore point, for she had come to love music, love it with a passion that few equaled. She would listen to pop and rock, country and blues, and ballads. Her collection of albums and CDs had grown impressive over the years, especially during these high school years. She was growing up, developing her own tastes, and music was her constant companion. Throughout the long hours she spent alone, learning this and that, reading and studying, her music was always with her, never left her alone or let her down.

She would try to sing along, sing with the words, her voice sounding more like the wail of a cat whose tail had been caught in the proverbial rocking chair. Her singing would actually scare small children, make grown-ups quake, and often draw a look of concern from her parents, as if she had been hurt and was crying out in pain. So she learned to sing along silently, quietly, or only when she was alone.

But dancing to the music eluded her. She would try to move, try to catch a rhythm, but her body simply would not respond in the right way. The rigidity would creep across her muscles. Her balance, tenuous in the best of circumstances, would desert her.

Yes, dancing was out. And although she was getting better at feeding herself, the simple act of picking up a glass of juice and drinking from it without a straw was still beyond her.

Thank goodness for straws, he thought.

But whatever the restriction, whatever the barrier, she found a way around it, or over it, or a way to avoid it altogether. So it was with her homework. They would sit, her mother and her, minutes and sometimes hours at a time, and perform this strange dance, this strange ballet of dictation, and writing, and language, and shorthand. Katie would dictate, would pound keys on a large, adaptive calculator, would construct complicated equations in her head, and her mother would write, patiently, lovingly, sometimes frustratingly, on a sheet of paper, would set down the figures and shapes and numbers that Katie could speak, but not write down for herself.

Standing behind the refrigerator, eavesdropping, lost in thought, his heart warmed to the sight of these two in their complicated dance, their waltz of numbers and language and yes, math.

She can dance after all, he thought to himself, a dance of her own making, her own choosing. Make it a tango or a waltz, change the tempo, change the steps. It really didn't matter, for she was dancing all the time, dancing to her condition, dancing to her challenges, dancing… in the end, just dancing.

Dancing to the beat of her heart.

"Dad," Katie asked one afternoon.

It was a lazy, late spring day, her sophomore year almost completed. The trip to Disneyland with Amy, her best friend forever, went well. They spent three days at the park, three glorious days of being princesses, of reveling in the magic and the wonder. Katie was a pro now, knew the ins and outs of it, how to get her magic pass, which rides to take and when. Amy was delighted to find that they could go to the front of any line, the front of any attraction. She had been to Disneyland before, but not often, and never like this. It was as if they were celebrities, stars basking in the fame of just being there, and being princesses.

Softball and school took up the rest of Katie's time that spring, that and learning how to socialize with others, other students who now seemed more likely to want to include Katie in some of their adventures and outings. But the school year was ending, summer was coming, and in her voice as she called to him, her father sensed some frustration.

"Dad," she said again.

He looked up from the paper he was reading.

"Yes, Katie, what is it?"

"Well, I'm tired of always asking you for money," she began. "You know, for clothes and movies and things. And summer's coming, and, well, I just thought..."

Her voice trailed off. He put down the paper. Something was up, something was on her mind.

"Yes, Katie, you just thought?"

"I'd really like to get a job."

There. She said it. It was out.

A job.

A summer job.

What could be more natural, more usual, than a high-schooler wanting a job for the summer, he thought. But this was no ordinary request. What kinds of jobs were available to teenage kids with time on their hands and no spending cash in their pockets?

Slinging hamburgers and pizzas at a fast food joint immediately came to mind. But for Katie that was out. She simply couldn't do it. Mowing lawns and doing landscaping, many boys and even some girls would find that a lucrative pastime. But not for Katie and those rigid muscles of hers. Babysitting? He felt she could do it, but would any parent really feel comfortable with that, with the possibility of emergencies and the need to hold small babies?

He thought back to the first job he'd ever had. It was a classic piece of Americana, a paper route, he riding his bike in the early hours of the morning, wrapping and throwing, wrapping and throwing, trying not to break windows or tear up the grass. He quit that job in indignation when he was told he could no longer ride a bike. Turned out the owner of the paper was on his route and grew tired of seeing bicycle tracks in the dew-laden grass of his yard every morning.

"Can't ride my bike!" he exclaimed to his handler. "Why that's, that's…" he stammered searching for the right words. "That's un-American… I quit."

And off he rode in triumphant indignation.

Later he worked at a hospital, his doctor-father providing the opportunity, an opportunity he took advantage of and used to become a full-fledged x-ray technician, working summers and weekends while he finished school. He knew the value of a job, the responsibilities that came with it, the learning and growth and maturity that would be gained. But for the life of him, he couldn't think of what his daughter might be able to do.

He gave up, thought of a diversionary tactic to gain time, and turned back to his daughter.

"Well, Katie," he asked. "What did you have in mind for a job?"

"I was thinking," she responded slowly, thinking, "… that I'm good with numbers, good with math. Maybe I could do something like that, you know, for you. Maybe I could be a bookkeeper at your store."

Now the words came faster, they seemed to rush out of her as she spoke. She'd obviously been thinking a lot about this.

"You know, you always have to go in and do the books, do the accounting at the store, in between your travels. And you always come home so tired. Maybe I could help? Maybe I could learn to do the books for you."

Hmmm, he thought. This was an interesting notion. And right out of left field. It caught him completely by surprise.

"Perhaps you could, Katie, perhaps you could. Tell you what, let me think about it and tomorrow we can go down to the shop and see about that. It just might work, yes it might. You might be able to do something like that."

He was warming up to the idea.

"Katie May," he continued, smiling, "Bookkeeper extraordinaire. Tomorrow. Let's look into it tomorrow."

This could be interesting, very interesting, he thought again. Another milestone crossed, another barrier surmounted. Katie didn't simply face up to, or recognize, her problems, she came with the solutions too, her own solutions, and they were as often as not, very, very good solutions. Yes, his daughter was certainly becoming an interesting phenomenon.

"Dad," she said again, her voice lifting at the last, as if asking a question rather than making a statement.

"Yes, Katie."

"So, how much does it pay?"

Oh yes, he thought, this was going to be very interesting indeed.

It was cozy.

The room was cozy, small and intimate, and personal. Leather chairs lined the sides of the room, with solid oak tables in between. The walls were sponge painted in many colors, the reds and greens creating a richness that suggested an almost indulgent quality within. There was a bar. It defined one corner of the room, running at right angles to the wall. Six stools nudged up to its rich oak paneling, their seats and backs covered with the same rich leather that encased the easy chairs along the wall. Behind the bar was a mirror lined with glass shelves, their contents a selection of different shaped and colored bottles, premium liquors and wines, single barreled bourbons and single-malt scotches.

It was the room he had always wanted. A room possessed of serenity, made for quiet conversation and the leisurely contemplation of the world's mysteries. It was a respite from the busy world outside. Branching off from this room was another, a room that continued the richly painted walls and offered another lounging area with more chairs and tables.

Capping the end of this second room was a glass enclosed humidor, its walls lined with cedar shelves stocked with the finest cigars from around the world. And in front of this humidor were two counters filled with merchandise, gifts, drinking and smoking accessories, pipes and exotic tobacco blends.

It had a name, this saloon, this area of peace and tranquility located in an old historic building in the middle of the small town in the mountains. It had a name. But no one called it by its name. It was simply referred to as "the club," and it was a locals favorite on the downtown bar circuit.

Katie's father built this little side-business, an avocation really, several years before, when Katie was much younger. It was a labor of love that grew several times over the years. His wife worked it at first, ran the business while he traveled around the world for his consulting practice. But the business soon outgrew just one person.

He did not work it full-time, could not give it the attention it really deserved, because he was so busy traveling for his real work, his consulting practice. But he had his wife. He had good employees, several who had been with him for years. They served the drinks, sold products out of the store, and created a comfortable, welcoming environment that seemed to anchor the center of the little town.

Katie was right when she said he was always tired when he came home from the road. But tired or not, he would go to the store, do the books and the accounting, meet with his employees, try to be a good owner, if almost an absentee one. And tired or not, he went willingly, happily. For it was his, this little saloon, his own creation, a world he could escape to, a world he could lose himself in, sinking into a plush leather chair, a cigar in one hand, a properly mixed cocktail in the other. Now his daughter was asking to be a part of that world. She was asking to go to work at her father's business, a time-honored tradition, the family business, handed down from father to child.

This and more he thought about as they sat in the little office on the second story of the building where the bar was located, sat in front of the desk, his daughter and he, talking about how the books were kept, and what she might do to help keep them. Katie was seated at the computer desk, the familiar keyboard in front of her, the screen filled with numbers and forms he had created for the purpose of accounting for the store's revenues and expenses.

"You see here, Katie," he said, patiently. "This is the daily sheet. It records all the activity for the prior day. From it you create the deposit that goes to the bank." He turned and waved at a pile of slips on the side table. "These are the deposit slips and here is the envelope where you put the receipts that record the day's deposit."

"Yes," Katie replied. "I see. Dad, these are all handwritten forms."

"I know, Katie. That's something I just don't see you doing. A lot of this requires that you write it all out, by hand."

He was speaking slowly, teaching, trying to make her understand the problems they faced in getting her to do this job, this summer job that she wanted so much to do.

"But Dad," Katie replied excitedly. "I can do all of this on the computer. I know I can. I can convert these to computer forms, print everything out. I just need some time, but I know I can do it."

"Okay, Katie, tell you what. You work alongside me for a few days and see how everything works, and then we'll see what you think you can and can't do. Okay?"

"Okay, Dad, let's get started."

"Now?"

"Yeah, Dad, right NOW!"

So Katie began what was to become a steady job for the next three summers, and even for the school years in-between. She followed him, shadowed him for the next month while he did the work, filled out the forms, processed the payments, signed checks and paid bills. When he was not there, she would work on the computer, slowly, patiently converting the paper forms into computer files, her arms once again flying above the keyboard like some deranged hummingbird, moving this way and that, her muscles rigid, her fingers plunging from one key to the next, her strange brand of typing getting the job done.

She got paid for those hours of work, not much, minimum wage at first, but it was a job, and she was possessed. The very first payroll she learned to process included her first paycheck, the first sign of her independence, her ability to earn, to create, to complete productive work, valuable work.

"Dad, the paychecks are ready for you to review," she said one day. They were in the office. He'd just flown in from a long consulting project and had not even gone home yet. Payroll was due, the forms needed to be checked, the hours entered, the deductions calculated and made, the checks processed and signed.

"Katie, have you already printed these out?"

"Yes, Dad," she said proudly, "and signed them too. I went to the bank with Mom and they put me on the account's signature card. I can sign them too."

"Really," he replied incredulously. "Your mother put you on the account?" He was flabbergasted. He'd had to argue with his wife for a week just to get his own signature on the account. She did not give up control of the purse strings easily.

"Yes," Katie replied. "See... here, and here."

Her father looked at the checks in question. They were properly filled out, the time cards checked and banded, the deductions made, the amounts filled in, the checks printed on the computer. And there, on the signature line of each check, the marks wobbly, twisted, barely readable, but legal, were the letters KM, her legal signature, the exact duplicate of the letters written on her signature card in the bank's files.

"Well I'll be damned," he said, more to himself than to her, or anyone else for that matter.

As summer progressed, the days growing longer and hotter, he found himself doing less and less. Katie completely computerized the entire accounting process for the shop, developed a system for just about everything. Tax reporting forms were available for downloading from the state, deposit slips too, from the bank. The daily forms were developed into a spreadsheet. The office began to take on a different look, what with two separate printers, a large, oversized calculator, a special chair with better supports for Katie's posture. Above the desk, affixed to the wall crudely with duct tape, hung a calendar featuring the ball players from Katie's favorite baseball team. Files were reorganized; many were discontinued as the filing system became more and more computerized.

He began to enjoy the freedom, freedom from the drudgery of bookkeeping work. He would come home, tired from a trip to some far off place, tired from work, and find that there was nothing for him to do but read reports, check results, and make the occasional correction or the occasional decision that required his experience and knowledge.

"Katie," he said after one such trip. "The head bartender says you've been changing things down in the bar. And he's wondering just who is running this place, me or you?"

He said it with a grin, lightly, but there was a serious edge to it. There could only be one boss, after all, one leader on the team. He wasn't sure he wanted changes being made in his absence, without his approval. It was, he thought, the danger of working with relatives, especially children. Lines of command were blurred, the distinction between personal and business was always a fertile ground for misunderstanding, for hurt feelings, for problems.

"Well Dad, the state auditor wasn't too happy with our control procedures on the sales tax reporting. So I wrote a new system that includes two audit checks. It makes for a better chain-of-command for the funds. Why, is something wrong," she asked innocently. She was smiling too, that great big wonderful smile of hers.

"No," he said. "No, you nailed it. I'm surprised I didn't think of it earlier. I went over it, but show me again just to make sure I understand it."

This was crazy, he thought. Two and half months and not only was she talking like a candidate for an MBA, but she was also already telling him what he was doing wrong. How had this happened? Of course he knew the answer, knew what the power of the Internet could accomplish in this modern day and age. When Katie was born the Internet was an obscure communications channel for scientists from far off universities and laboratories. A cell phone, if you could afford one, was as big as a suitcase, and required quite a few mental gymnastics to operate. Tabletop computers were fairly new, and laptops were still on some engineer's drawing board in some obscure lab somewhere.

But the world was changing, and with it, Katie's ability to make it over in her own image. She had been on a computer since the third grade, and been on the Internet almost from the beginning of its ascension into popular culture. He often thought how fortunate it was that she was born in this time, with these things going on.

Technology was making the world an entirely different experience for people like his daughter. He heard the stories, stories of the past, of how these kids were put in special schools, limited by the system, condemned to a life of putting round pegs in round holes in some special-needs workplace somewhere.

He vowed to never let that happen, researched the technology, stayed on top of new developments, continually asked how these new inventions could benefit his daughter and her quality of life. He spent a fortune on anything and everything that might help.

He tried the new voice-activated software programs that had come out in the last few years. If Katie could simply command her computer with her voice, then many, many problems would be solved. But that was not to be. The programs could not recognize the words she uttered, her speech far too garbled for anything but the human ear to be able to properly decipher.

But other technological breakthroughs were a godsend, including the Internet, especially the Internet. She researched basic accounting principles in a search engine and used the results to teach herself bookkeeping with no help, or prompting, from anyone. She would surprise him at times with her questions, and challenges about why he had set up certain procedures, and how she felt she could do it better.

The day finally came when he felt it prudent to reward this increased ability on her part.

"Katie," he said one day as they were sitting at home. "I think it's time for you to get a raise. What do you think?"

It was almost September, the school year was just about to begin, her junior year in high school. They were discussing her schedule and whether she could continue to work during the school year. Things had become so automated under her watch that it was fairly clear she would be able to continue doing the books and still carry a full load of classes.

"A raise?" she asked, puzzled. "A raise to what, and where?"

"No, a raise at work. A raise in pay. You know," he continued, smiling, "when you do well at work, you should make more money."

"Oh, that. Thanks, Dad, but Mom already gave me one. I'm making twice what you started me out at."

"What! When did this happen?"

"A few weeks ago. I just got my first paycheck with the new amount. Which reminds me, can we go to the mall later? I want to get some new school clothes," she said innocently.

"And Dad?"

"Yes, Katie."

"I'm buying."

A Proper Ambassador

He was sitting at the kitchen table, his wife standing just behind. Katie sat opposite, her eyes fixed on his face, her whole body rigid and motionless in the chair, her manner focused, intent. He held a letter in his hand and he was slowly reading it, as was his wife from her position behind him, her hair brushing his shoulder as she leaned in to read the words.

To the parents of Katie May,

We are pleased to inform you that your daughter has been selected by a committee of teachers for inclusion in this year's nominations for participation in the People to People Ambassador Program.

People to People Ambassador Programs offer extraordinary, life-changing, educational travel opportunities for students, athletes, educators, and professionals.

People to People's mission is to bridge cultural and political borders through education and exchange, making the world a better place for future generations.

People to People offers unique and engaging educational opportunities for your child to explore different cultures, make new friends in other countries and in their own community, and connect with extraordinary people and places across the globe. People to People programs are exciting, enjoyable, and activity rich. They are also highly educational and practical, helping students:

- *Earn academic credit*
- *Gain unique access to key people and places*
- *Develop leadership skills*
- *Gain an edge in the college admissions process*
- *Thrive in an increasingly competitive and globalized world*

Katie has met the requirements for nomination to this program and is being recommended to the national council for inclusion in this summer's student program. This program involves travel to New Zealand, Australia, and China for a select group of students from across the country, students possessing the highest academic and leadership qualities in their school.

Unfortunately, the regular People to People Program for which Katie is being nominated is not set up to handle disabled students. Therefore, we are requesting a meeting to be held between yourselves, a People to People representative, and the school committee to explore whether Katie is capable of participating in this opportunity.

If you are interested in exploring this wonderful opportunity for her, would you please call the admissions and records office to set up a time and place for the meeting. You will find the numbers below.

Thank you for your attention to this matter. This is a wonderful opportunity and we encourage you, in the strongest terms, to consider allowing Katie to participate in this program. We await your response.

Sincerely,

The Teacher's Ambassador Committee

In the strongest terms, he thought to himself. The words jumped off of the page at him, ***the strongest terms.*** That was putting it mildly, he thought. It would have to be that. This program was for normal kids, kids who could walk and run and climb, kids who could balance and handle all sorts of strenuous activities.

He knew that.

He had been to Europe himself, right after college, traveling around many different countries with a backpack on his back and a book on budget traveling in his pocket. It was strenuous, and demanding, and tiring. Not to mention the dangers involved. And this would include a large group of kids from all over the country. Kids who didn't know Katie, who hadn't gotten... what was the phrase, he thought... used to her and her ways.

He could tell she wanted to go, wanted to in the worst way. She came home from school excited, bursting with energy, her small body trembling even now as she sat in the chair opposite, watching him intently, looking for a clue as to his thoughts, and her mother's. Oh, she wanted to go. She was already there in her mind.

And yet, he hesitated. He remembered the doctor's words all those many years ago, an eternity ago it seemed to him now. "Don't coddle her," the doctor said. "If she shows an aptitude for something, then push her, get her involved." But this was different. This was something else. He wasn't sure he was prepared to go this far, to push her this far. Maybe later, when she was grown, when she had more of life's experiences under her belt, when she was stronger.

She was growing stronger every day it seemed, every month, every year. But still, he thought as he looked at her sitting there, her tiny body coiled on top of the chair, her muscles rigid and tense, this was a huge jump, a huge leap into territory he wasn't sure they were prepared for.

He turned to his wife, faced her, looking for a way to begin, to say something.

"Well," he asked her, "what do you think?"

He saw the look on his wife's face, and he knew that she knew, that he had taken the easy way out, the coward's way out, putting it on her plate, letting her speak first, getting her to commit one way or the other before he had to. She paused, gathering her thoughts, digesting the contents of the letter still clutched in his hand.

"I think it's wonderful," she said finally. The words came in a rush. "I think it is a great opportunity and I think we should pursue it."

"You think she's ready?" he replied, still biding for time. "Ready for something like this?"

"I don't know, I, it's all so sudden, I…" she stammered. "Yes, I do, I think she's ready. I know she is."

This wasn't exactly what he expected from her, this reaction. He'd always been the one to toss off the difficulties, to make light of the obstacles. He'd always been more the advocate for pushing Katie out into the world. His wife had been the protector, the one concerned with the dangers, the one showing caution. Now it was his turn to play that role.

"Katie," he said, turning back to her, taking the plunge, "I'm just not so sure. This is a big step. And it says here that this program isn't accommodating. You would have to step up, keep up, with kids a lot stronger than you. I just don't know if this is a good idea."

The look of hope that had settled on Katie's face as her mother spoke now slipped away, replaced by confusion, desire, and maybe just a bit of anger.

"Dad, I want to do this, I can do this, I know I can," she cried, her voice rising with each word. "They only chose a few of us at school, and I'm one of them. I told them I wanted to go, and that you would want me to go too. Please, can't we just talk to them? Can't we try?"

She was pleading now, her words growing more incoherent as the emotion took over control of her vocal cords. It was one of the things that worried him. Excessive emotion would cloud her thoughts, take over her body, take away what little control she had. It was emotional times like these when she would fall and hurt herself, or become caught up as she tried to talk, her voice growing more and more garbled.

"Katie," her mother said sternly, "I want you to go to your room and start on your homework. I want to talk to your father about this alone. Do you understand?"

"Yes, Mom," she said, her voice trailing away, the emotion draining out as she realized this was probably not going to happen.

It took her several minutes to get organized, to grab her school backpack, heft it onto her back, get balanced, and make her way out of the kitchen and off to her room. The silence was awkward, tense, both parents looking at each other, at Katie, and then at the walls, or at nothing at all.

As she reached the passageway between kitchen and hall, Katie stopped and turned. She faced her parents one last time.

"I really, really want to do this. Please, don't stop me."

Then she turned and was gone.

He did not want to do this, to put her in this program, to put her in what he saw as harm's way. Why, he wasn't quite sure. He was afraid of rejection, afraid of what it would do to Katie if they refused to take her. And he was afraid for Katie. What if she couldn't keep up, couldn't meet the demands of the trip? You couldn't just put her on a bus and send her home. Not from Australia. Not from China, for chrissakes. It scared him. And she would be beyond their reach, beyond their ability to do anything should something happen.

But his wife was adamant, forceful in her response.

"You're the one who's always telling her she can do anything she puts her mind to. You're the one who took her to Disneyland, taught her to believe in the magic. Now you're going to refuse her this, this first big challenge, her first opportunity to go out in the world and accomplish something on her own?"

"It's not the same," he argued. "Disneyland is one thing, traveling to see relatives is one thing, but this, this, it's, it's different. What happens when something goes wrong, when she can't keep up? What if she falls, gets injured? She'll be half a world away."

"I know," she responded. "I know, and it scares me, scares hell out of me. But it's time we let go a little more. We can't smother her forever, we can't always be there. And this program, it's really something. She'll have chaperones, aides, people to help."

"And what if we say yes, and then they refuse her, refuse to take her. What would that do to her? It's too risky. I don't like it."

"You're not the only one to make this decision. You're not the only one who has a say. Have you talked to your daughter, really listened to her? Do you really think refusing her is somehow going to help her? You tell her no and you shut her down. Hell, this world has done a great job of shutting her down every time she turns around. I just can't believe you feel this way. You just don't see it, you don't get it. This is her chance, a chance to do something on her own."

It made sense. It was a piece of everything he'd been led to believe, had told himself for years, but still he hesitated, still he argued. She was right, but she was wrong too. It was the same old fight between them, a fight that had gone on for years, ever since Katie's birth. It was the unknown, and the possibilities, the fear, and the joy. The guilt still lingered from her birth. Had they done something wrong? Was it somehow their fault? And if she went, and was hurt, injured, even lost her life, would they be to blame? Would it all be on them? Could they handle that, handle the strain? Could they survive that?

"What are you so afraid of?" she asked again.

"I don't know," he replied. He did know, but wasn't ready to admit it, didn't want to open up that can of worms. "I don't know. I just, I'm scared, scared for her. If she can't keep up, what it will do to her. If she's injured, hurt, what it will do to us? I just... I'm afraid."

"Look, I've always been the one to show caution, to say wait a minute, to hesitate. I've been terrified something would happen every time I let her out of my sight. I still am. But I learned. I learned to control it. We can't hold on that tight. I had to let her go, through my fears, a mother's fears. Now it's your turn. You have to let her go a little bit. You have to."

He knew she was right. Still, he didn't budge, didn't move. He said nothing, let the issue drift away unresolved. It festered between them for several days, the arguments growing longer, then shorter, sometimes just a word or a look. But it remained and was a part of everything they had dealt with from the beginning. It was fear, fear of the unknown, of what might be, could be, should be.

He simply couldn't sacrifice his daughter for the sake of trying to be normal, to have a normal child, a normal childhood, a normal life. He pulled back, regressed from his progressive self to one that wanted to protect his child, coddle her, keep her from the world, sew her up in a protective cocoon and keep her from all risk.

Still he knew that path was wrong, was stagnant, would lead to just the things he feared, that Katie would spend a life not living, not trying, not being allowed to succeed and yes, fail, on her own terms.

In the end, that was it, that was what made him resist, the fear of still not understanding her place in the world, her condition, her burden as she made her way through life. She was different, no matter how they tried to pretend, tried to make things seem normal, she was different. And he really had no understanding of that difference, was afraid of it… hadn't come to terms with it.

It seemed there would be no solution, no answer to this dilemma. And then, just as it seemed the whole thing would swell to bursting, would blow up in all of their faces, the matter was settled, settled by Katie herself.

He was puttering around in the garage. It was a Saturday and he was home for a time, not on the road working, had been home since that fateful letter arrived so many days before. His wife was out running errands, would be out for most of the day. He took Katie to work, to the shop for her daily bookkeeping chores. She would always call when she was done and they would come, one of them, to pick her up and bring her home.

His cell rang. It was Katie. She was finished with work and ready to come home. He dropped what he was doing, hopped in the car and made the short drive to pick her up. On the ride home they didn't speak, they hadn't been speaking for several days now, the letter hanging over them, the decision still not made, postponed while he resisted his wife and daughter.

It was only when they arrived at home, when she hopped out of the car silently, making her way inside to drop off her backpack, only then that Katie faced the situation, faced her father and his fears. She came back into the garage as he was turning to come inside, his chores done.

"Dad," she said. "Can I just say something to you? Without you talking? Would you just listen, please?"

"Yes, Katie," he said slowly. He was suddenly calm. At that moment he did not fear his daughter, welcomed her reaching out to him. "Yes, Katie, I'll listen."

"Dad, you know I really want to go on this trip. I'm not stupid. I know what the dangers are. I know I could get hurt, or have trouble keeping up. I know it will be a lot of strange kids, and places, and sit… situations."

The words came tumbling out, Katie stumbling over them as she tried to make herself understood, tried to get him to understand.

"Dad," she spoke again. "I'm not handicapped."

"Eh," he stammered, startled. "What's that Katie?"

"I'm not handicapped, Dad."

"No?"

"No," she replied. "This is just who I am."

The words came out simply, clearly, laid out before him like some truth that he'd never understood.

"THIS IS JUST WHO I AM." She was yelling now, her words loud, urgent, pressing upon him. "This is just who I am. I'm not going to change. I'm not going to be anyone else. This is me…. this is me."

He stood, motionless, paralyzed by the simplicity of his daughter's statement. Who I am. She had learned this truth, he realized, grown into this truth, where he had not, had never even been able to comprehend it. He was normal, life came easy to him. It must be tough, he thought suddenly, to have to deal with all she deals with and still have to educate others, including her own parents, about what it meant to be her, to be this way.

She was, he realized, teaching him more about life than he would ever teach her.

This is just who I am.

The words hung between them for what seemed an eternity, but was only a moment.

There is no normal.

He understood that now, at this moment, with his daughter staring at him intently in the garage, the two of them squared off, facing each other, like boxers in a ring. There is no normal. There is no abnormal.

There is only what is.

You take whatever you are given, and you do the best you can with it.

Katie understood, had learned that simple truth. She may be different, but then so is everyone else, so is everything else. There is no normal, only what is. The truth was so simple, yet so powerful and complicated and confusing.

He came out of his reverie, his daze, and looked at this daughter, looked intently as if truly seeing her for the first time in her short life.

"Okay, Katie," he replied slowly. He understood now, understood the meaning of those simple words.

"Okay," he said again, as if talking to himself, "you can go. Your mother and I will do everything in our power to see that you go."

And at that moment, he knew it was true, knew he would never again be able to deny his daughter anything, anything she wanted to do. For it was, as she had said, simply a case of knowing who she was, a lesson every person had to learn at some time in their life, a lesson that some never learned, no matter how normal they seemed to be.

For once he realized that his daughter had been first, had learned it before most others ever do. She'd finally done something ahead of time, ahead of the "normal" people.

"Thank you," she said quietly. "Thank you very much."

She turned and left him there, standing in the garage, standing alone.

And for a long time he didn't move.

The room they were sitting in looked familiar and, in fact, was familiar. It was the same classroom-turned-conference-room they sat in so many times before when going over Katie's progress in school. This time however, the crowd was different.

There were only a select few people in the room, including Katie's mother and father, the principal of the school, the special education consultant that worked hand-in-hand with Katie at the high school, and one of the teachers from the Ambassador Program selection committee. Katie was there as well, sitting between her parents, her head bowed, her body motionless but rigid with tension. There was one other person in the room, a stranger. She was the regional representative for the People to People Program.

Well, Katie's father thought to himself, here we go. This meeting was the culmination of everything that transpired over those days of fighting and arguing about the invitation to join People to People. He made the call, arranged for the meeting, told the school officials they were committed to seeing that Katie had an opportunity to participate, to become an ambassador, a student ambassador, one of the few selected from all over the country.

Unfortunately, this meeting was not going well. Maybe that was all of a purpose too. People to People wasn't any surer of this than he had been. They were… resistant… hesitant. Could she keep up? Would she hold back an entire group? Was it fair to the other kids, to the parents who would spend a great deal of money to send their children on this wonderful adventure?

"I'm afraid that I must inform you, we are simply not prepared to take these kinds of risks," the regional representative said. She was sharp, almost edgy as she sat dressed in a grey tweed business suit, her hair pulled back tight, glasses perched on a long, hooked nose that seemed even longer for the way the spectacles sat, perched on that nose as if they were some predator awaiting some unsuspecting prey. Her hair was silver grey and made her seem older than she probably was, for her skin was smooth and her body thin and angular.

The perfect villain, Katie's father thought at that moment. A Cruella de Vil. But no, that wasn't really fair. She had a point. She had a lot riding on this decision. It could turn out very badly for her should any of the possibilities they were discussing become reality. There could be angry parents, their children's expectations ruined. There could be repercussions, censure, a loss of trust. At that moment, with the enormity of "what if" crashing over him like a wave on a beach, he actually felt sorry for her, sympathetic to her plight.

But in the end, that was of no matter. He'd made up his mind. His daughter, his wife, they were counting on him to win this battle, to make this happen. He must proceed very carefully, cautiously. He needed to read this woman, figure her out. He was committed. Failure was simply not an option. He would go to war if he had to.

"Tell me," he asked, "tell me again specifically what the concerns are?"

She looked up sharply, not annoyed, not angered, but cautious herself, maneuvering carefully. For her there were the issues of fairness, the legal issues of providing reasonable accommodation for the disabled, reasonable accommodation and access to the program. They could be sued if this girl went, they could be sued if she didn't. It was a very delicate situation.

"We are worried about her physical ability to make the trip," she said, ticking off the concerns one-by-one on her fingers as she spoke.

"We are worried about the medical requirements of her condition. Could they be met on the trip?"

"We are worried about the consequences if she injures herself."

"We are worried about the impact on the group if her

condition interferes with the schedule of the trip, as it is very tightly choreographed."

"We are worried about the lack of accommodations at many of the trip sites."

"We are worried about liability should something happen to her."

She finished her list, finished with a flourish, her eyes bright, her body poised for the challenge, the arguments she knew would come. She was not prepared for his response.

"I agree," he said simply. "I have the same worries and concerns."

"You do?" she responded, surprise, and perhaps a touch of relief, evident in her tone.

"Yes, I do. And if we cannot address those concerns, address those issues, I simply will not let her go. You do not have to worry about that. But I'm worried, worried about you, about your position."

"Worried? About me? I don't understand."

"I'm worried that should we address those concerns, you still won't let her go. That you have made up your mind already."

"I can assure you sir, I am willing to be reasonable, but you have to understand the position we are in." She sounded angry... no, not angry... defensive.

He sensed the danger, drew back, marshaled his thoughts. He had to get this woman on their side, on Katie's side. He settled on a new plan of attack, saw a different way to proceed.

"I'm sorry, I do not mean to imply you would not be fair. But I wonder if you know the real story here, the passion with which this little girl, my daughter, has met every challenge in her life, the things she has accomplished."

He paused, took a breath, continued.

"I have watched her fall down, again and again, and pick herself up. I have watched her learn to do things the doctors said she wouldn't be able to do. I have watched her fight to live in a world that challenged her at every turn. I have watched her smile her way through a world that was cold and cruel and unaccommodating."

He hesitated for a moment, and then continued.

"I truly believe we can address every concern you have. We can provide letters from her doctor assuring that she receives no more medical treatment for her condition. That it is stable. That she needs no special medicines or ongoing treatment. We can provide letters confirming her insurance coverage. We can provide letters from the school about her achievements, both academic and in sports. We can provide waivers of liability. But still I do not believe that will be enough, because none of those things truly speak to her heart… her will… her passion. Without that, you would still be unsure, still unconvinced, still likely to say no."

He paused, took a deep breath, and then rushed ahead, his words seeming to collide with one another as he tried to get them out.

"But let me tell you a story, if I may. Let me tell you a story, a story of my daughter, a story of love and courage and, yes, of passion."

So he told her. Told of that night in the hospital so many years ago. Of a little girl born dead, a mother dying. How he watched it, watched them fight for their very lives. He told of her smile, and how it lit up every corner of the world around her. He told of her learning to walk, of the bruises, the falls, of her determination in the face of pain and uncertainty.

He told of her first computer, of how her arms wove the air like an angry buzzing horde of bees, her fingers learning to hit the right keys, one at a time. He told of her at Disneyland, the magic of the place, the way she made it her own world, her own special place, a place where anything was possible.

He told of her role as manager of the softball team, of the fears she had to conquer, and the acceptance and unyielding devotion of her teammates as they responded to her will and determination.

He told of her academic accomplishments, the long hours spent at homework, of typing a paper that would take others only a few minutes and of how she kept at it for hours until it was finished, until it was perfect.

He spoke slowly, his words falling like soft drops of rain into a quiet pond, his tone even, measured, but possessed of love and pride and amazement for what he was saying, for what he was describing to this stranger sitting in a strange place. And the words came to life, came alive with their simplicity, their urgency, and their truth.

When he was done, when he finished, he knew he had won, knew the field had been swept of all combatants, the battle over, the enemy vanquished.

She was quiet, this People to People representative, her face heavy with the emotion of his story, her eyes wide and moist, her mind turned inward, her body filled with the passion of his speech. She was inside of herself, silent, possessed not of liabilities and problems and concerns, but rather with possibilities and challenges and courage.

Slowly she came back to the present, to this moment, in this room, gathered herself together. She looked from Katie's father to her mother, to Katie herself. Looked at the school representatives, themselves lost in the power of the story they had just heard, a story they had been a part of, and yet had never heard in its entirety.

Slowly, ever so slowly, she turned back to him, turned back to speak.

"I understand," she said slowly.

And at that moment he knew she did, knew his words had hit their mark, hit the bulls eye. She was on their side. She was one of them.

"You will have to provide me with all you have offered. I will need documentation. I will need the papers, the assurances, from the doctors and the lawyers, from you, her parents."

Then she turned to Katie, turned, smiled, and spoke directly to her.

"Katie," she said slowly, "do you really want to do this, to go on this trip, to represent your country on this journey?"

"Yes ma'am," Katie replied. "I really want to go." And then she smiled… that great, big, wonderful smile. And the room, as it always did when she smiled, turned brighter, grew warm with the possibilities that lay ahead.

"Okay," the representative said. She drew herself up, squared her shoulders, and spoke the words she knew she must.

"Then let's make sure that you do just that."

In the end, the deed was done, the papers gathered, the letters from the doctors, from the school officials. Liability forms were signed, a physical was performed, paperwork was checked off on a master list. The People to People representative was as good as her word, went to war for Katie's acceptance, made it happen, bent the other officials to her will. She now had almost a personal stake in the outcome, as if it were her daughter being considered for this wonderful trip.

A passport was secured, Katie's picture captured with her smile, a smile that made the passport seem more like a family portrait, a photo of a girl enjoying life immensely, a photo devoid of any evidence of disability, of physical deformity.

She was excited all during the months leading up to the trip, the spring semester of school crawling to a close, the days getting not only longer, but, it seemed to her, getting slower as well. Her junior year ended, tests were taken, the report card came back, no surprise, all classes passed with an A or A+, the teachers' comments reflective of all those that had come before, in prior years.

"Katie is a delight to have in class."

"Totally focused, excellent work."

"Superior understanding of the material."

With the end of the school year came the dying days of spring, the birth of summer, of days growing longer and hotter as the season of the sun settled over the little town in the mountains. Finally, the day came, the day when she was to join her fellow ambassadors at the airport, the day when they would take off on their adventure, traveling to New Zealand and Australia and China.

That day dawned clear and hot, the wind stilled, the evergreens quiet, the mountains seeming to have stopped time for just a few moments. Everything was quiet, almost foreboding. Katie's father thought that was probably appropriate, considering the day and the occasion. For while Katie was filled to the brim with excitement, her parents were possessed of quite a different feeling. Like the air and wind and mountains, they were quiet this morning, possessed of their own foreboding. She was leaving, leaving for an entire month, leaving on a journey that neither of them was certain would turn out well. There were so many unknowns, so many potential dangers ahead.

"You have all your papers in your carry-on?" her mother asked Katie... again.

"Yes, Mom," she replied patiently, but with no small amount of annoyance creeping through the buffer of her excitement. "I checked again. Plane tickets, passport, travel dossier from the program. I have it all."

Her father was busy loading the car with Katie's travel gear, a suitcase shaped like a large duffel bag with zippered compartments, a soft frame, and wheels and a handle so Katie could pull it behind her. They special ordered it from the Internet and Katie practiced with it for weeks, carrying a dummy load of clothes and books, walking to and fro, learning how to walk while pulling this big bag with all of that weight. She would not have assistance with her luggage. She was responsible for handling all of her gear, of keeping up with the others.

That was the biggest concern for her parents. They stepped up her physical therapy, her exercises and stretching classes. They doubled her yoga classes. They helped her learn to pull her bag while wearing a backpack, the sessions reminding them of those painful and tedious days of learning to walk so many years before.

There had been a big fight because of that. They wanted Katie to wear her pads again, pads and helmet that still fit, although just barely, on her small body.

"Katie, the pads could be the difference between staying on the trip or injuring yourself and having to come home," her father argued.

"No, no, no," she cried. "I am not going to wear those horrid things. They make me look stupid. Everyone will make fun of me. I don't care if I get bruised or scraped up. I can take care of myself."

She went on and on and they gave up fairly quickly. It was a battle they knew they couldn't win. In case of injury or accident, or if she simply could not keep up, then her chaperones were equipped with an emergency plane ticket that would whisk her home from wherever she might find herself. It was one of the conditions of her going, one of the many conditions they had to fulfill to make this trip a reality. It was a condition they also kept from Katie. Better if she didn't know, they thought. Better if she had no negatives in her mind at all as she prepared for this adventure.

But going she was, the day was here, the time drawing near. The ride down through the mountains to the city in the valley, a ride Katie had loved for years, was now a torturous journey through curves and bends that seemed to retard her progress, seemed to delay, again, her entry into this new adventure. Her parents were silent on the way to the airport, lost in their own thoughts, thoughts of the upcoming moment of parting, of letting her go in a way they never had to before. For them the ride was all too quick, all too sudden, was over all too fast.

They turned into short term parking at the airport, found a space near the terminal in a handicap zone. Bags were retrieved from the trunk, and the slow walk to the terminal was begun, Katie carrying her backpack and pulling her bag, one last practice session in preparation for the real thing. No, her father thought, not a practice session, for this was the real thing. This was the beginning step in a journey of a thousand steps, a thousand steps she would have to take all on her own.

Inside the terminal, the check-in counter was mobbed with kids from all over the region. They were wearing the same shirts, their ambassador shirts, bright red with the logo of the program on the back. Parents milled about, hugging their kids, checking and re-checking their bags and papers and tickets.

There were cries of welcome from the participants. They had gotten to know each other through the pre-trip meetings, meetings that had been held monthly throughout the spring semester. Katie attended, met the others, began to get familiar with them and they with her, with her condition. Some were immediately accepting, while others were hesitant. Who was this girl with the funny walk and the slurred speech? Who was this girl and why was she going? Could she go? Could she keep up? Like everything else Katie had been exposed to in her short life, there were those few who gravitated to her, and the many who kept their distance, stayed away through fear, or ignorance, or misunderstanding. It was all of a pattern, her father thought, as he surveyed the scene. Kids milling and talking and hugging, Katie standing to the side, alone, waiting for one or two of the others to hesitantly approach and say hello.

Nevertheless, this is it, he thought. This is the beginning of her great adventure. From here it could be a disaster, or something great, something wonderful. It was the future, the unknown future that consumed them and hovered over them for all these years. What would happen? What were the challenges? How would it all work out?

Then it was time. The trip leaders, the adult ambassadors, called the group to order and delivered their instructions. It was time to go, time to march through security, time to depart for other countries, other worlds.

Katie turned to say her goodbyes, impatient to get going, and yet, all of sudden not sure she wanted to leave. She hugged her mother, tears starting to form in her eyes, her manner turning serious, somber.

As they hugged, her father had to catch himself, catch the tears that threatened to overwhelm him as well. He thought back to the night he had watched the helicopter whisk her away to the hospital in the city, the night when his wife lay convalescing in a hospital room, the night when he felt so alone, so isolated, so cut off from life. He was feeling that way again, feeling isolated and alone.

Get a hold of yourself, he thought angrily. She's not leaving forever, just for a month. For cryin' out loud, it's just a trip, like so many others she's taken. Get a grip. You're like some old maid crying over spilt milk. He laughed, his anger slipping away as he realized once again how ridiculous he could sometimes be, how caught up in the moment he could get, how his emotions could run away from him.

As he shrugged off the pain of his daughter's departure, at that very moment, as she turned to hug him, he knew. He knew she would make it, knew she would come back, her face filled with delight, her heart filled with the places she had gone, the things she had seen, the people she had met. She would come back older, wiser, more self-assured.

He was not to know, at that moment, about all the challenges she would conquer, the fears she would face and vanquish, but he could feel it inside of himself.

That she would rappel down a cliff in New Zealand.

That she would dance in the rain and eat kangaroo with aborigines.

That she would climb, all on her own, to the highest point on the Sydney Harbor Bridge, to that point some one hundred and thirty five meters above the harbor.

That she would walk the Great Wall of China, walk on her own, keeping up with her peers, walk up and down the steps of stone that had been built so many thousands of years before.

That she would come back with stories of faraway places, and strange people, and stranger customs, with stories of friendships made, and enemies converted, of communities explored, and lands discovered.

He was not to know at that moment of all the wonderful things she would bring back with her, bring back inside her backpack and duffel bag, inside her mind and heart. That she would meet every challenge, finish the trip as one of the group, accepted for who she was, as well as for who she wasn't.

That she would be one of them, an ambassador... a true friend.

But he could feel it. That was enough.

She was going. That was enough.

She was on her way. She said her final goodbyes, turned, and strode down the terminal walkway with her fellow travelers, hips splayed apart, arms pumping furiously, legs working to keep up with the group ahead. She turned one last time, waved, and then was gone.

For her parents, the ride home was a long and silent one.

Very long... and very, very silent.

Driving Miss Katie

"Your daughter wants to learn how to drive."

"What," he replied. "What's that? Drive? Drive what? Drive a car?"

"No, she wants to learn how to drive a train. Of course, a car. Earth to Dad, come in Dad. She wants to learn how to drive a car."

Katie's mother stood with hands on hips, her expression one of annoyance borne out through long years of practice. She was used to having her husband annoy her when she spoke. She had to repeat herself often, as if getting his attention was akin to getting him to return from some other planet.

"Sorry," he replied, coming back to the present. "I guess my mind was elsewhere. What do you mean, drive? Did she speak to you about it?"

"Yes, last night. I brought her home from work at the shop and she brought it up. Said she's a senior now and couldn't she at least try to drive. She wanted me to talk to you. I don't know why, but I guess she's afraid of how you would take the news."

"Well, I don't know. Is that... possible? What do you think?"

"I think it's like everything else we've been faced with. Who knows anymore what she can and can't do? But this one really scares me. I don't know. I guess we should at least try. Don't you think so?"

"Well, I suppose I could take her out somewhere isolated and let her play around with it. That would give us an idea. But if she really has an aptitude for it, then we're going to have to get something better than the Driver's Ed they have here in school. Probably it would take a professional school, maybe there's an adaptive one that specializes in that sort of thing."

He paused for a moment, a worried look on his face.

"What are you thinking?" she asked.

"Oh nothing, well, yes, I was thinking about her learning to walk, about her walker, about the whole thing, how hard it was, hard on all of us. I was thinking that, well, here we go again."

"Yes, it was hard. And wonderful. And look where it got us, got her. Just think, if she could drive, she could be really independent, really on her own."

"I know," he said slowly, pondering the thought. "I know, that's what scares me."

They both looked at the other, their eyes locked, their minds in sync, thinking the exact same thing at the exact same moment. It was one thing to deal with this handicap, with the needs of their child, with the effort it took. But this slow process of letting go, of teaching her not just to live, to cope with the world, but to be in it, to be independent, on her own, was hard. Harder than anything else they'd ever faced.

"That's what scares me," he said again.

"Okay, Katie," her father said, "let's give it a try."

They were out of town, way out of town. School had begun, the first few weeks of classes already past, the summer days turning to fall, a chill starting to show up every evening in the little town in the mountains. Snow was not too far away, and yet there were still the prospect of many pleasant days and nights left before the cold of winter set in.

He picked her up from school, surprised her, took off early from the office where he worked when he was not traveling. He did not speak to her about driving, did not let on that he had spoken with her mother about the prospect, and about Katie's desire to try and learn how.

At first he didn't let on about where they were going, what they were going to do. He simply said they were going to take a drive. He wound the car along the roads out of town, to a place out in the country that he knew of, a place where there was a long stretch of straight road and little or no traffic around.

Upon reaching a suitable spot, he slowed the car, stopped, put it in park and turned to her.

"Give what a try, Dad?" she asked, surprised, puzzled, the look on her face almost making him laugh out loud.

"Why, driving of course. You want to learn, don't you?"

"Well… yes, I…" she stammered and stuttered, caught up in the enormity of the thought. "You mean I can really try? Try to drive?"

"Sure, but you're going to have to get out and sit over here. They don't make cars with steering wheels for the passenger seat." He was grinning now, starting to laugh.

"Dad," she said, exasperated, "knock it off. This is hard enough without you making fun of me."

But she was smiling too, that great big smile that once again seemed to make the world, or in this case, the inside of the car, a lot brighter.

Slowly she settled herself into the driver's seat. She'd never sat there before, had imagined herself sitting there, but never actually done it. He had her adjust the seat, fasten her seat belt, adjust the side mirrors, the rear view mirror. She did it slowly. It was all new to her. It took a while for the mirrors, her arms rigid and tense with excitement and trying to master a new movement. But in the end she had it right, could see behind her and to the side, was buckled in, the steering wheel just the right distance from her arms.

He instructed her on how to hold the wheel, both hands at the ten and two o'clock positions, like he was taught so many years ago as a teenager. He had her turn it first one way, and then the other, until she was comfortable with it, her hands crossing one over the other, her grip still too rigid and tight, almost frantic as she struggled with the unusual feeling.

"Now, Katie, I want you to familiarize yourself with something very important... the brakes. If all else goes wrong, I want you to know how to put on the brakes. You see the pedal to the left? Go ahead and put your foot on it and press it down."

Katie obeyed, pushing the pedal down with her left foot, her leg tense and rigid, muscles taunt.

"Good. Now, if I ever say stop, I want you to press down on the brake pedal immediately. Do you understand?"

"Yes, Dad."

"The other pedal is the gas. That makes us go. I want you to give that just a slight push and see how it revs the engine."

Again Katie raised her foot, her right foot, and put it down on the pedal. The engine raced furiously. Katie's leg, rigid and unyielding, had mashed the pedal to the floor. She let up immediately, jumped in her seat, her body straining against the seat belt holding her in place.

"Dad, I don't think I can do this," she said. Her whole body seemed to shake.

"It's okay Katie, calm down. Let's try it again. I know you have trouble with small movements, but try to depress the pedal just a little bit."

Katie tried again. Again the engine raced. Over and over, her Dad encouraging her, she worked the pedal with her foot, learning to adjust her muscles, learning to use her whole leg to control the amount of pressure she applied.

Unlike others, she had little control of her fine motor skills. She always learned to adjust for that by using whole arms or legs to control her movements. It was how she typed on the computer, her arms waving furiously, her fingers, like a plunger at the end of a piston, going up and down and around. The car was no different. It was a learning curve that took a great deal of effort. But slowly she began to get control, to be able to apply the gas only so much, and no more, using her entire leg as a piston, her foot and toes fixed and stiff.

"Okay, Katie," her father began again, "let's give it a try. I want you to put your left foot on the brake and keep your right foot just above the gas pedal. Slip the car into Drive using the gear shift lever here between the seats."

Katie did as she was instructed, her arm moving the lever past Reverse and Neutral, past Drive, all the way to the First Gear position. She tried again, moving the lever forward until it clicked into place. It was another unfamiliar movement she would have to learn to control. With the car in Drive, her father continued.

"Now let off the pedal and give it a little bit of gas. Keep your hands on the wheel and be ready to steer. I want you to drive forward, straight down the road."

Katie complied, or tried to comply, but the excitement carried her away, and with it her muscles. Rigid and tense, her right leg shot out like a ramrod, her foot mashed the gas pedal to the floor. The car leaped forward, the engine growling in response. Within seconds they were shooting ahead faster and faster, the car swerving and swooping along the narrow road, the trees looming on every side. He felt panic for a moment, his whole body paralyzed, his throat constricted, the words he wanted to shout frozen in his larynx.

Katie gripped the wheel in sheer terror, her muscles rigid and unyielding, her grip a death-like vise of pressure. She was locked in, her foot mashed to the floor.

For what seemed like an eternity, but in reality was only a few seconds, they remained frozen in place, as the car careened on down the road, swaying from side to side like some drunken sailor trying to find the way back to his ship.

"SSSSSSSStop…" he finally managed to shout. "STOP NOW!'

Katie's mind unfroze, her senses took over. Almost as if on autopilot, her father's instructions impaling her like a spear, she took her right foot off the gas pedal. Her left leg rose in one movement, and, with all the rigidity of her muscles, descended like some primeval horde of locusts upon the unsuspecting brake pedal lying underfoot. Instantly the wheels locked up, the tires screaming as they left tracks of rubber across the pavement. The car screeched to a halt, the front end falling to the right as the rear tried to catch it, and slid sickeningly to the left, in a textbook three-point slide.

Her hands and arms rigid on the wheel, Katie found herself immobile in the driver's seat as the car came to a crashing halt, completely sideways on the road. Her father, with no wheel to hang onto, was not so lucky. He felt himself flying forward, the windshield rushing up to meet him at a sickening pace. He had just one moment to think, one split second for his life to pass before his eyes, and then the seat belt caught, suspending him in midair, the cloth of the belt digging into his chest and shoulder with a force that would leave a mark for days to come. He slammed back into his seat, the cushion absorbing the shock as his body snapped backwards.

It took only seconds, mere seconds, but the moment seemed like an eternity. Slowly he let out his breath, exhaled deeply, his mind a blank, numb from the suddenness of it all.

Finally, after what seemed like more eternities, he gathered himself, turned to his daughter.

"Katie," he said slowly, "I think that's enough for one day."

The marks on his chest, indelibly burned into his flesh, remained for many days thereafter. It was, he thought, a somewhat ironic turn of events, that his daughter, who suffered so much from bruises throughout her entire life, should remain bruise-free, while he himself was marked and sore after that first fateful attempt at learning to drive.

Surprisingly, it did not deter them from trying again. They were like two children who'd discovered a secret pleasure, two kids sneaking away to indulge in a private game known only to them. The very next day they were at it, Katie once again practicing the unfamiliar motions required to adjust seat and mirror, to position herself for the optimal perch from which to try and control this three thousand pound lump of metal, plastic and glass.

He found a parking lot, huge and deserted, its edges bordered by the empty shell of a long ago failed mercantile, a national chain that went bankrupt, leaving behind this large space with no one to fill it. A parking lot was the ideal place to teach the art of driving. There were no limits to be wary of, no curbs or cars to contend with. It was a space where Katie could feel free to experiment, to try without fear of consequence, without fear of failure. She could experiment with gas, pedal, and brake, turn the wheel this way and that, her arms and legs rigid and straight. It was her way of mastering movement, her way of controlling a body that didn't understand the nature of control, that needed something else, something unnatural, to control gravity.

Only with the car it was different. With the computer it was all movement, grandiose, large, sweeping movements. With the car it was subtle adjustments, tiny calculations of space and force that made the difference. It took her an entire week, with several hours of practice every day, to be able to control the pedals with motions that would not send the car hurtling forward, or cause it to come to a screeching halt. It was another equal period of time for her to learn to control the movement of the wheel, to not send it spinning out of control, nor turn it the wrong way when she became excited.

The hardest part was coordinating the two together, the wheel and the pedals. Her father sat endlessly in the passenger seat, his arms braced against the dashboard, just in case, he would say to himself with an inward grin. He sat patiently, guiding, instructing, encouraging, and yes, occasionally screeching out commands in near panic. It became a game for the two of them. A way to pass the time. Every day after school, after work, they would descend upon this deserted parking lot for their nightly driving ritual.

Occasionally her mother would come, would sit in the passenger seat and take the role of instructor, offering up commands and directions while Katie worked feverishly to master the subtle movements that the car demanded. She offered encouragement and advice, happy that she was able to do so after long hours of writing her daughter's homework without the ability to contribute or participate, her fingers working like a blind and dumb dictation machine. This was better. It fulfilled her need to offer guidance, direction, motherly advice.

It was, they decided, a much better experience than learning to walk. Oh, it was just as frustrating. It was also fraught with more danger and a far more uncertain outcome. Walking was one thing, it required only one's own ability to keep at it until mastered, or the attempt abandoned. But driving was another thing altogether. Other people's lives were at stake. Other people's actions were involved. And other people would have a say, with driver's tests and examinations, in whether this was a successful experiment, or one doomed to failure.

After two months of on again, off again, practice, the sessions being woven between school and softball and work, Katie began to show signs of mastering the delicate art of driving. Her father began to think that it might be possible, just possible, that this was more than a fun way to spend time together.

"Katie," he said one evening as he drove them home from the vast parking lot, "you are doing very well. So well that I think it's time we looked into some professional instruction for you."

"What do you mean?" she replied, "Professional instruction?" You mean like a driving school?"

"Yes," he replied. "I found one down in the city that offers adaptive driving lessons for people with physical impairments. I spoke with the head of the school today. He would very much like to take you on as a student."

"Oh, could I Dad?" she exclaimed. "Could I really? That would be wonderful. When can we start? I could go after school, tomorrow. Mom would take me, I know she would. Tomorrow, can we go tomorrow?"

"Whoa," he replied. "Slow down a minute. We were just talking. I will have to make an appointment." He was amazed once again at her ability to charge ahead, charge through the fears and uncertainties that loomed always in front of her. "But I think we could go down this weekend and see about starting. Would that work? Do you have a softball game or practice?"

"No, oh no, I'm free. This weekend would be fine."

"Okay then, we'll go. I'll call him tomorrow and make the appointment."

They drove on through the neighborhoods, winding their way home, the car silent for several seconds. And then…

"Dad?"

"Yes, Katie."

"Can we go down early, before the appointment, or stay after for a bit? I want to go shopping."

"Sure, Katie, I'm sure we can take the time for that. What do you want to go shopping for? New clothes? Maybe some new shoes for school?"

"Uh, not exactly."

"Oh, then what for?"

"Well, I know several places we can go, we pass them all the time when going to the city."

"Places to go? For what? What did you want to go shopping for?"

"A car, of course. I'm going to need a car."

She was nervous, very nervous.

It was not a good sign, he decided. They were sitting in the lounge of the motor vehicle department, the big one in the city, Katie, her father, and her mother. It was not the usual drab government office. The carpet was new and blue, a pleasant light blue that reminded him of the mountain sky in the afternoons. The seating was modern, with padding and armrests. The walls were also painted a light blue. It could have been called the blue room for all he knew.

But Katie was very nervous before this, the ultimate test. They were waiting for the examiner who would give Katie her very first driving test. And the carrot at the end of this stick would be her very own driver's license.

It was not a good sign, this nervousness. Katie could not sit still, her muscles rigid and twitching, her arms stiff. He hoped it was just nerves, and that she was not having a bad day.

As time passed and Katie grew older, it became apparent to those close to her that she had good days and bad. On good days she seemed to be possessed of a wonderful control of herself. Her arms swung in unison, her voice was far more distinct and understandable. Her walk was self-assured, and, although not normal, seemed natural, her balance stable and centered over her body. On good days she maneuvered well through her world, activities like dressing and brushing her teeth coming more easily to her.

On bad days, the opposite was true. Those were the days when everything seemed harder, when she expended far more energy just to get through the day. Those were the days when her speech was slurred, hard to understand or decipher. Those were the days when she needed help with the simplest of tasks. Those were the days when her backpack would threaten to send her tumbling down the stairs at school.

On bad days she fell, sometimes several times during the day. That was when the danger came, when bruises showed, when ankles got sprained and muscles got strained. On bad days it seemed the world around her pushed back, fought her, tugged her this way and that. On bad days the things she couldn't do, couldn't control, seemed more ominous, more present, more formidable.

He hoped she wasn't having a bad day on this, the day of her driving test. The adaptive driving program she entered had been wonderful, the instructors well-trained and patient, most of all patient. They continued where Katie's parents left off, teaching her how to control the car through movements that accommodated her physical limitations. They began with a parking lot as well, a large paved lot behind their offices. From there they progressed to the side streets, where traffic was light and Katie could learn to assess and control her environment. Gradually they moved to busier streets, to thoroughfares and multi-lane expressways. Finally, they tackled the interstate highway that ran through the big city in the valley.

Katie went three times a week, her mother driving her to the city after school, waiting it out while Katie attended lessons, shopping, or just reading to pass the time. They would come home in the evening to a waiting dinner from her father. Those were fun times, and exhausting, as Katie had to use all her faculties and concentration in completing her lessons.

Finally, the time came when, with the school's help, they got her a learner's permit. She began to drive down to the school and back home as well, her mother sitting in the passenger seat, fidgeting and nervous, her foot pressing an imaginary brake pedal as she learned to handle the stress of having her daughter drive in traffic.

The months passed. Winter came and the little town in the mountains was blanketed in snow. Her father took her out during those times when the roads were snowed over so she could learn to drive in slippery conditions. He even had her turn circles in the deserted parking lot, the tires slipping over the snow and ice. The feeling of slipping terrified her at first, but gradually she got used to it, learned not to tense up and overcorrect. These motions she was learning were hard enough for the average person. For Katie they were even harder as she learned how to make the rigidity of her body work for her, and not against her.

School days slipped away, her senior year flying by in a whirl of events and socials and study. Some events Katie went to, as she was growing more into herself and gaining confidence when out with others. Often, however, she would pass up these social events as the demands of school, the softball team, and her driving, took all of her time. The holidays came and went, and still she drove every chance she got, working towards an uncertain future, the possibility that one day she might have her own license, her own right to drive in this car crazy society in which she lived.

Now that day had come with this test. They logged her driving hours and filled out the forms. In keeping with her schoolwork, the written test was not only passed, but with a perfect score, a 100 that she proudly showed off to anyone who asked. The requirements were met and the test scheduled. The time was now. But she was very nervous, and fidgety, and rigid.

"Katie, are you alright? Do you feel okay? We don't have to do this today if you aren't feeling up to it."

"No, Dad, I want to. I'm ready. I'm just nervous."

"It's okay to be nervous, but you have to try and control it. Try running through your yoga and breathing exercises. And maybe we could find a room for you to stretch in."

"Oh no, I'm fine. I don't want to go anywhere and I don't want to do any exercises in front of all these people. Stop embarrassing me, Dad."

Now that was a complaint the parent of any teenager had to be used to, he thought smiling inwardly. That was a very normal reaction in a very abnormal situation, and the thought comforted him, warmed him. Regardless of everything else, his daughter was still a teenager, a full-blooded, American teenager, with all the baggage that came with it. Somehow it comforted him to know that inside that little body, with the thin muscles and rigid limbs, there lived a perfectly normal, hormonally driven teenager, a teenager mortified at the thought of her parents embarrassing her out in public.

"Well, settle down," he replied, "Else we will have to postpone this until you're in better shape to take the test."

Finally, their number was called, and they got up to meet the examiner, to hand over the forms and paperwork and get the test underway.

"You must be Katie," the examiner said, not unkindly. "I understand you have cerebral palsy, is that correct?"

"Yes sir," she replied, uncertain of what his reaction would be.

He studied her paperwork for long moments, his brow furrowed in concentration, his mouth twisted into a permanent frown.

"Well," he said finally, "we'll just have to see about this. Do you think you're ready?"

"Oh, yes sir, I've been practicing for months. I have over three times the hours required for the test."

"Yes, I see. Well, we'll have a go at it then. You can take me to your car now. We need to inspect it."

He turned to her parents, a reassuring tone in his voice.

"We can take it from here. If you two will just wait in the lounge, we'll come and get you when we return."

"But I thought we could go with her," her mother said hurriedly. "Can't we tag along, sit in the back?"

"No, I am afraid that won't be possible. Only the applicant and examining officer are allowed in the car. I'm afraid this is one test she has to take all by herself. Do you understand?"

"Well, yes, I guess. Good luck honey, don't forget to look over your shoulder when changing lanes, and don't forget what I told you about checking the mirrors, and don't…"

She stopped abruptly as her husband took her arm and started guiding her to the lounge.

"Okay officer, we've got it. We'll just wait over here," he said.

He was smiling now, confident that his daughter was ready, happy in the knowledge that his wife was far more nervous than his daughter, more nervous than himself for that matter.

At first, the waiting was easy. They'd done all they could, had no more responsibilities, nothing to do but wait. But the waiting grew longer, first a quarter of an hour, then a half, then a full hour passed them by. They grew nervous again, worried. Had something happened? Had there been a wreck, an accident? What could possibly take this long?

"Maybe we should ask someone, check at the counter," Katie's mother said hurriedly, frustration evident in her tone. "This isn't right. It shouldn't be taking this long,"

"Okay dear, I'll check. I'm sure it's nothing, but you're right, it shouldn't take this long."

He had to admit he was worried, too. He returned shortly, the look he gave her no more reassuring than when he'd left.

"There's nothing for it, we just have to wait. They say the length of the test is up to the examiner. They have a radio and if something goes wrong they call in, and he hasn't. So we have to just wait it out."

"Well, I don't like it. If they aren't back in another ten minutes I'm going to do something."

He didn't want to imagine what that something might be, but he knew his wife, and it wouldn't be pleasant. He'd also learned, after all these years of marriage, to not cross bridges until he came to them. So he settled in and tried to relax, knowing the future would take care of itself. But he didn't like facing the prospect of going to war with the department of motor vehicles. And his wife's tone indicated she was ready to do just that.

Finally, the waiting was over.

Just as Katie's mother had reached her limit, had put her things in order and gotten ready to rise, to challenge the power of the civil servants behind the counter, Katie and her examiner walked in. By the looks on their faces he couldn't tell if she had been successful or not. Katie's face was blank, her walk slow and uncertain. She was tired, he could tell that, but he could also tell that she was doing everything she could to hide the fact. Perhaps the test wasn't over. Perhaps she was still in game mode, still focused, still performing for the examiner's benefit.

The officer's face wasn't much more illuminating than Katie's. He had a firm look, not altogether unpleasant, but set. Her parents rose as they approached, her mother reaching out to her daughter almost at once.

"My, you two were gone a long time. Is everything all right? Did anything happen?"

"No, no," the examiner relied quickly. "Everything is fine. Your car is fine and parked out front. May I speak to you two for a moment? Alone please? We can step into the office in the corner."

"Of course," her father replied. "Katie, why don't you sit here. Just rest and we'll be right back."

The examiner led them into a small office tucked into the corner of the lobby. There was a round table, the Formica dull and scratched, and four chairs arranged haphazardly around it, their plastic backs faded from years of use. They sat down, arranged themselves. The examiner hesitated, paused, looked over his notes and the paperwork in his hand. Finally, he spoke.

"That is one very determined young lady," he said not unkindly. "Very determined."

He paused, as if searching for the right way to begin, then continued slowly, choosing his words carefully.

"I must say I was very concerned with this particular examination, this test. Your daughter is physically challenged in a way that could be very dangerous to others were she allowed to drive on her own. The responsibility for that rests squarely on my shoulders, my evaluation, my decision as to her fitness to drive. Driving is dangerous, tens of thousands of people are killed every day across the world. It is not a right, it is a privilege, and it must be earned."

He paused again, searching their faces for acknowledgement, for understanding.

"I have to admit I wanted your daughter to fail. I threw every trick in the book at her. I had her in the car three times longer than normal. I tried to upset her, tried to scare her, to startle her. I had her driving in areas we normally don't go. I took her to blind corners and complicated intersections. I had her repeat certain procedures over and over again. I even had her parallel park three times. This is why we were gone so long. This is why we took so much time. I have been trying to fail your daughter, to break her down."

He paused again. Katie's father interrupted.

"And the result? Did you... break her down, as you say?"

"I'll say it again," he replied. "Your daughter is a very determined girl."

"Yes, we know. Believe me, we've lived with that for many years."

"Well then, no, to answer your question. No, I did not break her down. I did not get to her. She remained calm, she remained focused, she performed flawlessly. You are to be congratulated. Your daughter is an exemplary driver. I cannot fail her. She has given me no reason to do so. Nor am I prepared to act arbitrarily and deny her a license because of a feeling."

"So she passed the test?" her mother chimed in. "She passed?"

"Yes, I am going to pass her. However, I am going to recommend restrictions. For one, I do not want her driving with other teenagers as passengers for three months. I do not want her driving on the interstate for six months. Those are restrictions we often enforce on new teenage drivers. And I am going to require that she be retested every year for the foreseeable future. Should she continue to pass the test each year without problems, then over time I am sure you can get that restriction lifted. But for now, I believe it is best that we examine her yearly, more often if she is involved in any kind of accident or incident while driving."

"Is that really necessary?" her father asked.

He knew it was probably prudent, and he himself was not altogether thrilled with his daughter driving, just another thing to weigh them down, to make them worry whenever Katie would be out with the car. I suppose that's the price every father pays when their kids start driving, but with his daughter that fear would be magnified a thousand times, at least for a while. Still he had to ask. Restrictions were often prudent at first, but a pain in the ass down the road, especially trying to get them lifted. He could foresee a time when that would happen.

"Yes, I'm afraid it is, at least if you want me to pass her. You can always request another examiner, but I wouldn't advise it."

"No, no, that's fine. We'll go with what we've got here, now. Thank you very much."

"Then that's all I have. If you do not have any other questions we can go and let your daughter know."

They all got up, shook hands, made their way back to the lobby where Katie was sitting, an anxious and nervous look hanging onto her face.

"Katie," her father said, very seriously. "I'm afraid they can't give you a license just yet."

"No," she replied, and a world of disappointment was contained within that one simple word. "No?"

"No," he replied, a smile spreading across his face. "You see, they can't print out your license until they take your picture. Have to have your picture on a driver's license you know. That's the next step after," he paused for effect, "after you have passed your driving test."

"Oh," she said, and that was all she could say.

But the look on her face spoke volumes.

It was a look, her father thought to himself, that he couldn't describe, but one that he would remember for the rest of his life.

Graduation

"The prom is coming."

"Eh, what's that, the prom?"

"Yes, dear, the prom, senior prom. It's coming, and Katie wants to go of course."

"I would think so. Is there a problem?"

"Well, yes, I mean, she's going to need stuff. A dress. Shoes. Hair appointment. Then there's the transportation, the after-dance party, oh, it's a world of stuff you men have no clue about."

"Well, I suppose so. I mean, it seems pretty simple to me. You dress up, you go, you have a good time. What's so complicated about that?"

"You know, if I had another twenty years, I might be able to educate you on the subject. But I don't, and prom's coming, and we need to get busy. A senior prom is something you remember for the rest of your life. Katie hasn't been to many social functions, and she's never really been to a dance. So we need to make this special. I'll handle most of the arrangements, but I want you to take her shopping for the dress."

"The dress? Her prom dress? Shouldn't that be something you do? Hell, I don't know about dresses and such."

"No, but you're a man and she will want a man's opinion. That's what a dress is for. It really is a father and daughter thing, whether you know it or not. I want you to take her dress shopping. I want you to be patient. I want you to let her take the lead, where to go, what to do. And I don't want you making your silly comments. A prom dress is a very serious thing."

"Well, okay. You want me to give her my honest opinion? You

want me to be her advisor?"

"Yes, I do. Encourage her to get something that makes her look good, even sexy, in your eyes."

"Whoa, little too much information there. I don't think I want to get into the subject of sexy with my daughter. I've never even thought about it, thank god."

"No, but now it's time. She's eighteen and she needs a dress that says she's pretty, and that she's sexy and desirable, and most of all, that she has taste. Think you can do it?"

"Well, I'll try, but that's a tall order. How much do we spend on this dress thing?"

"As much as it takes. And don't you dare argue. A prom is a once in a…"

"I know, I know, a once in a lifetime experience. And I'm going to remember it for the rest of my life too, at least my pocketbook is. How come I get the feeling this is only the beginning of this deal? How come I get the feeling this prom is going to set me back a bundle?"

"Because it is, and you will pay it, and be happy about it. Comprende, Dad?"

"Yes, dear."

Yes, dear. He was amazed at how comfortable, how routine, how regular that phrase had become. Yes, dear. It was the foundation of everything he had learned about marriage in twenty years of living through it. Yes, dear. What a wonderful phrase, he thought to himself.

Well, if this prom thing was to be done, then he decided it might as well be done right. The right dress, whatever the cost, the right shoes, the transportation, dinner, whatever. He would support his wife and daughter, and make it as wonderful as it could possibly be.

"Oh, and there is just one other thing."

"What's that?"

"An escort."

"An escort?"

"Yes, an escort, for the prom. You generally go with someone. Honestly, I don't know how you men survive. Don't you remember your prom?"

"Well, now that you mention it, there was a lot of this special punch and, well, okay, no, not much of it."

"But you did have a date? You know, an escort?"

"Oh yeah, I had one alright."

"Well, that's what I'm talking about."

"You mean…"

"Yes, I mean."

"Like a companion, a partner."

"No, not exactly."

"An escort, an…"

"Yes, an escort, a date."

"You mean…"

"Boys, dear. I mean boys, as in a boy, a boy to go with."

It wasn't the first time the thought had ever occurred to him. But at that moment, it hit him. His daughter was eighteen. She was growing up. Behind the thin limbs, the rigidity, the spastic muscles and awkward way of moving through the world, his daughter was becoming a woman, and quite an attractive one at that.

But boys?

No way. They were not mature enough at this age to see through the surface to what lay underneath. For years he had comfortably put the idea of boys away, tucked it into a corner of his mind and labeled it "sometime in the future, but NOT NOW."

"Does she have a boy? I mean, uh, er, a date?"

"No, she doesn't. And that makes me very worried."

"Well, what can we do about that?"

"Nothing, I'm afraid. But you'd better think of something."

"Why me?"

"Because it's your gender dear, your sex. Figure it out, or your daughter may have a very un-fun prom."

"Yes, dear," he replied.

"Nope. It just doesn't grab me."

"Dad!"

"Hey, I'm just being honest. You want me to be honest, don't you?"

"Yeah Dad, but this is the latest style. What do you mean nope? What do you mean it doesn't grab you?"

"Let me tell you something daughter, style or no style, I know what men like, I mean, er, boys like. I was one, am one, remember? And I may not know style, but I know what looks good, and that doesn't. It makes your body look like a stick and your butt look like it took a trip to banana-bottom land. You can do better."

"Okay, okay."

Katie turned to go back into the dressing room. This was the third store and the tenth dress she had tried on. Her mother said to have patience, and he was determined to do just that. So they took the better part of the morning on this lazy Saturday in spring to find just the right dress for her senior prom.

Money was no object, he knew. But looks were. And he was determined to find a dress, current style notwithstanding, that made her look just right, made her look grown, and full, and ripe, and, well, like a woman, a full-grown woman. And it wasn't easy. This shopping thing wasn't easy.

For himself, he walked into a store, said I need that, that, and oh yeah, give me one of those, and he was done with it. But he knew about the shopping adventures of the fairer sex. He'd had to participate in those far more often in twenty years of marriage than he cared to admit. And he realized that it was good practice for this moment, this moment with his daughter, helping her to pick out a special dress for a special occasion.

Once again he thought of his wife's perspicacity, her insight into this situation. After all, wasn't shopping for dresses a mother and daughter thing? But no, she knew her daughter, knew him, knew what would make the moment special. She would handle the shoes, the accessories, the transportation, everything else. But the dress? Well, the dress was something special, and Katie was determined to find just the right one.

Once again he thought, I am enslaved by this little girl's determination, her willfulness. What had the driving examiner said? Oh yes, that is one very determined girl. No, woman, he corrected himself. One very determined woman.

So he sat in the dressing area of a store in one of the newest malls in the city in the valley. It was trendy, with bright colors, a lot of bling, and hip hop music blaring through speakers that seemed to be everywhere. The sales staff were all young, all hip, all decked out in the latest and most outrageous outfits to be found on the store shelves. He almost mistook one of the clerks for a mannequin, was about to make fun of it to Katie, when the employee actually moved and scared him half to death.

It was a cool place, a cool store, at least for Katie, but all it did to him was make him feel old, and getting older every day.

"How about this, Dad?"

Katie's sudden appearance broke in on his chain of thought, brought him back to the moment, to reality.

"How about this one?" Katie repeated.

He took in the dress, from head to toe, and knew she had found it, knew the quest for the perfect dress was finally over.

It was a light blue and the material seemed to shimmer, even in the harsh light of the dressing area. It had one sleeve beginning just below the elbow and traveling up the arm to the shoulder. At that point the top of the dress fell away, across the chest, under the opposing arm, giving the impression of a strapless gown held in place only by magic and a prayer. The line across the chest was slightly angled, low but not too low, and allowed just a hint of cleavage without exposing too much.

In the back, the dress fell to a point halfway down the spine, suggesting a backless gown, without really being backless. It was tight across the hips, tight over the belly and buttocks, and from there it flowed to the lower legs. The bottom of the dress mirrored the top in that one side was short, above the knee, while the other was long, falling to almost mid-calf.

Once again it gave an impression, an impression of being slit up to the hips without really doing so. It was elusive, he thought to himself. It suggested, it teased, it offered up something that, in the end, really wasn't there. It was mysterious and magical, and it fit her like the proverbial glove.

He couldn't help gasping. His breath caught, his eyes stared. He was transfixed. This was his daughter, his little girl, the one who had to wear a helmet and pads in hopes of learning to walk, who couldn't tie a shoe or write her name legibly without a computer. The little girl who lit up the world and his heart every time she smiled, yet had trouble getting through a day without falling down. Only she wasn't a little girl anymore, she was this woman; and in this dress, this prom dress, a beautiful woman, fully grown.

How did this happen? How did this come about? This little girl who sat transfixed at a birthday party while a little mermaid sang and danced and swam across the screen, this little girl for whom the world was a magical place of toys and dreams, this little girl had become a woman. She was graduating from high school, soon to go to college, to leave the nest and make a life of her own. The unknown future he and his wife had so feared from the moment she was born was now becoming the present. And it all hit him, hit him in that moment, at that place, with that dress… that shimmering, slinky, tight fitting dress.

"Dad?" Katie asked again, her voice growing in volume. "Dad? DAD?"

"Yes, Katie. Yes, I hear you."

He came back to the present, back to reality, shaking off the haziness of his thoughts like a drunk shaking off his desire for another drink.

"Yes, that's the one, that's it. No need to look any farther. That's the dress."

"You really think so?"

She was pleased. She knew how it looked, knew she'd made up her mind the moment she put it on, before she even left the dressing cubicle.

"Oh yes, I really think so. You are beautiful. That dress is beautiful. That's the one."

"Do you want to know what it costs?" she asked.

"Nope, don't care. That's it." He said it with finality, with an air of surety that he really didn't feel. And somewhere inside his male brain he just knew it would be the most expensive one of the bunch. Of course. It had to be. But he would be damned if he would let on to his daughter just how THAT made him feel.

In two weeks, the senior prom would be held. After that, the sports awards banquet where Katie would receive a varsity letter in softball for her work as manager of the team. And then graduation, just four short weeks away. To Katie, those four weeks would go by in a flash, would race through her life like a cannonball speeding to its target.

But to her father, the next four weeks would be the longest of his life.

Soon the world would come knocking, that was clear. College, career, and yes, men. In that dress it was clear that the men would come knocking, would discover this latent flower, finally blooming in a desert where no flower had bloomed before. But he would cling to these last weeks and days, these last moments of innocence when he still held her in his grip. And he would remember her at just this moment, just this time, with this dress, and all that it signified.

His wife was right. The dress was a father and daughter thing. He knew that now. Knew the transformative power of just the right fabric, in just the right color, cut to the body in just the right way. Knew the power of how it spoke to the opposite sex, how a simple dress could hide, no, not hide, but rather conceal in an honest way, the abnormal shapes of an abnormal body.

"Yes, Katie," he said again. "That's the one."

In the end it was settled.

Katie would go to prom with her very best friend forever, with Amy. Amy who lived in the big city in the valley. Amy who was one year older, and already in college. Amy would be her escort, her companion, her dance partner. It was a solution Katie came up with all by herself.

There was no boy, no boyfriend, no magical man-child calling up and asking her out. Her parents put their heads together, tried to figure it out. Maybe later, her father thought, later when the boys were more grown, more mature, and able to see Katie for the whole person that she was.

Besides, he thought, it was a different time, a different age. Boys and girls didn't quite date the way they had when he was growing up. They tended to travel more in packs. Oh, some would pair up. And there were those that had been together, inseparable really, since almost grade school. But Katie missed out on that part of school, of dating boys, of going through the rituals.

It was like everything else in her life. Things came later, if at all, and never when they normally should. It was as if her life was lived in a delayed state, as if some giant hand had pushed the pause button on some remote control, making her wait, and work for everything that might come to her. Walking, talking, driving, dating, these things were not regular milestones in an ordinary life lived in an ordinary fashion. These were things that had to be earned, fought for, conquered. And always later, much later, than normal.

So for Katie it was the most natural thing in the world that she would go to prom with her friends, including Amy, her best friend forever, and a few other girls that she had come to know, had grown to like and spend time with.

One was on the softball team, another a confidant in her math classes. Katie was taking a course load heavy in math and science her last two years in high school. She gravitated to those subjects as part of her wizardry with the computer, and she continued to get straight A's and remain at the top of her class. She made friends with some of the other "smart" girls, the ones who, like her, made all A's in every subject.

So they would go as a group, her best friend, her teammate, and her classmate.

The night came, the girls gathering at Katie's house, waiting for the limo they'd hired to whisk them away to prom and to another in a long line of senior year rituals. The girls giggled incessantly as they primped before the mirror, adjusted dresses and accessories, applied tons of make-up.

Finally, they pinned on their corsages and got ready to go. Katie's mother took picture after picture. Her father simply stood to the side and watched, took it all in, immersed himself in the moment, became involved only when the task of pinning on the corsages was assigned to his capable fingers.

Their chariot arrived. When they left, when the limo turned

the corner of their street and disappeared into the darkening sky of evening, he turned to his wife, a wistful smile on his face.

"Well Mom, you did it. A perfect evening. I just hope the dance goes as well."

"She'll be fine. That dress is beautiful. I can't believe you found it."

"I didn't, your daughter did. But I knew it was the one the moment I saw it."

"Yes, it's perfect."

"Did you see her smile? Did you see the excitement in her face, in her eyes? Of all the years she's been in high school, I can't remember a time when she was so happy."

"Well, in a few weeks she graduates. It's a coming of age for her. A time she'll never forget. Through all the hard times, the work, the disappointments, this is a time when all that goes away."

"Graduation. Then college. We're going to lose her, you know."

"Yes, I know."

There was a sadness in her voice, a wistfulness that even he could not ignore. He knew the time was coming, growing close.

"Well," he said, his own voice laced with sadness, "how about some dinner now?"

They ate in silence, each to their own thoughts. It was a special night for their daughter, one she would never forget. But for them it was the most ordinary of nights, the most prosaic of evenings, the two of them alone, eating dinner, the house eerily quiet.

It was, he thought to himself, a portent of things to come.

With graduation quickly approaching, it was time for Katie to think about the next steps in her life, to think about college, where to go, what to study, what accommodations she would need in this, the next step in her journey. Katie's father regaled her with stories of his own days in college, the good and the bad, and what it all meant to him. They agreed that picking a college was a major step in whatever the future held for her. So they would expend a great deal of effort on the project. It was another chance for them to do something together.

Their search for a college actually started almost a year before. They checked out several schools, explored them through the Internet, wrote away for brochures, studied classes and subjects, talked about the many possibilities.

With Katie's grades it was clear she could go almost anywhere she wanted. Oh, there would be the questions, the accommodations that would be needed. College would be a different environment, a challenge that even high school could not prepare her for. She would be on her own. She would be out there, making her way without the support of her family, her hometown, of all the people who had come to know her and understand her.

They checked out each school's adaptive programs, their handicap facilities and accommodations. They examined travel options, housing, food programs and workout facilities for her physical therapy. They had fun, spent hours poring over pages of information from the Internet, their evenings filled with the camaraderie of being together, of examining, comparing, challenging, even dreaming about the future. Father and daughter sharing moments, moments he knew would only serve, in the end, to take her away from him. Still, she was here now, still close, still a part of his world, and he could drink in her presence every night, marvel at the efficiency of her movements on the keyboard, laugh over a shared joke, and soak in that wonderful smile, her smile, the smile that was so quick to spread across her face and light up the room with a warmth that he could actually feel inside himself.

They finally narrowed down their choices to only a few schools. One in particular, the closest one, the university in the city in the valley, was becoming the clear choice. It had the programs she was interested in, science and math, and, most importantly, computers. She'd come to depend on computers for her schoolwork and they were a comfort to her. Although she had no idea what she wanted to do or study, she knew it would involve computers.

It was also close to home, just a bit over an hour's drive away, far enough to be strange and different, yet close enough to be comforting and familiar. Several of her friends would be going there, and many more acquaintances.

So they carved out a day all their own, Katie and her father, to explore its buildings and grounds, to poke into its corners and recesses, the student union, the dorm rooms, the cafeterias and classrooms. They made an appointment to talk with the head of the handicap and disabilities office of the school, discussed her options and the programs that were available to her.

They spoke to the admissions office staff, and to a counselor who felt Katie would easily qualify for several scholarships, academic scholarships, state scholarships, even a "women in engineering" scholarship, should she choose to major in computer engineering. Her acceptance would be assured, the counselor told them, her grades and accomplishments would see to that.

It was a long day, a tiring day, and a wonderful time for him to spend with his daughter. They completed their tours, finished with their appointments, the shadows growing longer as the spring day wound to a close and the sun sank lower on the horizon. Soon it would be time to return to the car, to make the drive back to the little town in the mountains, to talk about the school and her decision, about whether to go there and what to study.

They were ready to leave, had almost left the last building on their tour, when a room caught Katie's eye. It was off to the side, really only marked by a single door that seemed quite inconspicuous. The door suggested that it was only a small room, perhaps an anteroom to some offices, or a storeroom stocked with supplies. But something drew them to this door, and to the room beyond. Something in the air, something possessed of importance, some feeling said that the next few moments would be... significant, would have an impact on everything that was to follow.

Katie was the first to enter, the first to pass through this small door in a forgotten hallway.

"Dad," she cried. "Dad, come here. You've got to see this."

"What is it, Katie? See what?"

"Well, come see for yourself. It's really cool."

Her father passed through the door and was surprised by the size of the room. It was large, rectangular, and filled with displays. A museum, he thought? Perhaps a school display or project?

They were in the old administrative building of the university, one of the first buildings to be built over a hundred years before. It had been converted to offices and classrooms spread over the four floors of the building, with most of the rooms small and cramped. But this one was different. It had probably been several rooms in a past life, but now the walls were torn down and the room stretched almost half the length of the third floor of the building.

He began to walk down one of the rows of displays, working towards where his daughter was standing, transfixed, watching something he couldn't quite see from where he was. As he neared, he heard a voice, small and tinny at first, but growing in timber and volume as he approached.

There, perched in a display cabinet in front of his daughter, was a small television, and on that television played a video, a video of a long ago event. The former president of the United States, John Fitzgerald Kennedy, was standing behind a podium, his body filling the screen, his face lifted to the skies. And he was speaking, the words coming loud and clear through the speakers in the display cabinet.

"If we are to win the battle that is now going on around the world between freedom and tyranny, the dramatic achievements in space which occurred in recent weeks should have made clear to us all, as did the Sputnik in 1957, the impact of this adventure on the minds of men everywhere, who are attempting to make a determination of which road they should take. Since early in my term, our efforts in space have been under review. With the advice of the Vice President, who is Chairman of the National Space Council, we have examined where we are strong and where we are not. Now it is time to take longer strides - time for a great new American enterprise - time for this nation to take a clearly leading role in space achievement, which in many ways may hold the key to our future on Earth."

His words were strong and clear, coming to them through years long past, from another time, another place. The words of inspiration, of vision, came to them from a man long dead, a man murdered in the streets of a city in the middle of a nation, a nation that still mourned his passing, wishing for a return to a simpler time, when hope and dreams ruled the land, when the future seemed unlimited, when mankind seemed destined to reach for the stars... and beyond.

Katie's father watched his daughter as she listened, as she hung on every word, her eyes focused, her brow furrowed in concentration.

"But this is not merely a race. Space is open to us now; and our eagerness to share its meaning is not governed by the efforts of others. We go into space because whatever mankind must undertake, free men must fully share."

The time came back to him, the place, the long years ago. He'd been a child, no more than seven or eight years old, when this speech had been made, had committed a nation to a singular path. And it was only then that he realized that the room he was in was dedicated to space, to man's attempt to invade and conquer that last frontier, the universe of stars and planets, of vacuum and emptiness, of a void so great that mere humans had trouble even comprehending it.

All along the walls were displays, pictures of stars and galaxies, rocket ships, space vehicles, and satellites. And there was more, for many of the displays spoke to accomplishments made by men and women who had attended this very university. There were astronauts and engineers, physicists and doctors, people who had left the university and joined the effort to explore space, to map it, to understand it, to search for meaning in the far reaches of the universe. The whole room was a tribute to the efforts of these particular alumni of the university. Some worked for NASA, the National Aeronautical and Space Administration. Many worked for technology companies that built rockets and capsules and satellites. Some spent long hours in laboratories, performing research and pondering answers to questions that defied explanation, questions about space, and time, and matter.

He turned back to his daughter, still listening, still transfixed by the scene in front of her, captured by the words of a visionary long dead and buried. She knew who President Kennedy was, knew of his place in history, and the assassination that took his life and rendered a country speechless and heartbroken. But she had never seen this speech, never heard these words.

"I therefore ask the Congress, above and beyond the increases I have earlier requested for space activities, to provide the funds which are needed to meet the following national goals: First, I believe that this nation should commit itself to achieving the goal, before this decade is out, of landing a man on the Moon and returning him safely to the Earth. No single space project in this period will be more impressive to mankind, or more important for the long-range exploration of space;

and none will be so difficult or expensive to accomplish. We propose to accelerate the development of the appropriate lunar space craft. We propose to develop alternate liquid and solid fuel boosters, much larger than any now being developed, until certain which is superior. We propose additional funds for other engine development and for unmanned explorations--explorations which are particularly important for one purpose which this nation will never overlook: the survival of the man who first makes this daring flight. But in a very real sense, it will not be one man going to the Moon - if we make this judgment affirmatively, it will be an entire nation. For all of us must work to put him there."

The words rang out, spoken across the vastness of time past, their meaning and purpose relevant to all that had followed, all that had transpired, right into the present, to this moment when a man and his daughter stood alone in a room, listening to the words of a dead man talking.

Their fatigue vanished. They continued on into the room, into the myriad of displays and pictures, the stories being told with every new step in any direction. In this wonderful room, on the third floor of a hundred year old building, located in the center of this great university in the city in the valley... time fell away. They laughed at certain pictures, marveled at others. They wondered aloud at the stories of the men and woman who had gone into space.

At one of the displays there sat a picture of a far away galaxy. And perched in the corner of the display was a cut-out, a cartoon figure that had been affixed to the picture in a certain way, a way that brought a laugh to the both of them when they came upon it. It was a picture of Peter Pan. He was flying, or rather hovering, a gleam in his eye, a mischievous smile on his face, and he was pointing into space, towards the far flung galaxy centered in the middle of the picture.

"What did Peter Pan say Katie?" her father asked, grinning. "What were his words to Wendy and the boys as they flew off to Never Never Land?"

He couldn't quite remember, but he knew his daughter would know, knew with a certainly that she would know everything about that magical world of imagination that she lived in all her life, that Disney created, it seemed, just for her.

"Second star to the right, Dad," Katie replied. "Second star to the right, and on till morning."

"That's it," he cried, "That's the way. Second star to the right!"

They both laughed, moved by the thought of space and science and magic and make-believe all balled up into one fantastic universe of imagination and wonder.

It was a short while later, as they came to the end of the room, the end of their journey into this world of space and stars and galaxies, that Katie paused, stopped really, standing rigid and still before a picture of a space shuttle launching into the golden hue of an evening sky.

"Dad," she said quietly.

"Yes, Katie?"

"Dad, I think I know what I want to do."

"What do you mean Katie? Do what exactly? You mean where you want to go to school?"

"No, Dad, what I want to do… you know. With the rest of my life."

He paused and turned to look at his daughter, saw the seriousness of her expression, the focus in her eyes.

"I know what I want to do with the rest of my life."

Graduation!

The moment finally arrived, the day when the graduating class, Katie's graduating class, would take to the stage to receive their diplomas and start a new chapter in their young lives.

It was a sunny day, a glorious day, a day that dawned clear and warm and still in the little town in the mountains. Prom had come and gone, classes were over, the awards banquet for the sports teams was held just days before. Katie received her last varsity letter, a symbol she proudly displayed on a letter jacket ordered especially for her senior year. It draped about her small frame like a robe. And although graduation day started off as a warm day, with the promise of getting even hotter, she chose to wear it over her graduation gown, a proud symbol of what she had achieved.

She would drive herself to graduation. After getting her license she made a habit of driving whenever she could, to and from school, to the store, out to dinner with her parents. She could take her friends now, they could ride in the car with her, in fact, two of them would ride with her to the ceremony.

They were graduating on the football field behind the school. It was the perfect setting, with the snow gone and the green grass of spring pushing up through the ground, well-tended and fresh. The school staff worked for days to set up the stages and chairs for the event, roping off sections for students and parents, with other relatives and friends relegated to the bleachers that lined the field on either side.

Her school was big, there were over three thousand students, as it was the only high school in town. Her graduating class was made up of over five hundred seniors. With that many students, the ceremony, the procession, and the awarding of the diplomas, would take several hours.

But not for Katie. She would be up on the stage, one of ten students who had earned the honor of being the best of the class, the best in grade point average, the brightest of the whole school. Katie was number seven. Of over five hundred students, only six had earned a grade point average higher than her. The long years of study had paid off, the work on the computer, the accommodations her parents had fought for, all had paid off. She was an honor student, a top ten graduate.

Her parents arrived early, seeking a spot up front in which to watch and take pictures. For them this was not just a special moment in their child's life, it was a moment they had not even been sure would happen. It was a moment they had only dreamed about, never wanting to take any of Katie's accomplishments for granted, never assuming that she would achieve any of the rites of passage that normal children go through as they grow into adults.

Although early to arrive, it seemed to her father that the time passed much too quickly. It seemed they'd only settled into their seats when the procession started.

"Here they come," his wife shouted as she caught sight of the first of the cap and gown attired students marching slowly to the strains of the processional hymn being played by the school band.

"Look," she cried, "Katie's there, right in front, just behind the girl with the ponytail. Do you see her? Can you see?"

"Yes, I see her," he replied.

She was walking quickly, trying to keep up, her arm clasped in the hand of a fellow student walking with her, helping to steady her. Her legs, stiff and straight, lurched forward with an eagerness that showed her excitement, her arms, rigid and stiff, were swinging from side to side as she fought for balance walking with the crowd of students pressing around her.

The graduating seniors took their seats, the procession winding along as each row was filled. It took some time, but once again it seemed only moments to her father, watching, taking it all in, trying to absorb the moment through his very pores, so as not to forget a single thing about this occasion.

As the last students took their seats the band quieted, the crowd grew silent, and the field was still. Every seat was taken. The bleachers were almost all filled, expectant relatives and friends perched atop the worn and splintered wood of the rows and rows of seats.

The principal took the stage, stepped up to the podium, and began his remarks. After him followed the superintendent of schools, her voice clear and strong in the morning air. Then came the valedictorian, a tall girl with long brown hair and spectacles clinging to her face, a friend of Katie's from her honors courses, the top student in the entire graduating class. Her remarks were brief, she was awestruck, nervous before such a large crowd of people. But she finished strong and was met with a rousing ovation by all.

Finally, it was time to hand out the diplomas, to call each student by name and have them walk across the stage to receive the vaunted sheepskin, the diploma, proof that they had finished something, proof that they had met the requirements for graduating from high school.

The students began to queue up at the side of the stage. The honors students, with Katie included, were the first to cross. One by one they walked forward, arms outstretched, one hand grasping the rolled up document, while with the other, they shook hands with the school board president. As the seventh student to receive a diploma, Katie's turn came quickly. Her name was called and she started her walk across the stage, her legs splayed apart, her muscles rigid, her whole manner nervous and fidgety.

She was worried, worried about this walk, worried she might fall in front of all these people, her peers and their family and friends. The thought of falling haunted her for over a week as she realized more and more what she would have to do. She lost sleep, and that made her days even more difficult to get through. For when she was tired she was far more susceptible to having bad days, days when her body did not want to cooperate.

She stood, took her first few steps across the stage, and at that moment, the sound hit her, a groundswell of applause and cheers coming from all corners of the football stadium. The crowd was cheering and clapping, many of them standing, others taking the cue and also standing, until the entire stadium was filled with the sight of it, a standing ovation from all in attendance.

The sound rolled over the field, rolled over all who stood on it. It propped Katie up, bolstered her as she moved across the stage, and a huge smile, that wonderful smile, the smile that had lit up so many rooms, so many places, so many people throughout her life, that smile began to play across her face.

She reached out with one stiff arm, grabbed the diploma in her outstretched hand, lifted the other to shake the hand of the president, and at that moment, her father would swear later that it was so, the earth seemed to stand still, its rotation quieted, time immobilized, as Katie May, the little girl who had been born dead, graduated from high school, seventh in her class, an honor student, a People to People ambassador, a varsity athlete, and now, an alumnus, with a diploma, a transcript… and a future.

College

"Hello, who is this please?"

The number on his phone was an unfamiliar one. He didn't recognize it, although the area code indicated it was located somewhere around his hometown.

"This is Amy. I'm sorry to bother you but I'm calling about Katie. I'm worried and I wanted you to know what's going on."

"Hi Amy," he greeted her warmly, and then his voice turned serious. "What's going on, what's the matter?"

"It's Katie. She hasn't answered her phone for two days now and none of her friends have seen her. Me either, and I'm getting worried."

"I see," he replied. He was not at home, but on a road trip working with a client. In fact he was halfway across the country but scheduled to fly home the very next morning. "Do you know what's going on?"

"Well, the first year of school isn't really easy. Like there's a lot of adjustment you know. We've been trying to help her with it, but you know how focused on schoolwork she is. We have to drag her out of her dorm room just to get her to have some fun or take a break. Now I think she's having trouble with her classes. I can't get a hold of her you know, and I think she's holed up in her room."

"Trouble with her classes? That doesn't sound like Katie."

"No, it doesn't. But she's taking way too many classes for her first year, especially with how long it takes her to do anything. I wanted you to know. Maybe you could talk to her, like get her out of that room or something."

"Well, I can try. I knew she shouldn't have loaded up her schedule like that, with six classes and all of them advanced."

"Wow, like I know, it's really way too much. I don't even take five classes and I'm a sophomore. But really, whatever, I just wanted you to know. I really think you should talk to her."

"I will, Amy, I will. I come home tomorrow and I'm going to see her first thing when I get in. I really want to thank you for calling. You truly are a great friend."

"Hey, it's nothing. Just don't tell her I snitched on her... okay?"

"Okay," he replied, smiling. No matter the age, it was always the same. You could feel concern for someone, but don't let them know you went around them to their parents, or their spouse or boss, or whatever the situation might be. Heaven forbid you should be labeled a snitch or a tattletale. "Don't worry Amy, your secret is safe with me."

The very next call was to his wife. Fortunately, she had her cell phone and she picked up on the first ring.

"Hi honey, have you heard about your daughter?"

"MY daughter? You mean OUR daughter, don't you dear," she replied, the honey-laced sarcasm dripping out of the phone into his ear. He could almost see the wry smile that must have crossed her face as she uttered those words... "Don't you, deeear!"

"Okay, our daughter. Amy just called. She's worried that she can't get a hold of Katie and she thinks she might be doing poorly in school. She thinks she may be holed up in her room freaked out. And she seems to be cutting off her friends. No one has heard or seen from her in two days."

"Oh no, I was afraid something like this might happen. I spoke with her twice this last weekend and she sounded strange. Not mad or unhappy, just tense, like she didn't want to talk. But why did Amy call you? Why not me? I'm her mother for chrissakes."

"Beats me, but let's just be glad she called. Listen, I fly in tomorrow around mid-afternoon so I can go over right when I get in. Do you want me to handle this? I can call if I need you to come down."

"No, I want to go to her now…" There was a long pause. "Well, on second thought, maybe you'd better. If it really is her schoolwork then you'd be the one to help her with it Mr. College-man. But I don't like leaving her alone, not for a whole day."

"I know, but I don't think it's anything life-threatening. I think she'll be alright till I get there."

"Okay, but call me as soon as you do get there. I want to know, I want to know how my baby is doing."

"I will, I promise."

"I'm serious. Call me. None of your 'I forgot' or 'I was busy' or other excuses."

"I'll call, I'll call!"

"Good," she replied, her words heavy with a sudden seriousness. "Something's wrong. I can feel it. I'm her mother and I know. I can feel it welling up inside of me. Something is very, very wrong."

And then the line went dead, the phone quiet and heavy in his hand.

Katie's preparation for college seemed a lot more complicated to her father than anything else they'd done. For the entire summer after her high school graduation they worked off and on while he was in town on the different aspects of her college life. First, there were the technology upgrades she would need for school. The computer had to be upgraded in both power and size, for Katie had set her sights on a computer science or mathematics major. She needed a new printer, along with some adaptive devices that she used. A larger keyboard, a dedicated number pad, a wireless mouse, all had to be investigated, tried, and purchased.

They made several trips to the university to work out arrangements for her accommodations. The adaptive and disability offices would be her headquarters. It was there she would take tests, speaking out the answers to a recorder much the same as in high school. But a lot of her work would be on the computer and she would need the ability to print from the classroom through online printers. It was all pretty complicated to her father, but Katie seemed to breeze through the arrangements with all the familiarity and comfort of a pro. She had been at this game for years now, and it was finally beginning to pay off. Her father found it less and less necessary to intervene on her behalf, except to sometimes interpret for her when she had difficulty making herself understood. That usually only happened on bad days, and with the summer break, she was having very few of those.

She selected a dorm that was close to her best-friend-forever Amy. Amy was already a sophomore and they spent hours together that summer talking about school, with Amy giving her the lowdown, all the ins and outs she had learned during her first year of college. They were like little girls again, enjoying sleepovers and giggling about, well, about everything under the sun, especially boys, or rather, men, as they now referred to the college-age boys they encountered.

The time came to move Katie into the dorm. It was late August, the summer months passing quickly, too quickly, her father thought. Soon she will be gone, out of the house, on her own. We're losing her.

Then he caught himself. That's a bit much, don't you think, he asked himself. After all, she would only be an hour's drive away, and sure to come home on many weekends and all holidays. Still, it wouldn't be the same. The more things change, the more we resist change. It was a vicious circle, he knew, and all a part of the journey through life.

We're losing her.

It was a hot August day when he moved her into the dormitory.

They had the room to themselves as her roommate, a student coming from a city many miles away, was not yet checked-in. However, the dorm hallways and public areas were teeming with activity. It seemed everyone else was moving in all at once. There were lines at the elevators, a constant stream of people moving up and down the stairwells, a multitude of cars, vans and trucks jamming the parking lot and loaded down with suitcases and pillows, computers and desks, refrigerators and microwaves. It was a tidal wave of young humanity converging on and enveloping this small dormitory perched on the edge of the campus.

Katie's mother helped handle the smaller items while her father sweated over the big stuff, the refrigerator and microwave, the boxes of computer and printer equipment and supplies, the results of all those weeks spent shopping during the summer months, shopping in anticipation of this day. He remembered just how much he hated moving, hated hauling boxes and lugging suitcases, trying to stuff too many things into his arms to save trips. And this is only the beginning, he thought. By his calculation he might have to move her, in and out, as many as eight to ten more times during her college career.

In the end it was done, her stuff moved in, her dorm room arranged, her clothes packed away, the bed made. She would spend several days pasting pictures on the wall, organizing knick-knacks, making the space feel like home. But now it was time for her parents to go, time to say goodbye, time to leave Katie to her new world and make the drive back to the small town in the mountains. Her mother held back the tears, but her voice was full and coarse, her tone muffled and sad.

"Okay baby, we'll get going now. Are you sure you don't need anything else?"

"No Mom, that's it. It seems I've got everything in here. I'll be fine."

"You're sure? What about some food for the refrigerator. How about that? We could go shopping… "

"Remember Mom, we talked about this. There's a store on campus right across the street from the dorm. I'm going there later to get some stuff. I'll be fine Mom, really fine."

"Okay, okay. Just give me a hug, honey."

The last words came out choked as she began to cry through her restraint. The hug lasted a long time, but finally she let go, turned and walked slowly, and alone, to the waiting car. Around her milled other parents saying goodbye, giving hugs, students waving and yelling as they welcomed each other back for another year, or recognized each other from a shared past, a common high school or summer camp.

Katie turned to her father, a big grin on her face. Her father grinned back, showing no signs of the sadness he felt at this parting. Only, he thought, because he was simply a better actor than his wife.

We're losing her, he thought again.

"Dad, you better take Mom out to dinner tonight. She needs something to take her mind off me. I was afraid she was going to cry."

"I know Katie, and she is crying, you can be sure of that. It's not easy for her, not easy for me either."

"Dad, I'm only going to be an hour away. I'll be fine."

"Yes, Katie, but that hour might as well be a week, a month, a year. It's a new thing for us, having you out of the house, and, well, we're going to need some time to adjust. Besides, now I have to handle your mother all by myself."

They were both smiling now, enjoying the joke, sharing the moment. But it was only a moment, and the time had come to say goodbye. A student called from across the parking lot, a young girl Katie's age, her arms full of boxes.

"Hey, Katie."

She smiled, waved and moved on. There had been several of those greetings during the move-in process. Several old acquaintances from high school were moving in, offering Katie a familiar sense of déjà vu, of having been here before, of having been the center of attention, like at her old school where there were so many who wanted to acknowledge they knew her, acknowledge her uniqueness with a hail and a greeting.

"Well, you certainly won't be alone. Looks like a lot of the old crowd is here as well."

"Gee, I hope not. I want to meet new people."

"Oh, you will. Don't worry, you will. So give me a hug, your mother's waiting. I'll check in on you in a couple of weeks and make sure everything is okay. You know to call with anything... with..."

"Yes, Dad, I know. It's okay."

He gave her a hug, strong but quick, and turned to walk down to the parking lot, the car, and his home in the mountains.

Katie turned, the dorm building towering above her, and walked up, slowly, cautiously... towards a new life.

Following Amy's call from the night before, the flight home was uneventful, except for the worry, worry that started to build pressure inside of him from the moment he'd talked with his wife. He tried to work on the plane, but had no luck and spent the time trying to occupy his mind with anything but the worry that continued to gnaw at him like some hungry rodent working over a stale piece of cheese.

The first two months of school seemed to go well. Katie would call, or, more to the point, dutifully answer her mother's calls, and those calls came almost daily at first. But slowly, a sense of normalcy returned to the household as everyone settled in to their new roles. Yes, the house was much quieter, there were no friends dropping by to study, no dramas from school to rehash every night. Katie's mom and dad were slowly getting used to having only each other around.

After hauling books and backpacks around her high school hallways and classrooms for four years, Katie was certainly acclimated to a wide-open campus and seemed to have no trouble navigating the different buildings and labs she signed up for. Her course load was heavy, with six lectures and two labs, all in computer and math subjects. Her father argued with her, told her to scale back somewhat, that it was too much, but she refused. She felt she could handle it. She felt she was ready. After all, she said, didn't she graduate seventh in her class, an honors student, with two college courses already under her belt?

Maybe, he replied, but college was different, it was more demanding, more work, and the professors were not babysitters, would not lift a hand to help students who showed no initiative or ambition beyond just skating by. You had to do the work, and then some. He tried to prepare her for a different type of school, told her of his time in college, of the adjustments, the difficulties. But she refused to listen. She knew what she wanted and she would be fine.

Perhaps that's it, he thought to himself as he got off the plane. Perhaps she bit off more than she can chew and she's in over her head academically. That thought hadn't occurred to him at all on the flight. She'd always been so perfect in school, so together. Oh, she would threaten a B or a C, but it never came to pass. He remembered thinking long ago about saving money for psychiatric help should she ever actually get less than an A in one of her classes. It was a standing joke between them.

Had the joke become real?

He hoped not. He hoped it was simply a matter of getting engrossed in her work, something she had a tendency to do, to shut out the world and focus, focus, focus on nothing but her work.

Once free of the plane it was only a matter of a few minutes to negotiate the parking lot, to escape into the afternoon traffic, and finally, to pull into the parking lot of Katie's dorm.

He waited for the elevator. She was on the fourth floor of the dorm building, but his instincts screamed at him to pass on the lift and take the stairs, to waste not a second of time in coming to his daughter's aid. Finally, the elevator doors opened, closed, and whisked him to the proper floor. Heading down the hallway, his heart pounding, his mind filled with the uncertainty of what he would find, he removed the key ring from his pocket, his fingers fumbling for the right key, the spare key to Katie's room. He would force his way in if he needed to.

His first knock was not answered. The second one, louder, longer, finally drew a response.

"Go away."

"Katie, it's Dad. Open up."

"Dad? What are you doing here?" Her voice was muffled and even more difficult to decipher through the closed door.

"I want to talk to you, about school. C'mon, open up."

"Dad, I'm fine, I'm studying and I don't have time for anything else. Please, go away. I'll call you later."

"Nope, not gonna. C'mon, open up."

He was just about to use the key, force his way in, when the door latch clicked, and slowly, ever so slowly, the door opened. Katie's face appeared in the crack between the door and the jamb, her eyes red, her face both puffy and drawn.

"Dad, please, I really don't have time for this."

"Yes, you do Katie, and we're going to talk... right now!"

He forced his way in, gently so as not to knock his daughter down. She turned and stumbled backwards, falling onto her bed, and at that moment, the dam burst, her emotions took over, she started to cry. It was only a sob or two at first, but then grew and grew, her cries getting louder and more anguished as she tried to bury her head in a pillow.

"Katie," he began, and then paused. What to say, what to do. What was the matter? He just didn't know, nor did he know how to proceed. He had not seen his daughter like this since the time when she was little and battling the cries of "spaz" and "geek" from the other children in her school.

Is that what had happened, he wondered? Had she run in to that same sort of reaction from the students at the university? Was she battling those demons all over again?

"Katie, please, tell me what's wrong, baby… what's got you crying so?"

Katie looked up, her tears falling from her cheeks onto the bed. She tried to speak, but he was unable to make any sense of what she said through the sobs that still wracked her body. Finally, she shook her head no and once again buried her face in the pillow.

Her father looked around the room, feeling helpless. He was looking for a clue, anything that might shed light on the mystery of why his daughter was in this near state of emotional breakdown.

His eyes wandered, looking about the space around him, finally settling on the desk where she worked. Textbooks were open, several of them, one stacked on top of another. The computer was on and there were several files open on the screen. It seemed as if she was trying to work on everything at once.

Then he noticed the papers lying about, papers strewn across the desktop, some lying half-crumpled on the floor next to her workstation.

He wandered over, selected one of the papers, picked it up and examined it, looking for clues, for any explanation as to his daughter's emotional state.

It was a test, a practice test. It was so labeled across the top of the paper. It was a practice midterm from her mathematics course.

He could tell the handwriting was from someone else, someone in the disability office, one of the volunteers who wrote for those who couldn't write legibly. The test was dated from last week. And across the top third of the page, in big, red ink, was a large C-. Following that, in smaller, red ink below, was a note from the professor. He read the note:

"This is substandard work for you. I expect better on the next attempt."

He glanced to the next paper on the desk. It was another practice test, this one in her basic computer languages class. It also was marked with a C and a note in large letters that said *"NEEDS WORK!"*

Below that was an essay from her English class. Neatly typed on the computer, it had been graded a B- with a note to the effect that it needed editing.

Slowly he began to understand. Slowly it came to him. Midterms, practice tests, essays, Katie was getting back the first real assessment of her college work since beginning her first semester. And by her standards, it wasn't good. Her father stifled the urge to laugh, to make light of it. He knew instinctively that would be the wrong approach.

"Katie, these tests, these grades, is that what this is about?"

Slowly, Katie raised herself off the pillow and to a sitting position on the bed. She nodded her head up and down, up and down, still unable to speak but slowly gaining control of her tears.

Her father paused, thinking, wondering. What was the best way to approach this? How to handle this? He stalled for time, stacked the papers neatly on top of her desk and then turned to join her on the edge of the bed.

He sat down slowly and put his arm around his daughter's

shoulders, inviting her to lay her head on his chest, to feel the comfort of his embrace. For quite some time they sat, quiet, neither one moving or talking, the afternoon shadows darkening the still room as the sun gave way to evening's grey gloom.

Katie's sobs were all but gone, her breathing measured and steady. He knew he could now talk to her, and make sense of whatever she had to say, make sense of whatever she was feeling inside. He decided on a course of action and turned to speak, pushing Katie away slightly so he could look at her directly.

"Katie," he began, "what are those books doing open on your desk? Why are all the files open on your computer?"

"I've been studying. I've been working on school."

"You have every class represented here," he said as he turned to indicate the piled up desk in the corner. "Have you been trying to study them all, every one, all at once?"

"No Dad, but I'm behind in every one of them. I have to."

"Katie, how long have you been here, in this room, studying?"

"I don't know. Two days, maybe three."

"When was the last time you ate?"

"I don't remember."

"When was the last time you talked to Amy? Or your mother?"

"I don't know, Dad… a few days… maybe… I don't remember." Her voice tightened again, her words tense, her mouth beginning to tremble. He backed off. He didn't want to upset her again, to let emotion once again take what little control of her body she had.

"Okay, Katie, it's okay. But I have to ask… why? Why are you doing this, working so hard? You're thin, pale, this isn't good. I've never seen you this way before. Tell me why?"

"You know, Dad, you saw, you saw the tests on my desk. I know you did. What do you think? That's why."

"Katie, running yourself into the ground isn't the answer. You can't keep this up. Besides, these are practice tests." He waved his arm in a sweeping gesture towards her desk and the papers littered there. "They aren't the end of the world."

"Yes Dad, they are. You don't understand. You don't get it. These tests, my grades, they're all I have. Don't you understand?"

"No, tell me. You explain it to me. Please."

"Dad, I'm just a geek. I'm a freak. I can't do anything. I can't play ball. I can't ride a bike. You know this stuff. Why are you making me say it? This…" She waved around the room frantically trying to get her words out, to make them intelligible through the rush of her emotions. "This… it's all I have. It's who I am. My grades. No matter what the other kids called me. No matter the stares I got at the store, or school, or the bullies that picked on me. It didn't matter Dad, it didn't matter. Because I had this. I had my grades. I knew I could be smarter than all of them. That made me… makes me… get through it."

She paused, her chest heaving in and out as she gasped for breath.

"I don't care about all that other stuff. It doesn't matter… as long… as long as I have this. But now I don't. Don't you see? Without this I'm nothing. I'm nobody. I'm the freak everyone thinks I am… oh god.…"

Finally overcome with the harsh reality of her words, Katie fell back on the bed, her knees pulled up tight around her chest, her arms, long and spindly, wrapping around them to form a protective cocoon as she once again gave in to her sobs.

The final light of day gave up its hold on the room, and the shadows of evening closed around them. There was no light on in the room and he let it grow dark. For there was comfort in the dark. It was still, and quiet, and neither of them spoke or even moved, the only sound the slowly diminishing sobs from Katie as she buried her head in the sheets of her bed.

Her father remained silent, let the emotion work its way out again. He knew his daughter, knew she was tough. Knew she would come around. It was only a matter of time… or so he hoped. She would come around. She had to.

The alternative was too much for him to even consider.

After a long interval of silence, after Katie had settled down once again, gained back control of her fragile emotions, her father stood up and ever so slowly started to organize the papers around her desk. He turned on the desk lamp, a tightly controlled beam of light illuminating only the books resting there, the shadows from the lamp casting gloomy and almost eerie shadows across the corners of the little dorm room.

"Katie, these are just mid-semester tests. You can fix this. You have time. We have work to do, but this isn't over. And you need help. I know you want to do it yourself. But you can't just withdraw from the world. You can't shut us out. No one can. This isn't about your condition. This isn't about your being a freak or a geek or whatever the hell else you think you are. I know you've been called worse by people who are ignorant, who don't understand, or who even hate. But that's not you. That's not who you are. And this…."

He gestured around her littered room, pointed at the desk and shook the test papers he held grasped in one hand.

"This is not who you are either.

"Dad, I…"

"No Katie, listen for a moment. Please, listen…"

He paused once again, then went on more forcefully, his words coming more quickly, as if being forced out in one long rush of air.

"Katie, this is not who you are."

He swept the room again with his arm, then reached out and grasped her arms, firmly, but gently, and propelled her from the bed. Still clutching her arm, he led her across the room, over to the far wall by her closet, over in front of a full-length mirror hanging just above an overflowing hamper of dirty clothes.

"This..." he said as he held her tight before the mirror and pointed at her reflection in it.

Katie looked in the mirror, stared at her own reflection for a long time. She was gaunt, gaunt and shriveled from the past days of inactivity and not eating. Her skin was grayish in pallor, her eyes sunken into their sockets. Her hair was a mess, her clothes rumpled, she was a walking disaster and she knew it, could really see it, see the damage of the last few days in her reflection.

"This is who you are, Katie," her father continued. "This."

They stood, the two of them, silent and still, staring into Katie's reflection for what seemed like hours but was only moments. And then it happened. The absurdity of her appearance, the raw misery of it jumped out at them like a lightning bolt. It struck them in revelation, overwhelmed them with the truth of the moment, of her reflection in the mirror. Her father was the first to acknowledge it, the absurdity, the first to speak.

"And if this IS who you are, Katie, then... oh my, you really could use a bath."

That's when the laughter began.

It started as just the slightest upturn, the slightest little up-tick in the frown that possessed Katie's lips. First one corner of her mouth twitched. Then the other. There was a slight pause, a dimpling of her cheeks. And then it rushed, full-blown, in the matter of an instant, rushed into being, growing into the reflection that stared back at them. It was Katie's smile... the smile... the one that brightened up everything, the otherworldly smile, the smile that defined her very existence, the smile that endeared, that possessed, that drew you inexorably into the secret delights of this delightful creature.

It was only a matter of seconds before the smile became a laugh, and before they knew it both father and daughter were collapsed on the floor, their bellies shaking, their sides aching as they laughed and laughed and laughed... and yes, laughed some more.

"That's who you are... a mess, a smelly, stinky mess," he finally cried once he could control the laughter that continued with each word he managed to speak.

"I am a mess," Katie replied. "Oh my god, I look horrible, I look like death. Dad! What on earth... what happened to me?"

And again they laughed and couldn't stop. It was as if a light switch had been flicked on, a circuit completed, a current allowed to flow uninterrupted.

"That's who you are girl," her father said again through his laughter. "Forget about the geek part. Forget about the freak part. You're a mess, you stink... and you need a bath, and that's WHO YOU ARE!"

Katie continued to laugh, and through the laughter, even cry. She was laughing one moment, crying the next, then laughing, until she finally wore herself out, lost the energy to even move as she lay quiet before the mirror, her laughter subsiding once again into just a smile.

"Dad, I'm a mess. Look at me. A mess. Oh my god, what did I do to myself?"

"It's okay little girl. It's okay. You just lost yourself for a moment. Maybe longer than a moment. But now you're back. And we have some work to do. But first, young lady, you're going to take a shower, a long, hot shower. Then we're going to get something to eat. And then I am a going to take you home..."

"But Dad, I..."

"NO. No ifs or buts. I know you think you have to get back to work. But I'm taking you home now... today... right after we get a bite. You can bring your books. Bring everything because we have some work to do over the weekend to straighten this mess out. And a fine mess it is too, Ollie..." he said again with a smile.

"Okay Dad, you win. Let me clean up, then dinner, then home. But, Dad?"

"Yes, Katie."

"Can we have dessert first?" she asked, smiling that old smile, that secret smile they shared between them. "Can we have dessert for dinner?"

"Of course, Katie… of course. After all, it's our way, isn't it?"

"Yes, Dad," she replied. "It IS our way."

On the drive home they were once again quiet. Katie kept her promise, took a long, long shower, cleaned up as best she could, did up her hair in a ponytail with her father's help and gathered up all her books and computer equipment for the long weekend at home. They had dessert for dinner at Katie's favorite grill, a college hangout that had a dessert selection far larger than the burger and fries offerings found on the menu.

As his car wound around the curves of the road leading to the little town in the mountains, and to their home, her father was glad for the quiet. He realized that he hadn't yet called his wife, and he knew he was in for a "talking-to" when he got home. But that was the least of his worries. He still needed time to think, time to plan. This thing with his daughter wasn't over yet. He had watched her retreat, withdraw from the world and everything she cared about. And all because of a failure that in reality was no more than a blip in the road, a blip other children had already faced, and conquered several times by their college years. Not Katie. She was, he realized, a stranger to failure.

Oh, she had faced restrictions, limitations, things she simply could not, and probably would never be able to do. But not failure.

Walking had been a hope, a dream, a possibility. And she had learned to walk.

Speaking, uttering words and sentences, that had been problematical. She still sounded garbled and was hard to understand, especially on bad days. But she had learned to talk.

Managing her high school softball team, participating in the ambassador program, traveling to far off lands, even getting and holding a summer job, all of these had been attempted and mastered. In none had she actually failed.

As he thought back through her life, through the few short years of her time on Earth, he simply couldn't think of anything she had attempted that had ended in failure. And he knew that it was not success that mattered so much in life as it was failure. For in failure we learn. In failure we grow and mature. In failure the emotions are reined in, controlled, and we move forward. We grow tougher, smarter, better. He knew this for a fact.

But not Katie, he thought. Oh, she's tough. Constantly falling and picking herself up, her little body often covered in bruises, that would make you tough. Being bullied or called cruel names in school, that would make you tough. Having to fight and strain and concentrate just to accomplish the simple tasks that others took for granted every day, that would make you tough. Having to prove herself in school, in those things she had succeeded at, that would make you tough. But not tough in the way failure makes one tough. Failure is the ultimate litmus test. It hones and refines, it breaks you down to your basic elements and requires that you build yourself up again. It is the fire that reduces to ash the dreams upon which a new phoenix is born, a new bird of hope and dreams.

And Katie had not failed, not really, not ever.

Now she was facing failure for the very first time, failure at something for which she was known, for which she had enjoyed innumerable success, a string of successes that had, unfortunately, left her defenseless in the face of that failure.

He would proceed carefully over the coming weekend, take

things slowly. They needed to solve this dilemma, to overcome this potential failure that so threatened her identity. More importantly, he thought, she needs to solve this problem. He must let her do it, let her find her way. He could guide, suggest, help, but he must let her stumble and fall and pick herself up again. Otherwise, the next time she may never come out of her self-imposed withdrawal, a withdrawal from the world around her, from those very people and things that she so needed. And that would be the ultimate catastrophe, to come this far and then fail, because failure was so crushing.

As the car rounded the last turn, and the lights of the little mountain town began to glow in the darkness ahead, he noticed storm clouds off to the west. They were low and grey and black, silhouetted against a rising full moon, a moon encircled by a hazy ring of moisture, a ring full of dark premonition and foreboding. He could tell they were in for a storm by morning. And he began to wonder, was this the foretelling of another storm to come? A future storm? Was this a portent of what lay ahead for Katie as she struggled on her journey? Was there a perfect storm waiting for her somewhere over the horizon?

He wondered, and as he turned the car towards the lights of home, a small shiver passed through every fiber of his being.

Boys, Boys, Boys

"Hi sweetie, how ya doing?"

He recognized the caller right away, even though his wife was the one doing the talking. She was using her "it's our daughter" tone of voice.

"Good. How's school? You studying hard, as always?"

"Uh huh... uh huh... uh huh. Wonderful."

It was interesting, listening to one-way conversations, he thought, trying to figure out the subject, what was being said, with only half of the conversation being heard.

"Really... really... reallllly!"

That sounded different he thought. Something must be up.

"Uh huh... at a party?"

"Really."

"What's his name?"

"Really. How long?"

"Uh huh."

"Stayed the night? All night?"

Now it was his turn to say "really," although all he did was think it. What was all this? Spent the night? That could be a lot of things, some good, some bad.

"How many times... uh huh. Dinner? Really."

"Engineering? No, computers. Well, that sounds nice. Where is he from?"

"Uh huh... really... oh my."

This was getting interesting. He had half a mind to go pick up the extension, but he knew that would be a mistake. His daughter and wife were warmed up now. They were in sync and he didn't want to interrupt. He knew he would get the story soon enough. But he had to admit, the suspense was killing him.

"I see. Did you put your foot down?"

"Good girl. That's how I would've handled it."

"Oh, another one? But you don't feel the same way?"

"Well, these things always seem to come in rushes. I remember... well, better not go into that now."

"Uh huh."

There was a long pause.

"Uh huh."

There was an even longer pause.

"Well, I don't know. You really have to go with your feelings. But hey, take it slow. Show some interest, but not too much. You know?"

"Uh huh."

"No, don't play games, but, well, you want to keep some control."

"Uh huh."

Control? Games? What on earth were they talking about? Was this some school strategy? Some professor who wasn't cooperating with Katie's program? A friend gone haywire?

"Well, I think that's wonderful. But be careful. Very careful. Go slow."

"Uh huh."

"Okay, are you coming home this weekend? No... I see."

"Let's talk then. Okay? Okay. Bye, honey. I love you. Dad says hi."

Dad would like to say a hell of a lot more than that, but he knew to keep his mouth shut. At least if he wanted to know what the heck was going on.

"Bye, bye."

She hung up the phone, a strange look on her face. It almost seemed as if she was trying to decide something, perhaps whether to speak with him or not. Finally she came to a decision, made up her mind, and turned to face him.

"You'd better sit down," she said absently, staring off into space.

"I am sitting down," he replied testily.

In fact, he was sitting down. He was sitting at the kitchen table going over some work papers when the phone rang and she answered it. She turned again, looked down at him, the confusion exiting her face like water pouring down a drain.

"What is it?" he prompted. "What?"

"I think your daughter has a boyfriend."

And at that moment, he was very glad he was sitting down.

Katie's first year in college passed without much more in the way of drama. Her father talked with her well into the late hours on that fateful night, the night he had confronted her, the night of her breakdown. They spoke of lots of things, friends, school, professors, what her problems were. And all weekend they worked on the problem, her problem, the failure that confronted her in every class she was taking. In the end, he advised her to drop two classes to make more time for the others. She simply couldn't take a full load. Her mind could do it, but her body could not. She needed time, time to work, time to think, time to overcome the inherent slowness of her motions. A lesser schedule would do it, he advised.

Not surprisingly, it worked. She dropped her hardest classes, the most time-consuming ones, rearranged her priorities, and went to work. She spoke to her professors, followed the carefully laid-out plan her father and she had developed. And when the call came, the call he was expecting, the call about her first semester grades, he knew she had made the right moves, chosen the right path.

She had overcome her failure, made a plan, and set things right.

"Dad," she said in a rush. "Dad, my grades were just posted on the Internet. I got all A's. We did it."

"No, Katie, we didn't do it, you did it. And I am so proud of you."

"But you were right. I just had too much to do."

He knew it was probably more than that, but now was not the time to go into it. Now was a time to celebrate. To ritualize the experience. And he knew just what to do.

"So, you nailed it. You got a perfect scorecard. Bottom of the ninth, two ahead and you got the last batter swinging. Let's celebrate."

"How?"

You know, dessert. Let's go have dessert."

"Dessert? But what about dinner?"

"Katie, its dessert for dinner, that's the plan. You pick the place and I'll be down in an hour. Okay?"

"Okay!"

And that is exactly what they did.

The spring semester rolled around with pretty much the same result. Straight A's and a class load that was smaller than normal, that gave her time to do the work. As summer came, they decided she would move back home and attend summer classes at the small community college in the little town in the mountains. The classes would transfer and they would help to make up for her light schedule during the school year.

He dutifully moved her out of the dorms, moved her back into the house, and when summer was over and her sophomore year beckoned, he dutifully moved her back into the dorms. It seemed to him, as he carried the umpteenth box of pictures and books and, well, junk, he thought, that all he did these days was move his daughter in and out, in and out. He was getting very tired of moving. In fact, he hated moving, always had. But it was necessary. Katie couldn't do it for herself. It was, of course, beyond her. And so, he picked them up, the boxes and cartons and bags, and moved them in. Picked them up, and moved them out, from spring to summer to fall and back again to spring and then summer.

Her second year she was able to move into a larger apartment-style dorm with Amy and two other girls. It was just the thing to bring Katie even more out of her shell. Although she still spent the majority of her time studying and working on class projects, she found time to go out with the girls, to socialize, to broaden her circle of friends and acquaintances. The other girls nagged her and cajoled and persuaded and finally began to drag her away just a bit from the incredible focus and single-mindedness Katie put into her schoolwork.

Her father was relieved, for still the foreboding of another storm hung over him, the idea that one day Katie would face another test, more severe, more daunting, and he wasn't at all sure how she would fare when that time came.

As her second year came to a close, she decided to remain in the city and room with Amy in an apartment. She and Amy would have the run of the city for the summer. They could explore, meet with friends, and for once, Katie would really be out on her own. They ate out often, mostly dessert, and it became their favorite thing to do. She was beginning to develop her own life patterns, her own rhythm.

And she was getting more confident, her father thought. He could see it in her walk, in the things she said and did, in how she carried herself. There was a newfound independence that seemed to engulf her like an oversized blanket.

She again took classes during the summer. It was, he thought, a year-round effort for her. There was little in the way of a vacation, or a break. Perhaps a few days here and there, the two-week break between semesters, but otherwise, she remained a full-time student.

It was that summer, the summer prior to her junior year, the dawn of that summer to be precise, when everything changed.

"A boyfriend? You're kidding me."

It was all he could think to say, the only reply he could make at the moment. A boyfriend? Really? That word "really" just kept cropping up, whether in his wife's conversation, or his thoughts.

Reallllllly!

"Yes, a boyfriend. And I don't want you freaking out. It's about time she got one. I was worried, although I never really spoke much about it. It's just what she needs."

He wasn't so sure about that. How would a boyfriend affect her schoolwork? How would a boyfriend affect the carefully constructed friendships she had managed to build with other students, her roommates and classmates?

How would a boyfriend affect his life?

That was the real question. That was what tugged at him almost immediately. The weekend trips home, the times they spent together. Would this new boyfriend supplant that, eliminate that, take her out of his life forever?

Oh, stop it, he thought to himself angrily. You're acting like a drama queen. Maybe she's right. Maybe this is the next in a long line of milestones, like walking, and driving, and living on her own. It was only natural. And about time. Every other milestone had taken longer than normal, had been delayed by the challenges she faced. Now here was another one.

Boys were something most girls started to deal with as early as elementary school. And certainly by high school they were immersed in the subject. But for Katie, it took college, and the maturity of that age, to put her in this position. He wondered about this boy, this man who had matured enough to see in Katie what really mattered. Who was he? What was he? What were his intentions?

Now you're thinking more like an ordinary father, he thought. Katie's maturity through those first two years of college had fundamentally changed her. She was more confident in social settings, more forceful in her dealings with others. She stood up for herself. And physically she was changing, filling out, her body taking on the long and graceful lines that reminded him of her mother, his wife.

Let's face it, he thought, she had become beautiful, a beautiful, sexy, desirable woman. Of course her motions, her speech, these would change the illusion, change the image. But only to those for whom superficial beauty was the only thing of importance. Anyone with any depth of character and insight would see through those superficial anomalies very quickly. It said something for this nameless boy, this man whom Katie had fallen for. He must have that insight, that maturity.

The thought warmed him as he contemplated this new development over the days and weeks that followed. Until, of course, the father in him kicked in. And then he would simply clamp down on the one thought that would dominate his mind.

He'd better not hurt her, or I'll kill him.

※

"Dad?"

"Yes, Katie."

He was working in his office, the one in the city. He'd been on a long road trip and just returned home the day before. And it was a full day at the office. He had expense receipts to turn in, reports to write, all the follow-up work that his trips out to clients demanded once a project was completed.

"Dad, what are you doing?"

"Just working, Katie. Working away. Why? What's up?"

"Well, it's almost noon, and Matt and I wanted to come by and take you to lunch. You haven't met him yet. Can you, please, can you come to lunch with us?"

He could hear the earnestness in her voice, almost as if she were pleading. And it was true, he hadn't met him yet, the new boyfriend, the first boyfriend, the only boyfriend.

They had begun to see each other often. The relationship, according to his wife who kept up with all things domestic while he traveled, was growing every day. After that fateful phone call where he first found out his daughter had a beau, he learned more about the beginning of their relationship.

Katie was going to a series of summer parties, one every week on Thursdays. They were impromptu parties, a group of friends would gather at the apartment of a student named Matt. That was the one, Matt. Katie started going to the parties as they did not conflict with her summer school hours. She had mutual friends, one a boy who had even expressed interest in her. She wasn't really interested in him, except as a friend, but the moment she met Matt, things changed. There was an instant connection, a shared feeling. What exactly the feeling was, they didn't know. He was an engineering student who chose to switch to computers, and had therefore fallen in with Katie's circle of computer science pals.

At the first party Katie attended, the attraction hit them both like a wrecking ball. They talked for hours, eventually ignoring all the others in the room, ignoring them until the party wound down, ignoring them until they all left. Still they talked, talked into the night, and on into the morning. She ended up spending the night with him. That got a rise out of her father until his wife assured him she slept on the bed while Matt slept on his couch.

Hmm, he thought, perhaps he's a gentleman as well. In this day and age, those were getting harder and harder to find. Now the time had finally come for him to meet this Matt, this man who had captured his daughter's heart, if only for a while. After all, who knew about first loves? His own had been turbulent and quick, and the heartbreak had been real. Katie, he thought, you are in for a real roller coaster ride, perhaps the first one you've ever really taken.

There were only a few weeks left before the fall semester would start, the fall semester of Katie's junior year in school. She located an apartment, a place with four bedrooms, a common area and kitchen, and three other girls, all of whom were students. It was a place where she could continue to grow in independence and confidence. She would have to move in soon. As a matter of fact, her father wanted to speak with her about that anyway, as he would once again have to go through the tedious and hateful job of moving things from one place to another. So lunch would be a good time for that subject as well.

They arrived soon after the phone call, Katie and her new beau. They'd been "in the neighborhood" so to speak. Immediately he was impressed with her choice. He was of average height, with a slim build and delicate features. He had curly black hair, and a face that was soft and gentle, a face that seemed both wise and kind. Behind his eyes was an intelligence that could be easily sensed. Her father knew anyone who tried to match wits with Katie would need that kind of intelligence.

The introductions went well enough, they made some small talk. He asked about school and their upcoming plans for the new semester. He then offered to take them to a small restaurant across the street that featured Greek dishes and offered a shaded patio in the rear.

The small talk continued as they ordered pastitsio and spanakopita and got their drinks, iced tea for him, a soda with straw for Katie. Matt ordered an iced tea as well.

"So, Matt," he found himself saying, trying hard not to sound pompous or overbearing. This new role as the father of the girlfriend was not coming quite so easily to him. He wanted to make small talk without seeming to interrogate the poor boy. "You're majoring in computers as well as Katie, or engineering? I wasn't quite sure which."

"Well, I was majoring in electrical engineering," he replied. "But I'm in the middle of switching majors. I prefer computers and so I'm going for a computer science major, same as Katie."

"Dad," Katie broke in, beaming, "Matt's folks have an

engineering company. They have offices all over the country, and even in Europe."

"Really," he replied with interest. "Europe, you say. What part?"

"Geneva and Paris," Matt replied. "It's a family business. Part of the family is on the East Coast and we have operations there, as well as out here in the West. And also over in Europe."

"What kind of engineering?"

"Mainly electrical engineering. A lot of technology and design. That sort of thing. You know."

Actually, he didn't. But he wasn't going to admit that.

"Of course," he replied. "Must be fascinating. You hoping to go into the family business when you graduate?"

"Well, I don't know about that. I would really like to follow my own interest. That's why I'm switching to computers. I'm interested in robotics and the artificial intelligence robots need to operate. Of course, my dad wants me to go to work for him, but I don't know."

"Well, I'm sure he only wants what's best. It can be hard sometimes to let go. I know. I have tried to stay out of Katie's decisions about her future, but then again, that's what we dads and moms do, we meddle. It's part of the job, I guess."

They all laughed and then broke up the conversation as the lunch orders arrived. Once the food had been delivered, they continued to talk, the conversation flowed fairly easily and he was happy about the fact he could meet his daughter's very first boyfriend and actually hold his own, make small talk naturally and convincingly.

It was, after all, a delicate situation. He didn't want to be overbearing. This wasn't a high school fling. These were two adults. Matt being 21 and Katie being 20. He tried to hit just the right note of concern and interest without seeming like a parent. And for a moment, he thought he was going to pull it off. But, as with all well-laid plans, his backfired as the lunch ended.

It started when he went to the restroom to wash up while the

lunch plates were being cleared. When he returned, he found that
Matt had paid the lunch tab. It had been his intention to buy lunch
for them, but he was outfoxed by a worthy adversary. Based on what
Matt's parents did for a living, and what he had picked up in the
conversation, it was clear Matt could afford it. This was no poor
college student after all. Still, there was his pride as a father, a pro-
vider and protector of his child and her friends, a role he had always
played. So the move both delighted him (good move, kid) and dis-
turbed him (hey, it's my job to pay).

Then, as they were getting ready to go, he brought up the subject of moving Katie to her new apartment.

"Katie, we have to talk about moving you in to your new place
for the semester. You know I'm going back out on the road and will
be in and out for several weeks. We need to plan so I can arrange
to get it all done while I'm in town. When did you want to move?"

"Oh no, Dad," she replied, grinning. "You don't have to move
me in this year. Matt's going to do it."

Matt's going to do it. The sentence reverberated in his head,
rattled around his brain, and settled across the entireness of his
thoughts. Matt's going to do it. He didn't have to move her. Oh joy.
Oh wonder. He'd gotten out of it. Matt was going to do it.

It was at that moment that he knew what he wanted to say. He
knew he shouldn't. Knew it was a mistake. Knew it at least sub-
consciously, if not consciously, but he just couldn't help himself. It
flowed out of him like water from a fountain.

"Let me see if I've got this straight," he said. "You're a computer
science major with good grades. Your parents own a worldwide engineering firm. You clearly are smitten with my daughter. You have
manners and were obviously raised well. You picked up the tab while
I was in the bathroom… AND YOU'RE GOING TO MOVE MY
DAUGHTER INTO HER APARTMENT?"

"Well, uh, yeah," Matt said, somewhat bewildered by the turn in the conversation.

"So," Katie's father replied with a grin. "You have my permission to marry her."

"What on earth were you thinking? Have you completely lost your mind? Are you really that big of an idiot?"

His wife was yelling at him. No, not yelling, more like preaching. By the time he reached home that evening, the story had already been recounted, retold, dissected, analyzed and told again, to her mother, by Katie, over the phone... a very upset Katie.

"What," he replied in defense. "What! I thought it was funny. Hell, it was hilarious. The perfect line at the perfect time."

"The what? The perfect what? You are nuts, you know that? Funny? You thought that was funny? You have my permission to marry her?"

"Well, yeah. I mean, you had to be there. But it was funny. I was just kidding. C'mon. Can't you girls take a joke? Besides, I think Matt got a kick out of it."

"Matt got a kick out of it? No, Matt did not get a kick out of it, Matt was stunned. He's just met his new girlfriend's father and he's offering marriage. Once again, are you nuts?"

"Once again, I was just kidding. I thought it would let him know I simply approved of him... of them... of the whole thing... the whole... oh hell, I don't know anymore. I'm in over my head here."

"You sure as hell are, father."

"Should I call Katie and apologize?"

"No, absolutely not! I swear I do not know how you men survive past your fifth birthday. You leave her alone and let it go away. It would be best if you never mentioned it again. Do you understand?"

"Okay, okay, okay. I promise. I will never mention it again. And I will be more careful in the future about what I say. No kidding around. Geesh, you'd think I started world war twenty or something."

"Just let it lie. That's the best thing you can do."

"All right."

He retreated to his study to sulk. But the sulking didn't last long. As a matter of fact, within a few minutes he was smiling again. And then, laughing out loud.

Because he knew, deep down inside he knew, knew that he was right. It was funny.

Funny as hell.

As the year wore on, as the leaves fell, the temperature dropped, and summer ran headlong into fall, Katie's relationship blossomed. Oh, they had their issues. It was all new to Katie, although Matt had had girlfriends before. But for Katie it was a real eye-opener, learning all the ins and outs of handling a man, an unpredictable, strange, unfathomable man. She just couldn't understand why men thought so… well, so differently. It was as if they had a part of their brain with nothing in it, and they spent most of their time there.

Her father would try to talk it over with her, try to put into words the difference between men and women, the intricacies of the whole sexual politics game she was now trying to learn how to play. But it wasn't easy. And try as he might, he just couldn't make it comprehensible to her, why men behaved they way they did. Her mother was of far more help, as she had years and years of experience in dealing with them. Don't try to understand them, she said to Katie, don't try to figure them out. Just learn how to deal with them.

And that, of course, made sense to him, because his wife had been dealing with him for a long time, dealing quite well, he had to admit. They'd been together for many years now. While others broke up, fell apart, got cast alone on the rocky shore of divorce and abandonment, they stayed together. They were united by a bond they'd shared from the very beginning.

It started as love, moved into a shared mission of raising their daughter, and coalesced into a sense of being one, of being a family, a condition he could no more break apart than he could break apart pieces of his body and leave them behind. They were intertwined through everything they shared. Even the fear, the fear that led to fights and arguments, even that was a tie to bind them. Now Katie was beginning to get a glimpse into that whole world with this, her very first boyfriend.

Who knew if it would last, grow stronger, or fall apart, as first loves often did. But it didn't matter, her father thought with every passing week. She's in the game and that's all that matters. She's in play. She's learning and loving and crying and fighting and all those things that, in the end, he realized, made life worth living, made being alive so real and painful and wonderful.

So this too was another milestone, another in a long and winding journey through life, a life lived under conditions that were so different from others, far more difficult, and also, in their own way, wonderful. He realized that what Katie had become, what she had achieved, who she was, was a product of what she had endured, what she had suffered through, what she had overcome. It was then he began to truly understand what that first night in the hospital meant to his life, that night he'd lived through, with Katie lying dead on the table, his wife dying on another. He'd thought it to be the worst night of his life. But now he realized that it was probably the best, the finest moment he would ever know.

For from that horrible time had arisen a phoenix, a new life that would make its mark, a life that would impact the lives of all those affected by it. His daughter was a gift to the world, a gift to be treasured just the way she was. And it was becoming clear to him that he wouldn't have it any other way. It was not that he was actually condemning her to a life lived under the weight of her cerebral palsy.

Of course, if he could undo it, take away her deformities, he would. Wouldn't any parent? But he no longer feared her condition, he embraced it. He treasured it for what it was, simply a reality, a reality of the sometimes wonderful and often tragic diversity of life itself.

His daughter was teaching him more about life than he would ever teach her. She'd made him understand, years ago, standing in the garage, as she struggled to gain his permission to go abroad, that there was no normal… no abnormal… just whatever you were given in life… and what you chose to do with it.

For some reason, that thought warmed him. On the coldest of nights it was a warmth that spread through his being in a way that no blanket, no heater, no fire could ever do.

As winter made its inexorable journey across the landscape, the days shortened and cold, Katie's relationship continued to grow, and her schooling remained in high gear. She did not find it easy to balance the demands of a social life and the incredible workload demands of her academic program, but she managed, she handled, she coped. The nearby storm remained just that, threatening but never coming, hung up on the horizon, a foreboding, but not a reality.

Another semester came and went, her report card a sea of straight A's and commendations from professors, a growing group of professors who were beginning to understand the true nature of her abilities and talents.

Winter slowly gave way to the first signs of spring. The days were still cold. The snow still fell on the little town in the mountains and on the streets of the city in the valley. But the sun would peek its head out a bit earlier each day. It would say good night a bit later each evening. And the promise of spring began to unfold.

It was around this time that it became clear to Katie's father that she was learning the ropes in this new endeavor, this new journey into the politics of relationships and love. Although he was not present when it happened, he later got to hear the story direct from his daughter. For she was going on a trip, a trip to a faraway place. And she was going without him, without her father or mother, or any of her family for that matter. Other than her adventures as a People to People Ambassador, she had never really gone away on a trip of her own making. Although she was not really going away alone this time either. No, she was going with someone very special.

She was going with Matt.

"Dad,"

"Yes, Katie, what is it?"

They were at home, home in the little town in the mountains. Katie had come home for a weekend visit. The second semester of her third year was well underway, to the point where spring break was almost upon them.

"Dad, I'm going away for spring break. I'm going with Matt."

"What's that you say? You're going away? With Matt?"

"Yes, Dad, with Matt. We're going on a trip for spring break, if it's alright with you?"

Slowly the story came out. Matt approached her, told her it was that time in their relationship where he wanted to take her away. Take her on a romantic getaway, perhaps for a long weekend or, even better, for the week of spring break. And not only that, he told Katie, but he wanted to take her wherever she wanted to go. "We can go anywhere," he said, "anywhere you want to go."

Her father thought about those words, thought about their meaning. After all, this kid had a certain amount of resources. His parents owned a worldwide engineering company. They had offices in Geneva and Paris. He could read between the lines as well as Katie. When Matt said "anywhere you want to go" he meant... "ANYWHERE you want to go!"

Want to go to Paris? We can be there by morning. How about

Switzerland, or London, New York or Chicago? Even someplace exotic like Cancun or Cabo San Lucas? In Matt's world, anywhere you want to go really did mean anywhere. Anywhere in the world.

Katie looked at him with a straight face, thought for a moment, and then said the words that her father knew she would say, that he would have bet money on.

"Well, Matt, if you're going to take me anywhere for the very first time... then we're going to Disneyland."

"Disneyland!" he replied in disbelief. "DISNEYLAND?"

"Yes, Disneyland. And that's final."

And that is exactly where they made plans to go, to the land of magic, to the place where dreams come true... where if you can dream it, you can do it.

As she recounted the story, her father thought back all those years to the first time he'd taken her there, their first visit, and the couple with the little princess in the wheelchair. It had been a special time, a magical time, as had every trip they had taken there since.

"So, Dad," she said, "If it's alright with you, we're going to Disneyland for spring break."

"Of course, Katie. Of course you would. Where else?"

For a moment, neither of them spoke, just looked in each other's eyes, the understanding between them needed no words, no communication beyond their shared thoughts.

"Where else would you go," he finally said.

And as he said those words, he knew, knew deep down inside, that another milestone was being crossed off, another fork in the road that was her very unordinary life. Her first trip as an adult, her first trip with a man, her man. Bon voyage my daughter, he thought, bon voyage.

Second star to the right... and on till morning.

NASA

For countless, untold years, man has stared into space, stared at the stars twinkling in the night sky... and wondered. What lies beyond the bounds of this Earth? What mysteries await discovery in the sky overhead?

After thousands of years of wonder, of naming stars, of forming constellations, of writing great works aimed at the heavens, at postulating thousands of theories and conducting thousands of experiments... two brothers who owned a bicycle shop in Dayton, Ohio, took the first steps towards putting humankind up in the sky where those questions might actually be answered.

Orville and Wilbur Wright, building on hundreds of years of experimentation with balloons and wing-like devices, finally built a machine that could fly. Although not the first to build and fly experimental aircraft, the Wright brothers were the first to invent aircraft controls that made fixed-wing, powered flight possible. And on December 17, 1903, at Kill Devil Hills, Kitty Hawk, North Carolina, the first powered aircraft took off, with Orville at the controls, to fly a distance of 120 feet, in 12 seconds, and at a speed of 6.8 miles per hour.

Twelve years later, on March 3, 1915, The National Advisory Committee for Aeronautics, otherwise known as NACA, was founded to undertake, promote, and institutionalize aeronautical research.

Fast forward several years to a time when the world was at war. A madman in Europe had undertaken the conquest of the planet for his own evil designs. Eventually, after many years, and many, many deaths, that man was defeated by the combined military forces of the free world, most notably by those of the "very free" United States of America and the "not-so-free" Union of Soviet Socialist Republics.

During the war, some of the most advanced scientists of the age were gathered in Germany, at the bidding of that evil leader, to undertake the research and development of rocket propelled machines that would be capable of flying within, and above, the atmosphere of the earth. At the end of the war these scientists were assimilated into the two countries, some going to the USSR, and some going to the USA. In the group of scientists headed to America was a man by the name of Werner Von Braun.

On October 4, 1957, on the desert steppes of Kazakhstannow, at a facility now known as the Baikonur Cosmodrome, Russia launched into space a small metal object not much bigger than a basketball and weighing only 184 pounds. Sputnik One was the first satellite launched into a low Earth orbit, its mission to not only prove a technological first for the world, but also to measure the density of the upper atmospheric layer.

In the United States, the intent of the satellite's mission was accorded far more evil possibilities by those in positions of power. And so, the attention of America to its own space effort was intensified to a degree until then unheard of anywhere in the world. The race to space was on. As a result, on July 29, 1958, President Dwight David Eisenhower signed the National Aeronautics and Space Act, establishing NASA.

With the urging of the aforementioned Werner Von Braun, now a chief scientist at the National Advisory Committee for Aeronautics, NASA began operations on October 1, 1958, by absorbing the 46-year-old NACA intact, including its 8,000 employees, an annual budget of one hundred million dollars, three major research laboratories and two small test facilities.

Humankind's quest to finally reach out and touch the heavens had begun.

NASA.

The National Aeronautical and Space Administration.

The words rolled around in his brain as he heard them. Katie had returned from Disneyland, returned from spring break and her romantic getaway with Matt. The trip went well. They met up with friends and had a great time, as her father knew they would.

Now he was being thrown another curve, another milestone to contemplate. Katie was thinking about her future, about what she would do after school. She had actually been thinking about it for a long time, ever since that day years ago when they first began to explore going to college, when they stood in a room of the university administration building listening to a President long dead, listening to his desire to unite humankind in the quest to put a man on the moon.

Now it was time to make her dreams real.

"Dad, I wanted to let you know, I've applied for an internship at NASA."

"NASA? The NASA? The space agency?"

"Yes, Dad," she responded, patiently. "NASA. The space agency. They have a facility on the West Coast where they do research into things like artificial intelligence and robotics. I've applied to work there this summer for an internship."

"Well, that's... that's..." he didn't quite know what to say. "That's great! You're going to be a rocket scientist, eh?"

"Gee, Dad, I don't know about that, but it's something I've wanted to do for years. And now I'm sure. I sent in the paperwork yesterday and they promised to let me know by next week."

"Do they know, know about your... well, your disability?"

He hated asking questions like that, even after all these years. He'd taken to heart her statement years ago that she was not disabled, that this was simply who she was. But sometimes there seemed no other way to put it. Could she keep up? Could she work at a pace that would be required in such a demanding environment? Many of the same questions that had come up when she applied for the ambassador program came rushing back to his mind.

"Yes, Dad, they know. I've applied under a program that matches students with disabilities to internships. It's part of the program, so they know."

"Well, that's great. How can I help?"

"You can cross your fingers. Because I really want this. I really, really, really want this."

At that moment, he knew that she would get it too. He was coming to know his daughter well, very well indeed.

"Then I am sure you will get it, Katie. I'm sure you've done everything you need to be successful... after all... it isn't rocket science," he said, a grin slowly spreading across his face.

"DAD!"

There it was again, he thought, smiling to himself. The perfect line at the perfect moment. It isn't rocket science. And it wasn't rocket science after all.

Or was it?

He began to wonder if he would ever be able to use that particular phrase again.

ON June 3rd, some fifty years after NASA came into being, Katie May officially became a member of the quest to conquer space. She was accepted into the internship program at the Ames Research Center, a NASA facility perched on the southern end of the largest bay on the West Coast. She was assigned to a project that worked on artificial intelligence and computer programming. Her project was to research and help write computer code that would incorporate the concept of outliers in a distributive computing environment, a project designed to make computers think for themselves, and to act almost instantaneously to better control large rocket engines that provided the thrust that drove their payloads into the far reaches of the atmosphere, into space itself.

She tried over and over again to explain to her parents the nature of her work, but it was a hard undertaking. In the end, they simply took her word for it, that the hours spent in front of computer screens writing endless code and debugging endless lines of computer language were not the drudgery that they appeared to be, but rather exciting, fascinating and challenging hours that would help to change the world.

Once again, Katie would move, would transfer her meager belongings from one place to another, to exchange the relative comforts of her apartment in the city for the harsh four walls of a barracks dormitory on the old World War II military airfield that was now home to one of the most advanced research facilities in the world.

And once again, her father was spared the task of moving her, as Matt came to her aid and helped transition her from one world to another. She would be staying at the center for the better part of the summer, her internship scheduled to last all the way through August, to within a week of the beginning of her fourth year of college. They spent the weekend together, Katie and Matt, moving her in, exploring the city around them, enjoying the last few days together before they had to part. Matt had his own internship, in another lab, in a place many thousands of miles away. He would be working in his family's company in one of their overseas offices in Europe, so this would be the first time they had been apart since their relationship had begun the previous year.

The time came for him to leave and the parting was only slightly bittersweet, for they were both excited about the challenges ahead, of beginning to discover a little piece of the future that awaited each of them, a future far less uncertain now, but in some ways far more mysterious and vague.

Katie settled in to her new routine quickly. She embraced the work with an eagerness that her father could easily discern simply by the tone of her voice when speaking on the phone. In fact, it was only one week into the internship when she called him, concern written all over her voice.

"Dad, I have a problem and I need your advice."

He thrilled to still hear those words, knowing that there would come a time when his counsel was sought less and less, when she would guide herself without help through the problems and issues of her life. But for now, it was enough to know that she still needed him, still needed his guidance and counsel.

"What's up, Katie? How's the new job going?"

"Well, that's what I wanted to speak to you about. I have a problem."

"Tell me about it."

"Well, they assigned me my first project. It's a coding project. I have to work out a set of algorithms around a set of data in order to identify and recognize outliers."

"Outliers? What's an outlier?"

"It's a data set that falls outside the normal parameters of the data matrix in which it was generated."

"Huh? What? Data set? Matrix? You lost me, girl."

"Dad, that's not important. I'll try to explain it some other time. That's not my problem."

"Okay, sorry. So tell me, what is the problem?"

"Well, they gave me the project and let me know that they expected I should have it finished by July 15th, and to let them know if I needed more time. My mentor said that should give me the time I need."

"Uh. Well, you still have plenty of time. What is it now, June 20th? When did they give you the problem?"

"I was assigned it on the fifteenth. Five days ago."

"So, they gave you a month to do it. Well, what's the problem?"

"I'm finished."

"Beg pardon Katie, I didn't quite catch that last. Must be something wrong with the connection. Would you repeat that please?"

"I'm finished, Dad. Finished with the project."

"Wow, so much for the deadline, huh?"

"Dad, what do I do? Should I tell them I'm finished? I mean, I don't want to upset anyone, but I'm not sure they're expecting me to be done for several weeks. I don't know what to do!"

He could hear the concern in her voice. This was a new one for her, he knew. She'd always fought against deadlines, fought against the need to do large volumes of work in short periods of time. They had always shortened her course load in school so she would have the time to finish her work. And now, here was the opposite problem.

"Do you think they maybe underestimated your abilities, Katie? You know, like the speed with which you can do these things?"

It was just the opposite of what they'd worried about, talked about before she accepted the internship, her ability to keep up in the real world of work and deadlines and business pressures. It was one thing to ask for accommodations in an academic setting, it was another to actually be allowed accommodations in the competitive outside world, where business and science and politics moved at a speed that made allowances for no one.

"I think they have, Dad, and I don't know what I should do. Should I just keep pretending to work on it and wait for a while to turn it in?"

It was an interesting problem, he realized. How to go about handling it? In the real world, he would advise her to sandbag. Sandbagging... it was a great concept. He'd used it many times before. It would be simple to do, just keep telling them she was working it out, then kick back and enjoy herself for a few weeks, and still turn the work in a week ahead of her deadline. She would get a few weeks of ease, some downtime. They would get their work turned in well ahead of schedule, and she looks like a hero. Everybody wins.

Sandbagging, what a wonderful concept.

But he knew that was not the answer for this situation, for this world in which Katie now found herself. It was a world of very smart people working very hard on some very important and advanced problems, problems that could ultimately change the face of the world. So the only answer he could give her was the one he was sure was the correct one.

"Katie, I'll tell you what you do. Remember that teacher you had in the ninth grade? The one who kept exempting you from all the assignments he was giving the other students? The one who 'felt sorry' for you?"

"Yes," she replied slowly, not really sure where this was going.

"Well, take a few hours or days, whatever it takes, to make sure your work is right on, that you nailed it in every way. Then turn it in and tell them 'Hey, step it up, come on guys, is this all you got? Give me some more, give me the hard stuff. I can take it. I came to work!'"

He could hear his daughter laughing on the other end of the phone and he knew he'd hit the right button. It was an attitude she'd taken in school, in the classroom. Whenever teachers tried to give her the easy path, the easy way out, afraid perhaps that her disability made her unable to do real work, to meet the real demands of their coursework, well then she had challenged them in just the same way. She would turn in the work they assigned, plus extra work of her own, and then challenge them to step it up, because she was getting bored stiff with all the easy stuff.

That was exactly how she'd handled her ninth grade mathematics teacher, practically calling him out in front of the whole class and forcing him to assign her the advanced work he was so sure she couldn't do "in her condition." And that teacher had become not only her biggest challenger, but also her biggest champion in the school.

But this wasn't school. This was the real world, and she had not been brazen enough to make that decision on her own. He needed to reassure her that it was okay, that to challenge yourself, and those around you, was the only way to achieve excellence. And he knew his daughter by now, knew her well enough to know that her goal was simple.

She wanted to be the best... and she wanted to work with the best.

Nothing else would ever do.

A month and a half into her internship, Katie had an accident. Her father first heard about it with a phone call from the hospital where she was taken. On the other end of the line was a stern voice belonging to a resident in emergency medicine at a hospital not far from the NASA facility. After the introductions, he got right down to business.

"Sir, I'm calling because your daughter Katie is here under my care."

"What's wrong?" he replied instantly, every sense keyed up. "Is she okay?"

"Yes, yes, it's nothing major. She fell at the dorm she is staying in and it looks like she has fractured her wrist. It's a small break, a hairline fracture of the fifth metatarsal bone in her left hand."

"Oh," he replied, relief bunched up within that one syllable. "A fracture, a small one?"

"Yes, it's not large, but it can be very painful," the doctor replied. "Your daughter is handling it well so far, and I am inclined to try and not give her anything too strong for the pain considering her condition."

"Her condition?"

"Yes, her cerebral palsy. I am worried about her coordination under a strong painkiller."

"I see."

"She could fall again and reinjure herself."

"Yes, I can easily understand that."

"That's why I'm calling. Your daughter is a very stubborn woman. I understand that she has periods where she falls a lot and I am worried about her reinjuring the wrist, perhaps turning it into a major break or dislocation. That's why I want to set the wrist in a hard plaster cast."

"Is that normal for such a small fracture?"

"No, we usually put on a flexible sleeve that stabilizes the bones while allowing the patient enough movement to handle everyday chores and minor work assignments. It's much more convenient."

"So, what's the problem?"

"Your daughter is refusing the hard cast. She wants the flexi-sleeve. She says she can't work in a plaster cast and she wants to get back to her duties as soon as possible. Of course I am recommending strongly against it, but I'm having trouble with her. I was hoping you could talk to her, talk some sense into her. She runs a real risk of more permanent damage if she falls again and injures her wrist with such a flimsy cast."

"Well, you just may be out of luck there, Doc," her father replied, laughter welling up and spilling out of him before he could stop it.

"I really don't think this is a laughing matter at this point. This could be very serious."

"I know, doctor, and I'm sorry to laugh, but I can't help it. You see, you're talking to the wrong person. I gave up trying to talk her out of anything she set her mind to many years ago. She is one willful girl."

"Still, couldn't you at least speak with her?"

"I can try. Put her on."

He waited while the phone call was transferred to the treatment room Katie was in.

"Dad?"

"How you doing, babe? Are you in pain?"

"It's not too bad. I just feel so stupid. I was walking in the dorm and tripped on the doorstep. I've gone in and out of that room a hundred times and this never happened. I just feel stupid right now. And everybody's making a fuss. I'm fine. I just want to go back to work."

"Katie, the doctor has a good point. You could fall again and reinjure the wrist."

"But Dad, I can't work with that cast on. I'd have to quit the internship. He wants me to leave it on for three weeks. That's practically the rest of my time here. I won't do it. I won't quit. I'll be fine. I won't fall."

"I know, I know, it's a tough decision. But have you really thought it through? After all, you're still in pain and maybe you should think about this some more."

"Nope, I've made up my mind. I'll be fine. I just want to go back to work. I can handle the pain and I won't fall again."

"You can't guarantee that, Katie."

"Yes, I can. I will. Besides, it's my decision and that's it."

"Okay honey, you do what you have to. But remember the consequences if you reinjure it. You're going to have to be very careful."

"I know, I will. The doctor says he can only do this and release me if I agree to sign a form that says it's against medical advice and they won't be liable for anything that happens."

"Yes, that sounds about right. If you don't want to follow a doctor's recommended treatment, then you don't have to. But they will make sure you understand, legally, that they are no longer responsible."

"Should I do that?"

"Well Katie, if you want the flexible cast, then you're going to have to. Are you still sure?"

"Yes, I'm sure."

"Okay, put the doctor back on."

"Well, Doc," he said as soon as the other man was on the phone, "no luck. You're on your own. She's twenty-one and able to decide for herself, and that's what she wants to do."

"You understand she will have to sign a waiver of liability?"

"Yes, and she does too."

"Okay then, I will put on the flexi-sleeve and prescribe her some mild painkillers. But she should have her wrist examined within two weeks to make sure it is healing properly, and if she falls she needs to come back immediately for an evaluation."

"That's fine, just make sure she understands that. I am sure she can manage her care."

"Oh yeah, she can do that all right," the doctor replied. "She's a handful. Okay, she's more than a handful, she's a pain in the ass, but then I'm sure you already know that."

"Oh yes, I do. Just don't try to tell her she can't do something and you'll be all right. It's kind of been a guiding rule of ours for many years now."

"I understand. And, sir?"

"Yes."

"One more thing."

"What's that?"

"Well, that is to say, I mean…"

The doctor hesitated, as if not sure how to proceed or what to say.

"If I ever have a daughter, well… I just hope she turns out like yours."

"I understand."

"I hope you do. You're a very lucky man."

Yes, I am, he thought to himself as he hung up the phone.

A very lucky man indeed.

Second Star On The Right

Summer ran away like a lost love, the long, hot days making way for the cooler bite of fall. Katie's internship ended, successfully, and she returned for her fourth year at the University. She finished the internship with accolades and an invitation to return the following year. Her mentor had counseled her about going into research, rather than the more practical aspects of space exploration that occupied the other NASA facilities around the country. He wanted her to get a Master's and a Doctorate while working at the facility. Katie had nodded solemnly, not yet sure what she wanted to do, needing time away to explore her options.

She was only a month into the new semester at school when she called her father to talk over her thoughts, thoughts about the future, about space.

"Dad," she said when the moment seemed right. "What I really want is to go into space!"

"No way," he replied, almost too forcefully. "You are not going to Mars. Your mother would have a cow, not to mention the heart attack you would give me."

"Dad!"

"I'm serious, I know you. You're thinking about that Mars expedition that's in all the papers, the new direction of NASA. Well, don't even think about it."

He knew as he spoke that he was whistling up the wrong trail, or barking up the wrong tree, whatever the saying was. If she made up her mind, well then, that was it. But he hoped she was just kidding.

"No, Dad, I don't want to go to Mars. But I do want to go into space. So I'm thinking I might try a different internship next summer, one at their space flight center on the East Coast."

"The East Coast? Across the country?" he exclaimed. All of sudden, Mars didn't seem that far away.

"Yes. They actually work on the stuff that goes into space, the satellites, the shuttles, the equipment that they send up in them."

"Huh. Okay, what would you be doing?"

"Well, they have an internship on image processing. I would work on the computer programs that process data that goes to and from the satellites."

"You mean like the Hubble Telescope, things like that?

"Exactly."

"Well great, Katie, go for it. But the East Coast? First I had to figure out how to tell your mother you're going to Mars. Now I've got to tell her you're going even further away."

The East Coast seemed like such a distant world from where they were. The prior internship had taken Katie only four or five hours away by car. This one would take her all the way across the continent, to a world far different from the laid-back, wide-open spaces of the west where they lived.

"That's okay, Dad. I've already told her. And quit kidding around. I'll only be there for three months, and they have an open house so you can visit during the summer."

"Great, count me in. When do you find out?"

"I'll know in a month or two."

"Okay," he replied, thinking of nothing else he could say.

"Wish me luck?"

"No," he replied. "That's the one thing you don't need."

Fall came and fall went. Funny how that happens. Winter moves in and the world seems to turn a cold shoulder to just about everything. The snow fell, streets were clogged in the little town in the mountains, the snow berms towering over the roads and the now seemingly tiny cars darting to and fro, slipping first one way and then another.

Katie continued to phone in progress reports. She came home far less often now. Between the pressures of high-level senior classes, her still-hanging-in-there relationship with Matt, and the social life she was building, her time was limited, and her mother and father saw less and less of her.

She continued to excel in her coursework, but it wasn't easy. She was often stressed, or out of touch for days at a time as she continued to focus on her work. The fall semester passed with another round of top grades and accolades from her professors. Katie received approval for her internship at the new facility, the Goddard Flight Space Center near the nation's capital. It was only just across the country, but it seemed worlds away to her parents. They spent long hours on the phone discussing with her all the plans for moving, the travel, the flights, even the open house they would want to attend during the summer. They talked often, going over plans and itineraries.

It was during one such call that Katie broke the news.

"Dad, we need to talk."

Oh, how he dreaded those words. They always foretold something bad, a wife wanting to talk about "feelings," or an employee wanting to discuss the "injustice" of their situation, or a daughter changing her mind at the eleventh hour.

"Okay Katie, let's talk now. What's up?"

"I've been invited to attend a special program during my internship. It's called the NASA Academy for Future Leaders."

"Whoa, that's great! I think. What is it?"

"It's for people they want to single out for future employment. It's an extra program, in addition to the internship. It involves a lot of work, and I don't know if I should do it or not."

"Why? What kind of work? It sounds like a hell of an honor to me."

"Oh, it is, I guess," she replied, not quite convincingly. "We meet after hours to go over subjects and hear talks from astronauts and NASA scientists. We do field trips on weekends and I have to write a paper on top of my normal internship stuff."

"You get to meet astronauts," he replied, completely ignoring the workload she was worried about. "Real astronauts? From outer space?"

"No, Dad, they're not from outer space. Sometimes I worry about you. But yes, real astronauts who have been in space."

"Cool, you've got to do it. I want some autographs. And get pictures, too."

"DAD!"

"Okay, okay. Don't get your shorts in a bunch. I'm just kidding. Katie, how many of the interns do they offer this program to?"

"Not many. Maybe about one in ten. But most of them are Master's and Doctoral candidates. I'm just an undergrad."

"All the more reason to do it, Katie. It sounds like a great honor."

"Yeah, but it's a lot of work."

"And since when has that bothered you? This from the girl who finished classes on a Friday afternoon in high school and didn't quit working on homework until the beginning of class on Monday morning. Since when are you afraid of work?"

"I just don't know if I can do it. If I can keep up."

There, she had said it. The same subject they had been avoiding the entire conversation. Could she keep up? Could she fit in with all the other "normal" people? He thought long and hard for several seconds, seconds that seemed like minutes, even hours, over the phone. The failure of the past, the one that made her withdraw from the world, it continued to hang over his thoughts like the storm clouds that always seemed to loom just over the horizon.

"Dad, are you still there? Dad?"

"I'm here, Katie."

"Well, what do you think?"

"Katie, do you remember the People to People Ambassador trip you took?"

"Yes, what's that got to do with this?"

"I never told you, but they made me buy an open-ended plane ticket for you before you could go. It cost a small fortune."

"Why?"

"Because they said if at any time you couldn't keep up with the other kids, they were going to put you on a plane and ship you home pronto, and they wanted a plane ticket ready to go in case that happened. In fact, they were sure it would."

"I didn't know that."

"No, you didn't, and I didn't tell you. I didn't have to. I knew you wouldn't fail. I knew you would never use it. Katie, you can do anything you set your mind to. You know it, I know it. Now you've got to start truly believing it. Take the internship. Take it, and to hell with them. Keep up? You'll not only keep up, you'll leave them in the dust. Master's candidates? Doctoral candidates? Big deal. It's just another title. It's what's in your heart that counts, girl. And yours is bigger and fuller and brighter than any I have ever run across any-where in my entire life. Accept the invitation and go kick some ass."

"Okay, Dad, okay. I'll think about it."

He knew that was as good as a yes. As good as a "hell yes," but he didn't say anything.

"And, Dad…"

"Yes, Katie."

"I love you."

"I love you too, little girl."

Only he knew that she wasn't his "little girl" anymore.

Planning a move three hours away is actually pretty easy. You load up the car with the essentials, cram every nook and cranny full of the sentimental junk you thought you'd leave behind, make sure you can still see out the back window of the car, even if it's only just a little bit, and then one morning you take off and drive.

Moving across the entire country is a bit different. At least that's what Katie's father thought as they went over the plans for the umpteenth time. Winter had given way to spring. Katie had finished her classes for the year and the internship was only a few days away.

First there were the living arrangements. She would be staying in a sorority house on the campus of a school not far from the NASA facility. She would be provided transportation, so a car was not necessary. But how to pack everything one needs for a summer into just a few suitcases and still stay under the airline's weight limit? In the end, it was decided that her mother would fly out with her and help with the whole process. Matt was staying home to work on school projects. He would fly out to visit during the summer, or so he promised. But it was clear that Katie's relationship was being strained by the dictates of their different career paths. They both were beginning to understand that the inevitable was probably going to happen sooner or later. But both wished to make it later. She spoke at length with her mother about the relationship, but her father never pried, never stuck his nose in the conversation. Better to leave it alone, he thought. Let them work it out. It was one more problem he was glad he didn't have. Sometimes getting older had its advantages, he thought with a grin.

The trip out was uneventful. Katie got settled in to what she would describe later as the most grueling schedule of work she had ever undertaken. She was ensconced in a sorority house with fellow interns, girls, or rather women, who shared her interests and didn't give a damn about how someone walked or talked, or whether they could tie their shoes or had to use Velcro. For them, it was all about the work, the science, the projects that involved the mystery of space, of the universe, of creation itself.

There were undergraduates, Doctoral candidates, young adults from overseas, from the Far East, the West, from some of the most prestigious universities in the world. And she was one of them. She belonged. She was at the center of the universe, her universe, a world made up of dreams and wishes and, yes, of princesses.

She was assigned a mentor. He was an astrophysicist at NASA. She called home one night eager and excited, brimming with the news.

"Dad, I got my mentor today and you won't believe who it is."

"Really. Your mentor for the summer? Well, who is he, or she?" He could hear the excitement in her voice, hear it from across an entire continent.

"He's an astrophysicist, Dad, and a prize winning one, too."

"Really, what prize?"

"Oh, just a little prize they offer," she said. "He won it a few years ago, a little prize they call… the Nobel Prize for Physics."

"Katie, that's… that's wonderful. What did he do… you know… to win the Nobel?"

"He won it for work that basically proved a little theory they have."

"What theory?"

"You know Dad, a theory called… the Big Bang."

"Wow." His daughter was really playing this one out, and he could think of nothing else to say to that particular news. In fact, it left him speechless.

"Yes," she informed her father gleefully. "I'm working with the man who proved, beyond a shadow of a doubt, how the universe was created. He did it with his work in cosmic background radiation.

You know the radiation that fills space, but isn't caused by any of the stars or planets around them. You see… the concept of photon decoupling, the set of points in space and time where photons began to travel freely and…"

"Whoa, Katie… whoa. Little too much there, you're losing me. Why don't you explain it when we come out for the open house."

"Okay Dad, but I can't wait for you to meet him. He's really cool."

He didn't know how her mentor, this winner of the Nobel Prize, would take to being called "really cool," but he imagined if anyone could get away with it, his daughter could.

They continued to talk for what seemed hours as she filled him in on her new situation. Yes, the hours were long, the work harder than anything she'd ever done before. She was meeting astronauts, touring research and engineering facilities, visiting the air and space museums of the nearby capital, Washington, D.C., the center of the known world. And she absolutely loved every minute of it.

She took it all in. She worked late hours, wolfed pizza in her room with other interns, with other Academy members. She touched satellites being constructed for work in outer space, ran her hands along the surfaces of the parts being assembled at the space flight center. She explored equipment that had been to space and returned, its gleaming metal surfaces dulled from layers of cosmic dust and wear and tear. She watched as a roomful of technicians scurried about building the next big thing to go into space, a telescope that would supplant the Hubble, and look back even further into the mysteries of creation. And in between, there was the work, because along with the academy program, she had her regular schedule of work, long hours toiling on projects that might actually be used to help propel man and machine into the far reaches of the universe.

She made her own accommodations, went to bed late every night, her tiny body exhausted from the rigors of the day, but got up early every morning in order to be prepared, in order to over-come the physical difficulties that made every day so challenging for her, things everyone else took for granted, like brushing her teeth or putting on her clothes. She was never late, never held up the group, never slowed down. But it took a toll, she was tired al-most all of the time, tired but exhilarated, tired but thrilled, tired but satisfied.

It was, as she would tell her father later... the best summer of her life.

The time for the open house finally came. Parents of the interns were invited to attend a full day of activities, including a tour of the space flight center, presentations from the interns on their work, the introduction of their mentors. They even scheduled a barbeque out on the grounds, a simple affair with hot dogs and hamburgers, chips and dips, the tables covered with red and white checkered tablecloths.

It was there that Katie's parents got to meet her mentor, got to meet the man who had won the Nobel, who had proven the Big Bang theory of creation. Her father's first thought was that he seemed otherworldly, this astrophysicist, like an Einstein, but in a different way.

He was slight of build, with an angular body that seemed not to fit together too well. His hair was silver and grey, not so much dis-tinguished as disheveled, shooting in all directions, as if embracing the concept of gravity with a certain gusto not seen on most other people's heads. His voice was soft, his words measured.

He seemed at ease with the social setting, and yet his manner sug-gested awkwardness with the world at hand. It was no wonder, her father thought finally, that he made his home in space, in the reaches of a universe so grand that it was practically incomprehensible to all.

But not to him. Otherworldly was the right description, he thought.

The serving line moved ever so slowly as parents and interns, mentors and staff, made their way through, grabbing hot dogs and hamburgers, ladling on ketchup and mayonnaise and mustard. When finally Katie and her parents had made up their plates, her father carrying Katie's food for her, they were invited to sit with the great doctor at the end of one of the picnic tables.

It was a great moment for Katie, her father realized, a moment like no other, when her parents, the two people she most looked up to, was most close to, her two parents could sit with her at the pinnacle of scientific endeavor, at this little picnic table in the middle of a space flight center, with a man who would surely go down in history along with other greats, Einstein, Von Braun, Oppenheim. And he was her mentor, her guide in this summer of learning and working and discovering.

You need to say something, her father thought. Now is the time to say something, something appropriate, something to mark the occasion, to solidify Katie's moment in the sun, to validate it, to freeze it in memory. But what to say? What to say to this man who had won one of the most difficult, most coveted prizes in the world. What to say to this man who had proven, with his work in background microwave radiation and black bodies, the creation of the universe?

What to say to immortalize the moment?

No matter how he tried, nothing seemed to come to him. Nothing momentous. Nothing equal to the occasion. Finally, he said the only thing he could think of at that moment, the only thing that seemed appropriate, that seemed right. He opened his mouth to speak, turned to the great man as they settled in, and said...

"Hey, Doc, could you pass the ketchup... Please?"

They returned home from the open house, from the trip across the country to see their daughter's new world, this space center that her father couldn't help but feel was basically a summer camp, a camp with far greater things at stake than just getting the kids out of the house for the summer. They'd only just settled back in to their normal routines, Katie's mother back to her schedule, her father back on the road for his consulting business.

He had just returned from one such trip. It was only two weeks since the open house, when Katie called to once again "have a talk."

"Dad?"

"Yes, Katie. How's it going? You almost wrapped up there?"

"Yes, we have two more weeks. Dad, I have to tell you something."

"Sure, Katie. Hey, have you got your airline tickets ready to go?"

"Yes, Dad."

"Have you started packing yet? Bet you've got a lot of junk... I mean souvenirs, to bring home, huh?"

"No, Dad, I'm fine. I can pack. Dad, I have to tell you something."

"Okay. You sure you don't want your mother or me to fly out and travel back with you?"

"No, I'm fine. I mean, I can handle it."

"Of course you can. How about your classes? Did you get registered on time?"

"Yes, I... DAD! I HAVE TO TELL YOU SOMETHING."

"Okay, Katie," he replied, his face splitting into a huge grin. He had learned by now not to take his teasing to too great a length lest his daughter come unglued. "Fire away. I'm done with the third degree."

"I've been offered a job. Not an internship. A real job!"

"Really. Doing what?"

"NASA, Dad. I'm going to work for NASA."

A Perfect Storm

"When are you coming home?"

"Tomorrow. I'll be home tomorrow around three in the afternoon. Why?"

"Something is wrong… terribly wrong… with your daughter… with Katie."

He could hear the fear in her voice as she rushed to get it all out, fear with maybe even a little bit of terror mixed in.

"I need you to see your daughter, to find your daughter. I need you to come home. I don't know what else to do. I need you… NOW!"

"What's happened? Is she injured? Is she hurt? What… what is it?"

"No, I don't think so, well… maybe… I don't know, but I'm worried, worried sick. She's gone. Disappeared. I can't find her. I can't reach her."

He was talking to his wife from across the country. He'd been on the road for six days on a long project with a large client. With the job done, it was time to come home. His flight left in the morning. The cell phone seemed to heat up in his hand as he listened to his wife, her tone growing increasingly frantic as she spoke.

"Please, calm down. Tell me what you know. What's going on?"

"Don't tell me to calm down! She hasn't answered my phone calls for three days now. Nothing. I've left several messages and now her voicemail is full."

"Maybe she's lost in her studies. You know that's happened before."

"No, it's more than that. I called Amy and she hasn't seen her in three or four days, or talked to her on the phone. She tried knocking on the door to her apartment, but there was no answer."

"That doesn't sound good. Not at all. And you tried to see her?"

"Yes, after I heard from Amy, I drove down to her place myself. Amy said her roommate is out of town for two weeks, so Katie is alone."

"What happened?"

"I knocked and knocked and there was no answer. Nothing. I don't have a key. I couldn't get in. I've been back twice today and there's nothing, no answer."

"Do you think she's in there? Do you think she's at least physically alright?"

"Who knows? If she is, then she hasn't been out of that room for days. She's missed classes, labs. I am at my wit's end. I called Matt. I spoke with him. They had another fight, about her leaving, about her new job. He hasn't spoken to her in over four days."

"Did you try…" he stammered for a moment, not wanting to ask… afraid to ask. "Did you call the police? The hospital?"

"No, I wanted to speak to you first. I just don't know what to do. You fly all over and I'm here alone. You haven't been here, you don't know what's going on with her school and the new job and Matt… even her friends are having trouble with her. I need you here. I need you to handle this. I need you to help, to try and see her the moment you get in tomorrow. Go to her apartment. Whatever… I don't know what to do. I'm worried half out of my mind."

"Of course. I fly out first thing in the morning. I get in with plenty of time. I'll head there first thing and call you as soon as I know anything. You say you have no idea what's going on?"

"None, only that Amy said she's been a recluse and no one has seen her much for weeks."

"Okay, I'll keep trying to call her and head there first thing when I get in. You know I have an extra key to her apartment. I knew I should have left it with you, but somehow it ended up on my key ring. So, if she's there and won't open the door, I can get in. One way or another I will get to the bottom of this, okay?"

"What else should I do? What else can I do? I'm going crazy here."

He thought quickly. If she were with the police or in the hospital they would have been notified. Someone would have called. And then the feeling arose in his mind, started as just a thought, a speck of an idea, and grew and grew, mushrooming in mere seconds to form full grown within his brain. He knew she was home. Knew she was barricaded in, shutting out the world, shutting out everything.

Why?

He wasn't sure, but he had an idea. She had done this before. He remembered her freshman year, when she locked herself in the dorm for two days after having gotten back her practice exams. It was her way of coping, of dealing with things, to withdraw, to retreat from failure. She had reached adulthood, turned twenty-one, but inside, in many ways, she was still a little girl, still emotionally fragile, still insulated through her condition from dealing with the feelings and trauma of the real world, the world that fought her at every turn.

"I don't want you to worry," he said, turning his attention back to the phone and his wife. "I'm pretty sure she's still in her apartment. Just to be sure, you can call the university medical center and police. See if they have had any reports on her. But don't report her missing. Not yet."

He was sure, sure as he ever had been, that she was home, home alone, isolated, cut-off, shut-out from the reality of whatever she was going through. And whatever it was, he knew it involved some kind of failure, the one thing his daughter had not learned to deal with, could not accept, failure at anything she put her hand to, failure at anything she tried to accomplish.

"Don't worry," he said again. "Everything is going to be alright."

"Well, I am worried, and I'm not going to stop until I know what's going on. I'm her mother for chrissakes. Don't tell me not to worry. You travel all over and I'm left here to deal with all this, so don't give me any of that soothing crap. Just get home and get involved."

"Okay, okay. I'm on it, honey. First thing. I'll call as soon as I know."

"I'm sorry, it's just… I'm upset. I don't mean to take it out on you but this is serious. Please, this has never happened before, and I just don't know what to do."

"I'm sure she's fine. I'll call you tomorrow."

"No, she's not fine. I'm her mother. I know. Please hurry home."

She paused, then uttered one more phrase, simply, and with complete conviction, before hanging up.

"She's not fine."

Now he was worried, worried sick. He tried to call that evening, tried more than once. She didn't answer any of his numerous calls. Her voicemail only announced it was full and temporarily closed for business. During the long flight home, he tried to read, to sleep, to type on his computer… but nothing worked. There was nothing to distract him from the worry and the constant workings of his mind as he thought of all the bad things that could happen.

Maybe she was sick? Incapacitated? A plethora of ideas ran through his mind like a runaway train careening down tracks leading nowhere. Her upcoming job, the stress of school, her boyfriend, the changes that were happening so fast… too fast.

He went back through the last several months in his mind, from the time Katie had called so excited, so breathless, so full of this new job she had been offered, of her dreams of space, of her dreams of working for NASA actually coming true. Sitting in his aisle seat, flying through the air at 37,000 feet, winging his way home to whatever troubles awaited, his mind began to drift, to go back in time, back to a time that was supposed to be simple and easy.

Back to a time that was supposed to be simple… but wasn't.

"Dad, just leave me alone, okay?"

She was crying, sobbing almost uncontrollably, her little body wracked with anguish, with the spasms emanating from her pain.

She was only eight years old and she'd come home from school with tears in her eyes.

"Katie, please, tell me. What happened? What happened at school?"

It took a while, took a long while for her to calm down, to stop crying, to nestle in his arms while he tried to hug away whatever pain possessed her at that moment.

"They called me a retard, Dad. The boys on the bus called me a retard."

"What boys? Who did this? Your classmates?"

"No… they're older. They're in the fourth grade. They made fun of me. They've been making fun of me for days."

"Katie, why didn't you tell me? Why didn't you say something?"

Classes had only been in session for a few weeks. She was riding the bus to and from her school for the first time, and until now her parents thought everything was going well, wonderfully well. They were wrong.

"I didn't want to. I didn't want anyone to know. I just hate them. Why? Why are they so mean?"

"Katie, I don't know why some people are so mean. They're little, they're kids, they don't know any better. They can't handle someone who's different. And you are different, Katie. You're not like them."

"Why? Why do I have to be different? Why, Dad, why? I don't want to be different."

"I know, Katie, I know. But you aren't just different. You know that. You're special, you are a special little girl... a princess. Remember?"

"I don't want to be a princess, Dad. I just want to be the same... the same as everybody."

"Oh Katie, no you don't. You want to be just who you are. You're smarter than them. Look at how well you do in school. You're brighter and tougher. You're precious. They just don't know it yet. But they will. One day they will. One day you'll show them just how special you are."

Katie was silent for a long time. She sat motionless, thinking, the tears having dried up, her face set in concentration. They sat together for what seemed hours, hugging, thinking, silent. Although outwardly calm, he was crying inside, crying for what he knew his daughter was going through, what she would have to go through for many years, the taunts of others, the finger-pointing, the harsh words.... retard... geek... spaz.... the words of spite and venom, so full of misunderstanding and hate. He continued to cry inside for his daughter long after she had stopped, long after she had settled comfortably into his arms, her mind full of what thoughts he could only imagine. Finally, she stirred, looked up at him from where she sat nestled in his arms.

"Dad, can we have something special before dinner? Can we have some ice cream?"

She was smiling now, smiling the smile, her smile, the smile that made everything brighter.

"Sure, Katie, let's do that. Let's have some ice cream before dinner. And you just forget about those hateful boys and the things they call you. They just do it out of ignorance."

"I won't forget, Dad," she said as they got up and made their way to the kitchen. "I'll forgive them... but I won't ever forget."

❧❖❧

The plane's engines continued to drone on and on, the sound filling his ears, numbing his brain, putting him in a trance-like state, a stupor from which his thoughts continued to wander through the past, to wander through moments he'd shared with his daughter.

"I can't believe I'm going to work for NASA, Dad. I just can't believe it."

They were at the airport, Katie and her father. He was picking her up as she returned from her second internship, the job offer still fresh in her mind. She told him how it had all come about on the ride home.

"I still can't believe it," she said as they pulled out of the airport parking lot. "I was there with Doctoral candidates from MIT and Johns Hopkins, Master's students from Carnegie Mellon, from schools in Japan and Italy. And they asked me. I'm the only one they offered a job."

"That's incredible, Katie, truly remarkable. Tell me everything. Tell me what happened."

"I was on the team doing image processing, programming you know, for the satellites like the Hubble, the stuff we talked about. My project leader said he had an opening coming up. And he wanted me to apply for it. He wanted me for his team."

"Really, just you?"

"Yes. He said he was amazed at not only what I had achieved in school and in my work, but how I did it while overcoming my condition."

"Your condition?"

"Yes, my condition. That's what he called it. My condition."

"I see."

"He said if I could do that, why then I could do just about anything and he wanted me at NASA, he wanted me on his team. He asked me to put a resume together, to apply for the position. That it would open up in the new year after I finished my last semester and graduated."

"So, you've applied? You made a resume? I thought you already had the job? You've only applied?"

"No, I didn't have to. A few days later he asked me to send over my transcript from school, you know, all my courses and grades and stuff."

"So you did?"

"Yes, it wasn't hard. It's all on the Internet, on the computer. I sent it to him and in one hour Dad… one hour after I sent it to him, he called me back."

He remembered how she stressed the "one hour" as she spoke.

"Really. One hour?"

"Yes, one hour."

"What did he say?"

"He said forget the resume, forget the application. He said the job was mine if I wanted it. To just let him know."

"Katie, that's wonderful."

"He said, of course I have to finish school. I have to maintain my grades and graduate. Without that, he wouldn't be able to do this. He would have to put it out to bid, invite other students. But with my grades, he could get that waived. Dad, I'm in. I just have to finish everything… finish strong."

He thought about her words, about the tone of her voice as she spoke, the look in her face as he drove along the winding roads back to the little town in the mountains and home. Through the excitement and the joy, she also sounded worried. Worried about finishing right, finishing school at the top of her class. Everything hinged on that, or so she seemed to think, so she had been told.

He came to the present suddenly, came out of the stupor he was in, found himself back on the plane, the plane that was winging him back to home and trouble, trouble that awaited him at the end of this journey. Was that it, he wondered? Was it her schoolwork? Was it the job? Was she in trouble?

Had she lost the job... ?

The whine of the jet engines kept up their reassuring tone, lulling him back into the recesses of his seat, the plane swaying gently through a light but steady turbulence the pilot couldn't seem to avoid. The plane flew on, seeking its destination, seeking home and the unknown. Once again, he drifted away, away to the past and his thoughts...

"I spent two hours on the phone with your daughter today. It took me a half hour just to get her to calm down enough so that I could understand her."

His wife was standing in the doorway to the garage, hands on her hips, a determined look on her face. She hadn't even waited for him to get inside and put down the suitcase he was carrying.

"Really," was all he could think to say.

"Yes, she's having trouble again, trouble with Matt, and it's getting serious."

"Trouble? I thought they were getting along great."

"You know, you really need to pay more attention to things. I know you have to go winging off for work every other day, or so it seems, but that's no excuse.

"Are we going to go through that again?"

"No, no. But things are not good and haven't been for a while. You know, this job she keeps talking about is going to take her away. Take her all the way across the country."

"I know. We've talked about it over and over again. How we'll miss her. How we'll have to deal with the distance."

"Yeah, but you never stopped to think about her boyfriend.

About Matt. What about that? What about her relationship? You know about long distance relationships, how they don't work out."

"Now I do feel like an idiot. No, I didn't think about it. Of course, it makes sense. They have to deal with it, too. Not just us, is it?"

"No, it isn't. And this is her first relationship, her ONLY relationship. I know you think your daughter is full-grown, but in many ways, she is still just a child."

"I don't know about that."

"Well, she is. Don't you understand? She should have gone through this years ago, when she was a teenager. She's never been faced with it. Never learned to deal with it. And I don't think Matt is any better at it than she is."

"So, what's happening between them? What's going on?"

"Well, he's withdrawing. Underneath everything I think he's pissed that she's going, doesn't want to admit it, or deal with it."

"Did something happen?"

"Yes, he's acting cold and distant. He's been ignoring her calls for days. And Katie really doesn't know what she's doing either. She talks about them seeing each other throughout the year, of making trips back and forth. But I think they're both beginning to realize just what this means... and they can't handle it."

"You think she's in love?"

"I know she's in love, I don't think it. But I don't know what kind of love. Full grown 'I love you and want to commit to you' love? Puppy love? First love? Who knows. There's no book for this sort of thing, no how-to manual. But it's affecting everything. She's moody, she's mean. I've never heard her say such mean things before... and to me, her own mother."

"I'm sure she doesn't mean it, but yeah, I've noticed she doesn't seem very happy when I talk with her."

"That's not the half of it. I've been on the phone with her every other day for weeks. She cries, she yells, she yells at the littlest things, things that shouldn't matter."

"And you think it's all about this… about her relationship, about Matt?"

"I know it is. What I don't know is what we can do about it. And I'm afraid. Afraid she'll blow off the job. Afraid she won't. I don't want her to go either and I'm having a hard time hiding my feelings about the whole thing."

"You know we have to let her go. We've talked about it."

"I don't care. She's not like everyone else. I don't care what you say. She's not normal. And I don't know if this really is for the best, if she can handle it."

The words hung over him, oppressed him with their truth. Be careful what you wish for, he thought, you just might get it. This job, this offer should have been the culmination of her dreams, and instead it was pitting everyone she loved against her… her mother, her boyfriend, her other friends.

"So, what do we do about that? What can we do?" he asked plaintively.

"I don't know," she replied, frustration clearly evident in her response. "Nothing, I guess. We just have to be there, to listen. But I am trying really hard not to call her boyfriend and lay into him. You men can be such cretins at times."

"I don't think that's…"

"No, that's right, you don't think. None of you do. We're going to have to wait and see. Sound familiar? We're going to have to just take it one day at a time, like everything else in her life. But mind you, this isn't going to go away."

He looked at her again, saw the anger in her face, saw the way she tried to control herself, to keep from lashing out again and again. And as much as he wanted to put it all aside, to chalk it up to just young love and the lessons of life, as much as he wanted to believe that everything would be alright, he knew better.

Like she said… this wasn't going to go away.

The sound of the engines winding down and the sudden change in the plane's angle once again pulled him from his thoughts and brought him into the present. They were starting their descent. For better or worse, for whatever would come, the time was drawing near and he felt pulled towards it, pulled inexorably towards whatever crisis awaited, a crisis that had loomed over him, not just for the last twenty-four hours, he realized, but for days and months, and yes, probably for years and years.

Whatever it is, he thought, we'll get through it. I know we can, if I can just figure out what it is.

That's the problem, I really have no idea. As the jet settled onto the runway, he thought again that it could be anything… or it could be everything.

The plane touched down at exactly three o'clock on what was turning out to be a cold, late fall day. There was a chill in the air and the clouds looked steely grey and menacing, as if promising snow. The holidays were only a few short weeks away. As the plane taxied in, he reached into the pocket of the seat in front of him to retrieve his cell phone and turn it on. He would try again, try to call Katie, just as he had been doing ever since he hung up with his wife the prior evening. Once again, there was no answer, just the steely voice of a robot telling him her inbox was full.

He rushed to baggage claim, fumed and paced while waiting for what seemed like an eternity for his bag to come down the conveyor belt, and then rushed to his car. It was only a matter of a few minutes to negotiate the parking lot, to escape into the afternoon traffic, and finally, to pull into the parking lot of Katie's apartment building. He felt an overwhelming sense of déjà vu as he got out of the car. This had happened before… this had happened before.

Okay, he thought to himself, calmly now, don't blow it. Whatever it is, take it slow. He reached into his pocket to recheck that he had a key to her place. One way or another, he would force the issue and see his daughter. That is, if she was there. Please god, let her be there. He didn't want to think of the alternative.

He climbed out of the car, locked it, and headed into the building. She was on the third floor, but the elevators were slow and he didn't want to wait. So he took the stairs, climbing them two to three steps at a time, his breath coming in gasps as he neared her door.

Now, after what seemed like a journey of a thousand days, but was only a few hours from the time of that fateful phone call last night, he stood before her door. There was no sound, no music, no radio, no nothing.

He knocked.

He knocked again.

Nothing.

"Katie," he called out. "Katie, it's Dad, are you in there?"

No answer.

"Katie, I know you're in there, so please answer me. I have a key and I'm going to come in anyway, so please answer me and open the door."

Still nothing.

He banged again, banged on the door with all the frustration of the last few hours.

A door down the hallway opened, two eyes peering out from behind the opening, questioning eyes. He ignored the eyes, ignored everything else around him, just continued to bang on the door like a fool, like a maniac.

Finally, from behind the door came sounds, ruffling and shuffling sounds. More than hearing them… he felt them.

"Katie, open up. I know you're there."

"Go away, Dad. Leave me alone, just leave me alone."

The voice coming through the door was muffled, strained, just barely audible.

"I'm not going to do it, Katie. You've got us worried sick. Even Amy is worried. Now open the door."

"Go away."

"Not gonna happen. Open the door."

"No."

"Okay, I'm coming in."

He started to put the key in the lock, fumbled with it for just a moment, pushed, and the door seemed to fling itself open. There was no one in the room. He stepped in, looked around, felt the emptiness. It was quiet… too quiet.. and still… too still.

He wandered down the hallway, looking, sensing, afraid of what he might find. Then he saw her, saw her in the bedroom, saw her laying on the bed, her head down in her hands, her limbs curled into a ball, her body rocking back and forth, her eyes averted.

"Baby, what's wrong?"

"Nothing. I'm okay, just please go away."

"No, I'm not going to. I told you. We're worried. You haven't been out, you haven't been returning calls. Katie, tell me what's going on?"

"Nothing Dad, it's just… it's just…. nothing. Okay?"

"Has someone been bullying you? Making fun of you?"

"No."

"Did something happen, happen in class or out in public?"

"No."

"Were you attacked. Were you raped, for crying out loud?"

"Good god, no, Dad. What a question."

"Well, Katie, if you won't talk, then I have to guess. How am I to know what's happened?"

He noticed she looked thin and drawn, her face seemed lined and her body even more shapeless than usual. Other than the rocking motion, she seemed powerless, unable to even get up off the bed, much less walk on her own two legs.

"When was the last time you ate?"

"I don't know. I'm not hungry."

"Where's your roommate?"

"She's gone. She won't be back till after the holidays."

Her voice was listless, her tone devoid of energy. The words were spoken without form and it was hard to understand her. He stood for a moment, not knowing how to proceed, what to do. Something was so obviously wrong. But what was it? None of his questions seemed to hit the mark, nor did he think she was lying to him. But something was dreadfully, dreadfully wrong.

What was it?

Déjà vu.

He cast about the room, searching for clues. He noticed several papers on her desk, some lying bent and crumpled and half covering her laptop. He reached over to the paper on top, smoothed it out, tried to read it.

Déjà vu.

It was a midterm test from one of her courses, an advanced course on artificial intelligence. As in the past, he could tell the handwriting was from someone else, one of the volunteers in the disability office. The test was dated from last week. And across the top third of the page, in big, red ink, was a large C-. Following that, in smaller red ink below, was a note from the professor. He held it at length and allowed his eyes to adjust to the small type and the subdued light of the afternoon sun peeking from behind the window of the room. He read the note:

"This is not senior-level work or what I have come to expect from you. I want to see better on the next attempt."

He glanced at the next paper on the desk. It was another test, this one in advanced robotics. It also was marked, this one with a big red D and a note in large letters that said, *NEEDS WORK! AT THIS PACE YOU WILL FAIL!*

He thought back to her first semester, to the practice tests that she'd had so much trouble with.

"Katie, these tests, these grades, is that what this is about?"

"Just leave me alone, Dad. Please, and you can throw those away or take them with you. I don't care."

Her voice remained listless and tiny, swallowed up by the space around her, just barely audible.

"Yes, Katie, yes, you do. You care a great deal. How long have you been here like this? Holed up in this room?"

"I don't know. I don't care."

Then he saw it. Saw the letter, the missing piece of the puzzle. It was laying on the floor next to her desk, laying slightly crumpled on the carpet. He picked it up, held it up to the light to read. It was from NASA, from her team leader from last summer, her future boss.

It began, *Dear Ms. Katie May...* He glanced once at his daughter, crumpled on the bed before him, and then continued to read, the words seeming to jump off the page at him.

> *We are in receipt of your latest progress reports from the university. As you know, your employment is conditional on your graduating and maintaining the high standards and grades for which we made the decision to offer you employment with this office. Should you not graduate as scheduled, we will not be able to offer you the position. Nor will we be able to circumvent the normal hiring and recruiting process should your grades fall below the level you have maintained to date.*

This is to inform you officially that we will have to open the position up to general recruiting should either of these things occur. Please advise us as soon as possible if your plans have changed, or if you feel that you will not be able to graduate as planned so we may begin to make other arrangements. Of course, we still wish to offer you the position and hope that the latest progress reports can be reversed or corrected.

You may contact us at the email address listed below. Please advise as soon as possible your intentions and how you plan to proceed. We hope the latest results from your coursework can be reversed before the semester ends.

We look forward to hearing from you...

He paused, and then started again from the beginning, seeking understanding, the words not making any sense, the meaning eluding him the first time through. She was being censured. Her work was falling off... failing... her high standards crumbling under the weight of everything going on in her life, everything grinding her down, her friends, her parents, her expectations, her boyfriend... it was all too much. She was sinking, sinking into an abyss from which she could find no escape, no relief.

It was the perfect storm he had sensed, had worried about for so long, the storm he felt sure was brewing over the horizon, a storm he'd hoped would veer off course and never arrive. But it was here, now, at this moment, and a cold chill began to run through his body from the bottom of his feet into the recesses of his heart.

"When did you get these papers back?" he asked slowly, having finished the letter for the second time. "When did you receive this letter?"

"Monday. I got it Monday."

It was now Thursday. She had been like this for over three days. He quickly thought to himself. Started to speak, hesitated… then plunged in.

"Katie, I know this is a lot… a lot to take in. A lot to deal with. But this isn't the answer, this retreating from the world, from us, from the ones who love you."

She said nothing, didn't move from her position on the bed.

"We can fix this, Katie, you know we can. We've done it before. You've done it before."

His words were soft, but firm. He was trying, trying as best he could to sound positive, to offer hope.

"I know we can fix this. You've never failed before. You're not going to fail now."

Finally, she spoke, her words still just barely a whisper.

"You don't know, Dad. You don't know anything. Just leave it alone."

"I'm not going to leave it alone, Katie. I'm not going to leave you alone. You have to face this." His voice was rising, his tone increasingly strong, even harsh.

"No, I don't. I don't have to do anything. I don't want to do anything."

Now her voice started to rise, her head raised, her eyes started to glow as they bored into him.

"I'm just a spaz, Dad… a retard… a geek. Now leave me alone."

Now her words were biting into the air. They began to have weight, to pierce through the heaviness in the room. She was getting worked up, getting angrier and louder as she spat out the hateful words from her past.

Perhaps this was what she needed, he thought. To get mad. To get really mad. He decided to try a new tack.

"A spaz huh… a RETARD! Sure, Katie, that's just what you are. This is just the proof we need. It confirms it, doesn't it? Doesn't it?

Nothing you've done up to now matters, only this. Is that it? Is that really it?"

His voice was rising too, growing angrier, louder, filling the room.

"You're just a geek and you really can't cut it, can you?"

That did it. She came roaring to her feet, her whole body rigid and tense, the misery of the past four days seeming to rush out of her, propping her up. She pointed her finger at her father, her arm outstretched and rigid, muscles straining against the damaged nerves that wove through her arm.

"You don't know. You just don't know," she screamed at him. "This is all I have. This… this is all I am."

She stomped over to the table, grabbed up one of the tests with the big red C- on it. She held it tightly in her grasp, thrust it into his waiting face, thrusting it at him as if to impale him on the point of a sword.

"This is who I am. It's all I've got. Without it… I'm a nobody. I can't walk right. I can't talk right. I can't even hold a stupid glass in my hands without spilling or breaking it. I'm a freak, Dad, a freak. And this, my grades. My schoolwork is all I have. NASA. The job… it's all I have… it's all I had. It's the only thing, the only thing. And now it's gone. And Matt's gone. And my friends are gone. It's gone. It's all gone."

She was sobbing now, crying, yelling, and crying some more, her little body wracked with the pain of letting it out, letting the build-up of the last four days run out of her, run out like a river pouring over a precipice into a waiting pool below, a deep dark pool.

"Don't you understand, this is all I've got. This is all I am. Without this, I'm nobody."

She fell back on the bed now, her body bent into a curve, her hands grasping at her knees as she started again to cry, her tears falling gently onto the bed sheets.

"I'm nobody," she yelled again.

Her father stood very quiet, very calm. He dared not speak, dared not risk saying or doing something that might make it worse. He knew she needed this, needed to get it out, all the emotion, the buildup of the last few days and weeks, the pressure. And then it hit him. It wasn't just a buildup of the last few days and weeks. It wasn't college. It wasn't the grades. It wasn't her friends. It wasn't Matt.

It was everything.

It was her whole life. It was years of having to fight and push, of going to bed exhausted every night, of always having to question whether she could do something, participate, achieve any of the things she set out to do.

It was everything.

It was all the years, the frustration, the taunting, the stares. She was an outsider, an outcast, a hanger-on in a society that adored physical beauty and seeming perfection, that promoted it in every magazine, every TV show, every movie. He understood, really for the first time, just how important her schooling had been, how critical to her own sense of self, of who she was, of her self-worth.

He always assumed, like his own experience with school, that she simply did her best, was gifted, and focused more on school than anything else because it was what she could do on her own. He hadn't realized that, throughout the years, it had come to define her. It made her over in her own image of herself. It was her claim to fame, her strength... her one thing.

And now that thing was threatened. It was being taken away. Her job at NASA, her top scholar position, all of it was being taken away. These grades, these tests, they were laughing at her, telling her she couldn't measure up, that she was no good.

And if that was true, if it was all gone, if reaching for and achieving your dreams led to this, then what was to become of her? What would she do? How would she cope? How would she live?

It was all too much. He could see that now. This was not just a silly outburst from someone with too much pride to admit they needed help. No, this was about her identity, about her life, about her very survival. He knew now what he had to do, how he had to proceed. It would not be easy. It might take time. But the next few hours and days would be critical. He knew his daughter could recover from this, could rebound. But the alternative also hovered in his mind like a heavy blanket shutting out all light. She could truly lose it, truly lose all she had built in the few, fragile short years she had been alive. She could retreat to that world of mediocrity, of being disabled, of being handicapped.

She could give up.

And that, he was afraid, might kill her, or at best, put her back in a wheelchair, or put her in a corner, grasping at her knees, slowly rocking away her life in a pool of self-pity and doubt.

Katie continued to lie on the bed, the sobs crashing over her body like waves onto a beach. He stepped over to the bed, sat down beside her, silent, his arms reaching out to caress her back and shoulder. It was only the work of a few seconds, but he was successful. She raised herself just enough to fall into his arms, into his embrace, sobbing, crying, letting it out.

They sat for what seemed hours, silent, hugging, the only sound an occasional sob from his daughter. He was prepared to go on sitting there for as long as it took. But finally, finally Katie straightened up, her face red, her eyes rimmed with tears, puffy and black.

"I'm sorry, Dad... I'm so sorry..."

"No dear, no, don't be sorry," he answered softly, holding her once again. "Just let it out... let it go."

They sat without moving, huddled together for another eternity that was only a matter of minutes. Slowly, the light in the room dimmed, the evening shadows beginning to play across the walls opposite the only window in the room. They didn't move, didn't notice the growing darkness, just sat and slowly hugged, sat and hugged, he and his daughter, not speaking, not wanting to move, not wanting to let the moment go.

Time fell away and he began to feel as if she was a little child again, a precocious princess, a little girl trying to make her way in a cruel world. He wanted this time, this moment, to last forever, to never let her go, to shut out the world as she was doing and just exist, quiet, silent, alone, just the two of them.

But he knew it had to end. He was in danger of doing just what his daughter had done, of retreating, of slipping away. And he needed to fight, needed to bring her back. Slowly he cast about for any thought, anything that might help.

Then he had an idea.

"Katie, get your coat, we're going for a drive."

"Dad, I…"

"No, don't argue. Just do it. We're going for a drive. We're not going to see anyone, talk to anyone. Just you and me. A quiet drive. Private. Okay?"

She nodded. Slowly she came to her senses, as if coming out of a deep sleep. She stood, tottered for a moment, and then gained her strength, gained her balance. He had the feeling at that moment that she had not even stood up during the long hours she'd been alone in her self-imposed exile. He waited while she grabbed a coat, and then followed her out of the bedroom, followed her down the hall, moving slowly, the shadows growing longer, the lights off. They felt more than saw their way across the living room to the front of the apartment. With one quick motion, he opened the door and passed outside, his daughter following slowly, passing through the entranceway and out into the world.

It was the first time she had passed through that door in four and a half days.

It was only a matter of minutes for them to navigate the elevator and lobby, to cross the parking lot, to get in the car, to buckle themselves in. He pulled out slowly, not really sure where he was going or what he was going to do. He was hoping for a sign, for some opportunity to present itself. He was hoping, in short, for a miracle. But he knew that first and foremost he had to get her out of that room, get her out into the world, to see things from a different perspective. Maybe that would be enough, he thought. And then he quickly dismissed the thought. It was a start, but something else would be needed.

He would look for a sign, something that would bring her back to the present, to the moment. Something that would allow her to draw from the wealth of experience and knowledge she had acquired during her short life. Something that would bring her back to herself, her old self, her real self… her fighting self.

He pulled onto the main thoroughfare that divided the campus from her apartment complex. The neon lights from the bars and school hangouts that lined the road were just coming to life. Evening continued to advance and the town was quickly growing dark. They continued down a long hill, across a freeway that dissected the city and on into the main downtown area. The lights of the buildings were coming on, their harsh glow softened by the reddening hues cast off by the setting sun. The car was quiet. He left the radio off and they did no talking. They just drove and drove and drove. He turned onto one street and then another, aimlessly, just driving, letting the car find its own way.

They made it to the south end of the city, turned and retraced their steps. They worked into the western foothills where the mountains began and the valley floor left off. They climbed a hill and slowly worked their way to a ring road, a road that highlighted the lights of the city against the setting sun and the reds and purples of the evening sky. They came back down and around to the east side, the car quiet, each one lost in their own thoughts.

Slowly the dark consumed what little was left of the day. The lights of the city were now a harsh backdrop to their aimless wandering. The car seemed to have a mind of its own as they turned from one avenue to another, the tires making a soft squishing sound, the engine quietly humming, the air around them stilled and quiet. Katie sat, not moving, just staring out the window, her shoulders slumped into her chest, her head sagging into her shoulders as if trying to find some way to disappear, to vanish into the dark of the night.

They had been driving for perhaps an hour, perhaps more, when it finally came to him, the sign he had been waiting for, hoping for. A sign of destiny, of hope, a sign that would turn the tables, that would bring them into the present, bring them back into life. It started out as just a bright light in the distance, brighter than the other lights around it. As they neared, it grew in shape and form and substance. It was more than just a vision, it was a real sign, a marquee with a great deal of writing on it. As the sign grew nearer, he could make out the letters perched upon it, and then the words that the letters formed.

Finally, he was able to read what was written, was able to make sense of the letters that stared out at him. There, he thought. There it is… the answer. He slowed the car, began a turn into the parking lot that surrounded the sign on all sides.

"Dad, where are we going?" Katie asked suddenly, pulling herself from the self-imposed stupor that had consumed her all during their long drive to nowhere.

"We're going to see a movie, Katie. Would you like to see a movie?"

"Not really," she replied.

"Well, we're going anyway. I want to see a movie and I need the company."

"All right."

She said it simply, without any emotion, without any tone, as if she was lost in some other world.

He pulled in under the sign, a marquee for the largest movie theater in the city, a metroplex with ten screens. The sign held the names of all the movies that were showing that evening, along with the times they would be shown.

The last movie on the list, at the very bottom of the marquee, that was what had caught his eye. That was the sign he'd been looking for… his miracle.

It read, "Walt Disney's The Little Mermaid."

The title was followed by the time, two showings only, one at 2:45 PM and one at 7:30 PM.

He looked at his watch as he pulled into the nearest parking spot.

It was exactly 7:20 in the evening.

They took their seats just as the previews started to roll. He made sure Katie was comfortable and told her he would be back. He was going to get popcorn and a cherry slushy, her favorite movie snack. Once in the lobby, he quickly pulled out his cell phone and called his wife.

"Honey, I'm back and I'm with Katie."

"It's about time you called, what's going on, what's…"

"Not a lot of time to talk now. But she's okay. She's been holed up in her room upset about her grades, the job, Matt. She got her midterms back and they weren't good. And she got a letter from NASA, a letter about her job. There's a lot to tell, but later. I got her out of the room. We're at the movies."

"The movies?" she practically shouted into the phone. "What the hell are you doing at the movies? What about this letter…

WHAT'S GOING ON, DAMMIT?"

"Trust me, it's the right thing to do. It's her favorite Disney movie, the first one she ever saw. I'm trying to get her mind off of school and on to something else."

"Well… I don't know. Will that work?"

"Yes, it's got to work. It's magic, Katie's magic. I need to get her in a better place and then talk with her. I'm going to stay here tonight, stay with her. I'll call again when I can, but I won't be home until tomorrow."

"I want to come down. I want to. Where are you? I want to see her."

"I know honey, I know. But not now, please. Tomorrow. Wait until tomorrow. Give me some time alone with her. I need some time alone. You asked me to help solve this thing. Now you're going to have to trust me."

"Alright. But call me. Let me know what's going on."

"Will do. Gotta go. Gotta get some popcorn."

"Get her a cherry slushy. It's her favorite."

"I know. I've got it covered. Love you, bye."

He got back to the theater just as the movie previews were ending. He could see that Katie was watching, although from her expression he couldn't tell what she was thinking, or if she was even aware of the movie. But she dove into the popcorn, took her slushy and started to drink. It was a good sign. He settled in to watch with his daughter the tale of Ariel, the little mermaid, and the magic that somehow he knew she had lost touch with.

Once again, the familiar scenes played across the screen. Sebastian the crab conducted, the crustaceans played their instruments, and Ariel sang, sang with a voice as pure and sweet as only the Imagineers at Disney could imagine it. And slowly, surely, as if by magic, they were transported to that world beneath the sea. The real world, the world of school and grades and difficulties, of NASA and boyfriends, of shattered nerves and rigid muscles, the real world simply dropped away, the cares, the worries… everything simply fell away.

They laughed at the antics of Sebastian and Flounder the fish. They recoiled at the menace of the sharks and the evil of the sea witch. They cried at the beauty of love, the love between a mermaid and a man, a princess and a prince.

Time fell away. Katie was three years old again, the look on her face one of awe and wonder. Her father too, felt young again, strong, full of the future and the possibilities of life. It was as if the past eighteen years were a dream, a memory of something vaguely familiar but not real. He was back at that birthday party, watching his daughter, barely three years old, watching her discover the magic of life, the possibilities, the wonder.

He held her hand, not the hand of a young woman, but the hand of a little girl, a child. Her fingers grasped his, her grip rigid and unyielding, her hand tensing as the drama unfolded.

They laughed, they cried, they lost themselves in the moment. It was tender and sad, funny and happy, painful and pleasurable. It was all those things, and he felt closer to his daughter than he'd ever felt. They were sharing this one thing, this magic that had defined Katie more than any schoolwork, more than any other accomplishment. They clung to it like a lifeline, like a life preserver tossed to a drowning man.

When it was over, when Ariel had become a woman, a real woman, and rode off into the sunset, to live happily ever after with her prince, still they sat, their hands entwined, their fingers interlocked. They sat through the ending credits, the music blaring through the speakers and then softly fading away. They sat until there was nothing left, nothing but the blackness of the theater and the tiny pinpoints of light defining the way out.

Slowly they rose, without speaking, without the need for words. Silently they left the theater. Silently they exited the lobby. Silently they found their car and settled in.

He put the key in the ignition, turned it. The engine roared to life. Only then did the silence seem to be broken. They pulled out and drove some more, aimlessly as before, just turning from one street to another. Looking for another sign, another thing to do, only now there was a warmth between them, a shared feeling, a bond that had returned from some lost and faraway place.

Finally, they passed a restaurant, one of a chain of restaurants, one of Katie's favorites. This restaurant had a large dessert menu, with ice cream and lava cakes and sweet tarts, all the things he knew Katie loved. He thought of the past, of a time when they would eat dessert before dinner, Katie's mother infuriated, yelling about spoiling her dinner and teaching her the wrong things, setting the wrong example. "I swear," she would say, "you two have no more sense than god gave a duck." They would laugh and wink, secure in the knowledge that it was just their way, their private way, a private world that only they had the key to.

"Hey Katie, how about dinner?"

"Dinner. Here?"

"Yeah, but not dinner, let's just have dessert. Let's have dessert for dinner."

For the first time that evening, she smiled... THE smile... Katie's smile... and once again, the world fell away as the smile grew larger and larger, filling the car with light, filling his heart with warmth.

"Dessert for dinner? That's just silly. That's for little girls, not me. I'm all grown up now Dad. But okay, let's do that. Let's have dessert. Let's have all of the desserts."

"You're on, every dessert on the menu. And if we don't finish them all you owe me a dollar. Deal?"

"Deal," she said, laughing.

And that's when he knew, knew for certain... knew in his heart that it was going to be okay. The perfect storm was over.

The magic was back.

Top Scholar

First I would like to start off by thanking the alumni association for this award. It is truly an honor to be recognized for all my hard work.

The forty-two steps were mastered. She did not fall, did not wobble, did not even hesitate. Now she was talking, speaking into the microphone, her voice hesitant at first, then growing stronger and broader, her nervousness apparent, but in check, her words filled with the emotion of the moment, and the difficulty of talking with vocal chords that didn't work quite right, that had never worked quite right.

Her father sat in the front row, flanked on either side by his wife and Amy, Katie's faithful and trusted Best Friend Forever. He knew this was a big moment for her, the biggest so far in her small life, and for once, he wasn't sure he even knew how to feel. It was as if he could run the emotions through his mind like a movie, playing them out one at a time, although they seemed to rush through him in one big wave of raw feeling.

There was the nervousness of waiting for her to be called, the anticipation of what was to come, the understanding of it, and the unknown and unknowing of it as well. There was pride, of course, pride for all she had done, pride for the fact that only eight students from among thousands had been chosen for this honor, and she was one of them, one of the eight, one of the few, the best and brightest of the bunch.

There was joy and happiness. She had made it, finished the first part of her journey through life, finished a part of the journey that to others was one of discovery, but to her had been one of pain and effort, of striving against a world in which she was an anomaly, an outlier, a measurement outside the norm, outside the bounds of what was considered usual… of what was considered normal.

And there was sadness, a great, growing sadness from deep inside him. She would be leaving now, would be going out into the world, the world of science and space, of work and play, of relationships, a whole new set of trials and tribulations, and with each year they would move farther and farther apart. He supposed this was the way any father felt at watching his child grow up, at watching them become independent, in no need of fatherly advice and support.

I would like to thank all of my professors here at the University. They have all been excellent teachers and have helped me when I needed it. I would especially like to thank my mentor. She is my favorite professor and an excellent advisor. Not only did she give me prudent advice on classes to take, but I could also come to her with personal problems or even just to chat. I am really glad I had her as a mentor throughout my time here.

Katie's voice grew stronger as she continued, her words racing across the room and reaching into the farthest recesses of the massive hall in which she spoke. She spent hours writing and rewriting her speech, going over the phrases, editing in order to make it as short and powerful as possible, while using as few words as possible, choosing only those words that would come easy to her during this time of stress and nervousness. For her words were like her walk, easier at times, harder at times. There were days when she spoke almost as clear as a bell, and others where one could barely comprehend her. Today was a good day, her father thought. Today was a day when her words were strong, and sure, and simple.

He thought back to those years of therapy his daughter had endured. He thought of her walker, once so shiny and new, now tarnished and bent, relegated to a corner of the hall closet, dusty and forgotten, its mission accomplished, its useful life over.

He thought of the voice lessons she had taken, the therapy for her muscles, her conditioning and strength training, all the work, all the toil, all the effort gone in to simply making the world a manageable place, a place that Katie could navigate through.

He thought of yellow school buses, shiny, yellow school buses. They always made her smile, made her light up at a simple glimpse through a window or car door. Had that been a foretelling of things to come, of the academic prowess she would exhibit in later life?

I would like to say a special thanks to my parents who taught me that I can do anything I put my mind to, and also encouraged me to be my best. I especially want to thank my Mom because without her I wouldn't be here today. She has dedicated her life to my success. In grade school, she would come with me every day, working on class activities that I needed extra help on. Throughout high school she wrote all my math homework, patiently waiting as I figured out the problems and told her what to write. She has truly been one of my heroes, and I want to thank her for that. Mom, I love you very much.

He glanced sideways at his wife and felt another surge of emotion, feelings of love and duty, of responsibility and obligation to this woman he had committed so much of his life to. He wondered how she felt at this moment, knew it must be hard, if the tears welling in her eyes were any indication, harder even for her than for him. She would remain close to Katie, as mother and daughter do over time. They spoke almost daily, talked endlessly on the phone about the trivialities of life that surge in and out of each day, each week, each month. They would continue to do so, he imagined, would continue to stay linked together on an almost daily basis.

He thought back to that day, so many years ago, a lifetime ago, when he watched as his wife lay on a table dying, Katie beside her, and for all intent, already dead. He shook himself from the image, the memory; it was too painful to dwell on. They had both come back to life, and he had decided long ago that rather than the worst day of his life, it was probably the best.

I would also like to thank my Dad who worked hard, took care of so many things at work so that my Mom was able to help me. I want to thank him for sharing with me the magic of Disney and the idea that anything is possible, that if you can dream it, you can do it. Were it not for that, I would not be standing here before you today. Thank you Dad, I love you so very much.

Now it was his turn to cry, to stop holding back, to let go of the wetness welling in his eyes. Yes, Katie, he thought, there is magic in the world, and you are the proof. He thought of their first trip to the land of enchantment, the hours spent wandering the park with that other princess, the little girl curled up in a wheelchair, her muscles tense and rigid, her body unyielding and motionless, as if frozen in place, and in time. Katie was lucky. They were all so very, very lucky. She could have been that other princess, that little girl who could think and feel, laugh and cry inside, and yet who could not control her body, could not even stand upright and simply walk across a room. Yes, Katie had worked hard, so very hard, and yet she had the potential within her to do those marvelous things, to rise above her body and achieve what others less fortunate could not achieve. Yes, she was lucky… very lucky.

He thought of another moment from the past, a time not so long ago, a time in the past year. Katie had been home for the weekend from the University. She was working, as always, on homework, and her father was reading the paper while he sipped his morning coffee. It was a lazy Sunday morning, a morning that was cold outside, with the snows of winter on the ground. A morning best spent inside, all warm and toasty and insulated from the cold.

He was reading an article in the paper, an article about another boy who was also confined to a wheelchair, who had a case of cerebral palsy far more severe than Katie's. He was a senior in high school, and he was fairly mobile, what with his motorized wheelchair and a special van that his mother had been able to purchase with assistance from the state. It was equipped with a lift and a special space for the boy's wheelchair. It was the only thing that kept him active, kept him in school, kept him connected to the outside world.

The article went on to point out the mother's plight. She was a single mom, trying to raise her son, along with two other children, working two jobs, doing what she could. The unsung heroes of our society, he thought as he read. There is no normal, he thought again, only what you are given, and what you do with it.

But it was all too much for her. The car payments were in arrears, she was going to lose the van on that following Monday, lose the only lifeline her son had to the outside world. The article suggested that donations could be made to help, that perhaps the community would pitch in, perhaps a little here and a little there, and possibly help her to keep this car, and her son's mobility, intact.

He showed the article to Katie, read parts of it out loud to her as she sat before her computer at the breakfast table. He saw the look come into her eyes, saw the tears begin to seep onto her face, felt her go rigid in the chair. And then it happened.

She smiled.

She smiled that beautiful smile, the one that lit up a room, lit up a snowy morning, lit up the whole world around her. And with that smile her chin jutted out in just such a way, the same way it had when she made the decision to manage the softball team in high school. The same way it had when she fought to attend the People to People Ambassador program. The same way it had when she took on the extra program of work at NASA. And he knew what was coming, could telegraph it, repeat it word for word before the words even left Katie's mouth.

"Dad, I'm going to pay to have his car returned. I know I have the money in my education account. And with my scholarship, I can save even more. Please Dad, let me pay it, let me take care of it."

"Of course, Katie, if that's what you want."

"Can you do it, Dad? Can you? Can you go to the bank and take care of it tomorrow? With my money? Not yours. Mine!

"Yes, Katie, first thing tomorrow I can go to the bank. I will. I promise."

And he had done just that. Gone to the bank and paid off the outstanding payments, deposited a bit more to help with the future. He had used some of her money as he promised, and even more of his own. And as he walked out of the bank, as he strode to his car, a feeling of peace and well-being rolled over him like a wave, for he remembered the last thing Katie had said to him before leaving to return to school the next day.

"Dad, about the van, you won't forget?"

"No, Katie, consider it done."

"And Dad, I want it to be anonymous. No names. Not mine, not yours. Anonymous!"

It was that which warmed him so. He knew in his heart that his daughter was all grown up. She was a woman, full-blown, a work of art the likes of which the world would be better for. And he knew that he was done teaching her, indeed he knew that she had taught him far more about life than he would ever be able to teach her.

She was all grown up.

Last but not least, I would like to thank all of my friends. I came to the University with an "all work, no play" attitude, and my friends quickly taught me that I need to have a little bit of fun. I would really like to thank my best friend Amy, who not only proofed my core humanities and English papers, but also dragged me out to get ice cream when I would start yelling profanities at my computer science homework.

He dared not glance at Amy, sitting so quietly beside him. He knew her face would be filled with tears as well. Amy had already graduated, already entered the real world of work and duty and responsibility. But she had never wavered in her support and friendship for this little girl who had so touched her heart and won her friendship. The rest of the crowd laughed in approval at Katie's intended joke. Even when she stumbled a bit over the word profanities, the meaning was clear, and helped to make more human this seemingly perfect specimen standing in front of them.

Finally, I would like to thank everyone who came tonight, your support has made all the difference. There are many friends in the audience whom I did not mention, many professors and helpers and advisors without whom I would not be standing here. I wish to thank you all from the bottom of my heart. Thank you, thank you, thank you.

And with that she was finished. The speech was over. The crowd rose as one, another standing ovation, the sound of their clapping ringing throughout the hall.

Katie stood motionless, unsure now of what to do, of how to exit. She was genuinely moved and trying not to cry herself. The University President sprang up to assist, to help her walk off the little stage at the front of the great hall.

And at that moment, Katie's father knew, was sure, as sure as anything he had ever been sure of in his life, as sure as the sun rose in the east, as sure as the world turned on its axis, as sure as his love for his daughter, he was sure that there would be many more to come… more standing ovations, more clapping, more accolades and awards.

Oh yes, he thought, there would be more of these moments, many more.

She was going to help change the world.

Of that he was sure.

Epilogue

The room was small, drab, and somewhat out of place for what seemed such a momentous occasion. Banks of computers lined the room, their screens set into worn and marked linoleum frames, the keyboards carelessly arranged on the counters below. The carpet was torn in spots, stains showing in haphazard patterns across the floor.

Along two of the walls were floor to ceiling glass windows looking out onto an even drearier hallway, their panes muted with dark tinting. Above the computer screens, on the far wall, was a large digital screen with a schematic of the world hanging in space and surrounded by smaller images and digital data readouts. The air was heavy and the lighting was dimmed, the multi-colored hue from the computer screens adding an almost ethereal look to the room.

One digital readout stood alone, fixed into the wall in front of the gathered crowd. On the screen were numbers slowly counting down. T minus 23 hours, 15 minutes… and counting.

A heavy pall hung in the air, for this was a moment in history. Seated in the room were fifteen of the brightest young minds in the whole of the National Aeronautical and Space Administration organization.

The Project Director, "the Chief" to the assembled team, a PhD in Aeronautical Engineering, Astrophysicist, NASA Scientist and Nobel Prize winner, Katie's former mentor, stood in the front of the room addressing the group.

"I want to welcome all of you to the official start of the James Webb Telescope Project, a project most of us in this room have been working on for over twenty years. As you can see from the clock behind me, we are less than 24 hours from launch. Tomorrow. at 5:32 PM precisely, at the European Spaceport in New Guinea, an Ariane 5 ECA with a cryogenic upper stage will lift off on its way to an orbit over a million miles from Earth. The payload for that rocket, as you all know, is the most advanced infrared telescope and data gathering satellite ever launched by man."

It was true. The universe was calculated to be around 13.75 billion years old. The Hubble Space Telescope had managed to pick up a galaxy that had formed within 480 million years of the Big Bang. That they had been able to peer back through time that far had been amazing, but the James Webb was designed to go back even further. It was designed to find the first galaxies that formed in the early Universe, connecting the dots that led from the Big Bang all the way through time to our own Milky Way. It would be capable of peering through dusty clouds to see stars forming planetary systems, forming the earths of space, connecting the Milky Way to our own Solar System. It was a true time traveler, peering back to our very beginning, our birth.

"Team A leader," the Chief continued, "your group is ready with telemetry and logistics?"

"We're good to go, Chief," the leader replied. He was also a PhD with a string of additional titles, but no Nobel Prize. "We've completed the final debugs and all systems are reading the test programs correctly. However, we won't know any more until the telescope reaches orbit and the structural array unfolds."

"Of course," the Chief replied. "I'm hopeful we will have no problems in that area... but you never know. Team B Leader, your status?

The Team B Leader, a PhD in Computer and Electrical Engineering from MIT, was the project data coordinator. "We're good, Chief. We may have to pull an all-nighter, but then all of us are used to that by now." That was accompanied by laughter that seemed to break the tension in the room. Everyone had been work-ing 20-hour days for weeks, some for months, in preparation for the launch.

The Chief continued, "I would also like everyone to say hi to the newest member of Team B. Katie May will be working with the team on the image processing coding necessary to the interpretation of all the data from the new telescope. Katie, this will probably be your last chance to greet the team as a whole, so take a bow."

Sitting to one side, at the edge of this group, her chair turned to allow her to stretch her legs and avoid cramps, Katie May felt a surge of electricity course through her body. She simply couldn't believe she was sitting here, a part of this group, a part of this project... a part of history.

She half rose out of her chair, her manner somewhat embarrassed and self-conscious, but her face breaking into that well-known smile.

She knew this was a solemn moment, a moment of seriousness in a room full of very serious people. But she just couldn't help smiling, in fact, laughing out loud, as she greeted the assembled multitude.

I can't believe I'm here, she thought to herself. At that moment, the image of Peter Pan flashed into her mind, and his all too familiar words went ringing through her consciousness.

"What do you think, Katie," Peter seemed to say, "a piece of cake? Tell them you've been here before. Second star to the right... and on till morning. Right?"

Katie couldn't help thinking about school, the long hours of work, her university mentor urging her on, paving the way, han-dling the accommodations she needed. Telling her, "Katie, one day you're going to help change the world."

She thought of her mother sitting at the kitchen table when she was twelve, patiently writing her homework by hand, putting down mathematical symbols on paper, symbols that were completely meaningless to her mother, but not to her.

She thought of her father, and his love for Disney and all things magical, for the most important thing he had ever taught her, the magic of wonder and imagination. She looked around the room and her confidence grew. She knew she belonged. She knew she was home. After all, she knew in her heart what everyone else in the room had also learned at some point in their lives.

If you can dream it… you can do it.

"That's right, Peter," she thought with an inward grin, "second star to the right.. and on till morning." She turned to face the group in the room. And for the life of her, she just couldn't help smiling… again.

Get ready Big Bang, she thought.

I'm on my way.

In a very large city in the western half of the country sits a sprawling, well-appointed hospital complex, a center of healing, a monument to the preservation of life. In this hospital, tucked away on the second floor, just above the emergency room, is the neonatal intensive care unit. It is a suite of rooms with one central space where newborns are brought to heal. These newborns arrive with all sorts of problems, from hearts not healthy enough to sustain life to congenital birth defects, from babies suffering the withdrawals of their mothers' addictions to ones with undeveloped organs and withered limbs, from premature births to genetic deformities.

Along one wall of this space, consuming almost the entire wall, and looking down upon the tiny bundles of life wrapped in blankets and nestled in their cocoons, is a bulletin board of pictures. Some of these pictures are Polaroids, some printed on fine Kodak paper, some simply printed out on a computer printer. But they are all pictures of children, some still very young, some in the early stages of adolescence, and some all the way into young adulthood. They are the survivors, those who once inhabited this room and made it out, made it into the world to thrive and grow.

The pictures are tacked on to the board willy-nilly, their edges overlapping. The messages written on them in ink and crayon, messages of "hello" and "I'm doing fine" are partly obscured by the haphazard way in which the pictures flow one into another. For you see, the board is not quite big enough to hold all of the pictures placed there so carefully by the recipients, the medical personnel who toil and strive in this room, who work to save lives, to preserve life and coax cures from the ravaged babies who end up here. The workers toil ceaselessly, sometimes winning, sometimes losing, but always trying, always working to undo what nature has so cruelly wrought.

Just to the right of center on this bulletin board, slightly below the middle of the board and prominently overlapping its neighbors, is the picture of a young woman. She is dressed in graduation garb, cap and gown, a long, flowing robe reaching to her ankles, a cap and tassel perched upon her head, the silk strings of the tassel falling to one side of her face. She is smiling, this young woman, with a smile that seems to spread across the whole of the bulletin board.

In one hand she is clutching a rolled up diploma tied with a string of red ribbon, while with the other hand she is waving at the camera. If one looks closely one can see that all is not quite perfect with this picture. But you must look very closely indeed. The hand holding the diploma is curled inwards, the wrist and fingers too rigid and vise-like to appear normal. The head is tilted on a neck that seems frozen in space at a not quite normal angle. It is barely noticeable, in fact, not noticeable at all to those who only casually glance at the picture.

Like the other subjects in all the other pictures on the board, this young woman is a past resident of this room. She was brought in one night, her body shaking and straining, her cries filling the air with their pain and misery. She is a survivor, and her picture is a reminder to all who work in this room, to all who come to visit and pray, to all who spend long hours trying to will their babies to health, a reminder that not all outcomes are bad, that not all efforts end in failure, that there are other possibilities… other outcomes for the future, and for what life may bring.

The picture is a message to all who gaze upon it. Have courage, you are not alone, and the future is brighter than you may think.

For there is no normal… there is only what you are given… and what you do with it.

Oh, and one other thing. There is hope.

There will always be hope.

The End

CPSIA information can be obtained at www.ICGtesting.com
Printed in the USA
LVOW08s1952110913

351757LV00005B/3/P